409 SMALL HOME PLANS

TABLE OF CONTENTS

CREATIVE HOMEOWNER®

COPYRIGHT © 2002
CREATIVE HOMEOWNER®
A Division of Federal Marketing Corp.
Upper Saddle River, NJ

Library of Congress
Catalogue Card No.: 20-01090766   ISBN: 1-58011-115-7

Creative Homeowner A Division of Federal Marketing Corp.
24 Park Way, Upper Saddle River, NJ 07458

Manufactured in the United States of America

Current Printing (last digit) 10 9 8 7 6 5 4 3

Front cover photography by Donna & Ron Kolb, Exposure Unlimited
Back cover photography by Charles Brooks, Brooks Photography

Photography by Glenn Wood

At Home on a Hill

Your hillside lot is no problem if you choose this spectacular, multi-level sun-catcher. Window walls combine with sliders to unite active areas with a huge outdoor deck. Interior spaces flow together for an open feeling that's accentuated by the sloping ceilings and towering fireplace in the living room. Thanks to the island kitchen, even the cook can stay involved in the action. Walk up a short flight to reach the laundry room, a full bath, and two bedrooms, each with a walk-in closet. Up a separate staircase, you'll find the master suite.

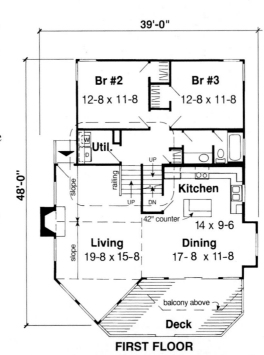

39'-0"

48'-0"

Br #2
12-8 x 11-8

Br #3
12-8 x 11-8

Util.

UP

Kitchen
14 x 9-6

slope
railing
UP
DN

42" counter

slope

Living
19-8 x 15-8

Dining
17-8 x 11-8

balcony above

Deck

FIRST FLOOR

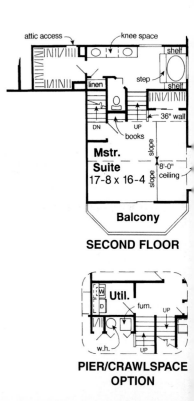

attic access   knee space

shelf

linen   step

shelf

DN   UP
books   36" wall

Mstr. Suite
17-8 x 16-4

slope   8'-0" ceiling

slope

Balcony

SECOND FLOOR

Util.   furn.

UP

w.h.   UP

PIER/CRAWLSPACE OPTION

Flooded with natural light, the dining room also enjoys the view through the French doors that open onto the back deck of this comfortable home.

Plan info

First Floor	**1,316 sq. ft.**
Second Floor	**592 sq. ft.**
Bedrooms	**Three**
Baths	**Two (full)**
Foundation	**Basement, Pier/Post or Combo/Basement/Crawl space**

The fieldstone fireplace provides a solid center to this home, and the large windows that rise two levels on either side flood the living room with incredible light.

Big Style on a Small Scale

This three bedroom home is perfectly designed for the price-conscious home builder with a sense of style and a demand for the finer things. The public spaces in this home are open, yet well-defined by thoughtful details such as the columns that delineate the vaulted living room. Floor-to-ceiling windows open the living room to the lovely little front porch. The kitchen is well planned and efficient and includes a center-island workstation. The dining area opens to a rear patio for backyard views and seasonal entertaining. The bedrooms in this home are in their own wing, allowing for privacy that provides a nice contrast to the open public spaces. The vaulted master bedroom is complete with a private bath and large walk-in closet. Two additional bedrooms each have ample closet space. A laundry facility — thoughtfully located close to the bedrooms — separates the house from the garage.

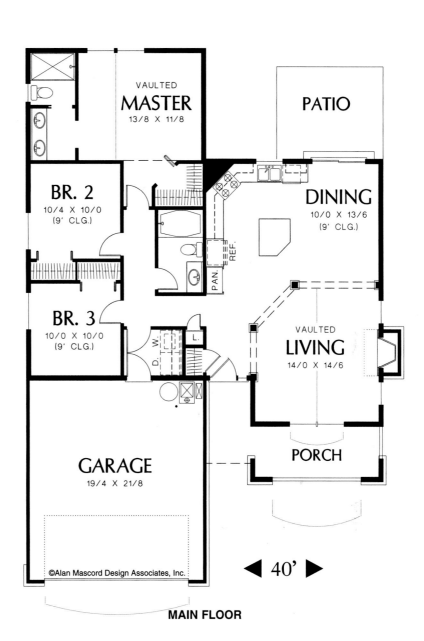

VAULTED
MASTER
13/8 X 11/8

PATIO

BR. 2
10/4 X 10/0
(9' CLG.)

DINING
10/0 X 13/6
(9' CLG.)

REF.

PAN.

BR. 3
10/0 X 10/0
(9' CLG.)

VAULTED
LIVING
14/0 X 14/6

D. W.

58'

GARAGE
19/4 X 21/8

PORCH

©Alan Mascord Design Associates, Inc.

◄ 40' ►

MAIN FLOOR

Plan info

Main Floor	1,275 sq. ft.
Garage	440 sq. ft.
Bedrooms	Three
Baths	2 (full)
Foundation	Crawlspace

Photography by John Ehrencle

Enjoy the Views

This home is a vacation haven with views from every room, whether it is situated on a lake or a mountaintop. The main floor features a living room and dining room with a center fireplace serving as a room divider. The kitchen flows into the dining room and is gracefully separated by a breakfast bar. There is a bedroom and a full bath on the main floor. The second floor has a secondary bedroom or library loft, with clerestory windows, which opens above the living room. The master bedroom and bath are also on the second floor. This home has large decks and windows on one entire side.

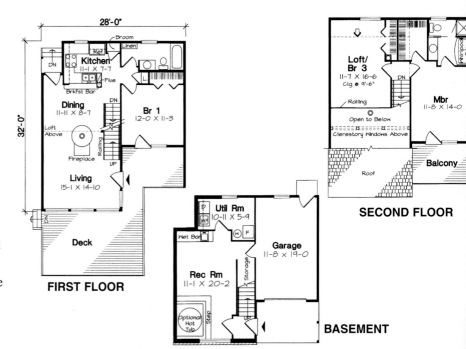

FIRST FLOOR

28'-0"

32'-0"

Broom

Linen

Kitchen
11-1 X 7-7

Ref

Flue

Brkfst Bar

Dining
11-11 X 8-7

DN

Loft Above

Railing

Fireplace

UP

Br 1
12-0 X 11-3

Living
15-1 X 14-10

Deck

BASEMENT

Util Rm
10-11 X 5-9

Wet Bar

W

F

Garage
11-8 x 19-0

Storage

Rec Rm
11-1 X 20-2

Optional Hot Tub

UP

SECOND FLOOR

Loft/ Br 3
11-7 X 16-6
Clg @ 9'-6"

DN

Railing

Open to Below

Clerestory Windows Above

Mbr
11-8 X 14-0

Roof

Balcony

Sunny and open, the kitchen and dining area are separated by the two-level breakfast bar, which offers a place to serve meals and a lower countertop for preparing them.

Plan info

Main Floor	**728 sq. ft.**
Upper Floor	**573 sq. ft.**
Lower Floor	**409 sq. ft.**
Garage	**244 sq. ft.**
Bedrooms	**Three**
Baths	**2 (full)**
Foundation	**Basement**

The spacious and clean floor plan keeps comfort within easy reach. Family members can enjoy games or television in the living room and still keep in touch with those in the kitchen.

Extraordinary Duplex

This pretty income property starts with a graceful façade made up of elegant columns, gabled rooflines and lovely bay windows. On the inside, the attention to detail and thoughtful arrangement of rooms raise this plan to a level well above standard duplex housing. Each house offers an entry with coat closet, bay windowed living room and thoughtfully planned kitchen. Three pleasantly proportioned bedrooms on the second floor share a full bath.

Plan info

First Floor	1,086 sq. ft.
Second Floor	1,086 sq. ft.
Bedrooms	Three
Baths	1 1/2
Foundation	Basement

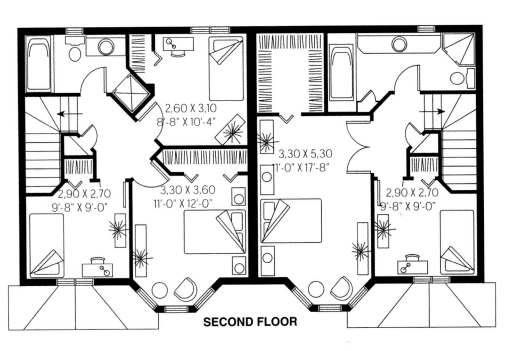

2,60 X 3,10
8'-8" X 10'-4"

3,30 X 5,30
11'-0" X 17'-8"

2,90 X 2,70
9'-8" X 9'-0"

3,30 X 3,60
11'-0" X 12'-0"

2,90 X 2,70
9'-8" X 9'-0"

SECOND FLOOR

FIRST FLOOR

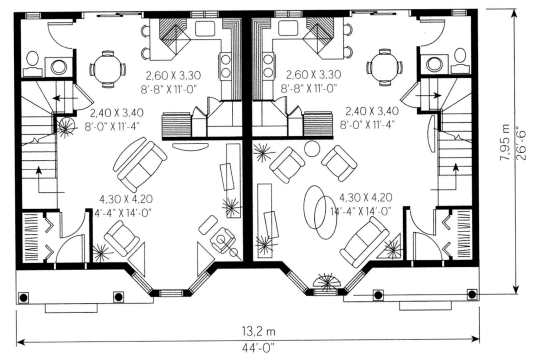

2,60 X 3,30
8'-8" X 11'-0"

2,60 X 3,30
8'-8" X 11'-0"

2,40 X 3,40
8'-0" X 11'-4"

2,40 X 3,40
8'-0" X 11'-4"

4,30 X 4,20
4'-4" X 14'-0"

4,30 X 4,20
14'-4" X 14'-0"

7,95 m
26'-6"

13,2 m
44'-0"

9

Plan no. 65125

Tremendous Curb Appeal

Plan info

First Floor	**1,324 sq. ft.**
Second Floor	**688 sq. ft.**
Basement	**1,324**
Garage	**425 sq. ft.**
Bedrooms	**Four**
Baths	**2(full)**
Foundation	**Basement**

Sure, it looks great from the front. But this home looks great from any angle. And the appeal doesn't stop at the curb. Step inside this open floor plan and enter a world of light and spaciousness. From the front entry past the generous coat closet, the rear of the home opens into a veritable conservatory of open spaces and big windows. The well-planned L-shaped kitchen includes a curved center-island work space and breakfast bar. The first floor master bedroom has private access to a bath and between the two is a generous closet that can serve as a dressing room. On the second floor, three bedrooms and a full bath make this home complete.

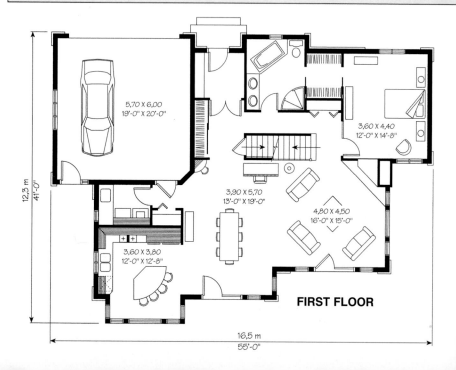

FIRST FLOOR

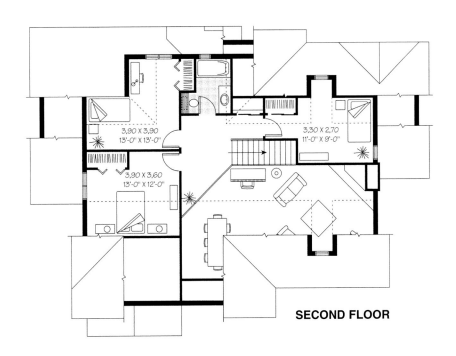

3,90 X 3,90
13'-0" X 13'-0"

3,30 X 2,70
11'-0" X 9'-0"

3,90 X 3,60
13'-0" X 12'-0"

SECOND FLOOR

Photography by Charles Brooks, Brooks Photogra

Skylight Brightens Master Bedroom

Keep dry during the rainy season under the covered porch entry of this gorgeous home. Off the kitchen is the convenient laundry room. The living room features a vaulted beamed ceiling and a fireplace. A full bath is located between the living room and the two secondary bedrooms. The master bedroom has a decorative ceiling, and a skylight above the entrance of its private bath. The double vanity bathroom features a large walk-in closet. An optional deck is offered accessible through sliding glass doors off the wonderful master bedroom and the living room.

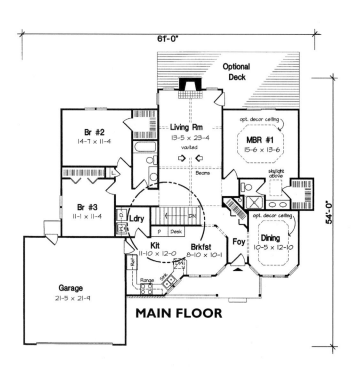

MAIN FLOOR

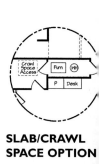

SLAB/CRAWL SPACE OPTION

French doors lead from the comfortable master bedroom onto the deck, providing views, light and easy access to the backyard.

Interesting angles define the lines in this kitchen, where the counter forms both a border between kitchen and dining room as well as a place for the kids to enjoy an after-school snack.

Plan info

Main Floor	1,686 sq. ft.
Garage	484 sq. ft.
Basement	1,676 sq. ft.
Bedrooms	Three
Baths	2 (full)
Foundation	Basement, Crawlspace or Slab

Plan info

First Floor	1,293 sq. ft.
Second Floor	629 sq. ft.
Garage	606 sq. ft.
Bedrooms	Three
Baths	2 1/2
Foundation Basement	1,293

Sweeping Staircase

This attractive two-story traditional offers many pleasant surprises. From the curb, it presents an elegant and traditional façade to the neighborhood while the rear elevation provides a delightfully extravagant sweep of stair rising to a private deck off one of the three bedrooms in this finely planned home. Interior spaces include a dramatic two-story dining room linking together the fireplaced living room and the bright breakfast area.

SECOND FLOOR

FIRST FLOOR

Photography by John Ehrenclou

Cozy Three-Bedroom

FIRST FLOOR

Covered Porch 13-7 x 19-5
Dining Rm 11-6 x 13-6
Kitchen 4-0 x 13-6
Brkfst 10-7 x 13-6
Living Rm 13-7 x 19-5 Flat Clg. @ 10'
Entry
Pantry
Porch
Garage 22-5 x 22-11

50'-4"
47'-0"

SLAB/CRAWL SPACE

Crawl Space Access

SECOND FLOOR

Master Br 13-5 x 15-6
Walk-in Clos.
Whirl-Pool
Flat Clg @ II'-0"
Attic Access
Br 2 13-5 x 10-11
Br 3 12-0 x 12-0
Linen
Bonus Rm 11-5 x 11-8

This cozy design offers amenities found in larger homes. A formal entry gives access to a lovely living room accented by a fireplace. The formal dining room has direct access to both the kitchen and the living room, perfect for entertaining. The kitchen includes a work island and a walk-in pantry. The breakfast area is open to the kitchen, and offers a laundry closet plus access to the rear yard. There are three bedrooms on the second floor. The master bedroom is part of a suite with a compartmented bath and a walk-in closet. There is a bonus room for future expansion.

Plan info

First Floor	988 sq. ft.
Second Floor	956 sq. ft.
Bonus	144 sq. ft.
Basement	976 sq. ft.
Garage	532 sq. ft.
Bedrooms	Three
Baths	2 1/2
Foundation	Basement, Crawlspace or Slab

Easy Living

Here's a pretty one-level home designed for carefree living. The central foyer divides active and quiet areas. Step back into a fireplaced living room with dramatic, towering ceilings and a panoramic view of the backyard. The adjoining dining room features a sloping ceiling crowned by a plant shelf and sliders to an outdoor deck. Just across the counter, a handy U-shaped kitchen features abundant cabinets, a window over the sink overlooking the deck and a walk-in pantry. You'll find three bedrooms tucked off the foyer. The front bedrooms share a handy full bath, but the master suite boasts its own private bath with both shower and tub, a large walk-in closet and a bump-out window that adds light and space.

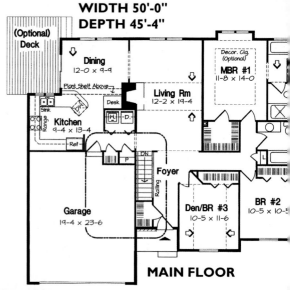

WIDTH 50'-0"
DEPTH 45'-4"

(Optional) Deck

Dining
12-0 x 9-9

Plant Shelf Above

Sink
Kitchen
9-4 x 13-4

Ref.

Desk

Living Rm
12-2 x 19-4

Decor. Clg.
(Optional)
MBR #1
11-8 x 14-0

Garage
19-4 x 23-6

Foyer

Den/BR #3
10-5 x 11-6

BR #2
10-5 x 10-5

MAIN FLOOR

Plan info

Main Floor	1,456 sq. ft.
Basement	1,448 sq. ft.
Garage	452 sq. ft.
Bedrooms	Three
Baths	2(full)
Foundation	Basement, Crawlspace, or Slab

Garage

Furn.

Crawlspace Access

CRAWLSPACE/ SLAB OPTION

tography by John Ehrenclou

Rustic Exterior

Although rustic in appearance, the interior of this cabin is quiet, modern and comfortable. Small in overall size, it still contains three bedrooms and two baths in addition to a large, two-story living room with exposed beams. As a hunting/fishing lodge or mountain retreat, this will serve your needs.

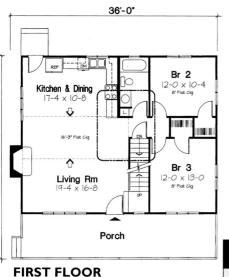

36'-0"

Kitchen & Dining
17-4 x 10-8

16'-3" Flat Clg

Living Rm
19-4 x 16-8

REF DW

Br 2
12-0 x 10-4
8' Flat Clg

DN

Br 3
12-0 x 13-0
8' Flat Clg

UP

Porch

FIRST FLOOR

FURN HH

Crawl
Space
Access

**CRAWLSPACE/
SLAB OPTION**

Open to Living
Room Below

Flat Clg @ 7'-6"

DN

Master Br
12-0 x 13-4

SECOND FLOOR

Plan info

First Floor	1,013 sq. ft.
Second Floor	315 sq. ft.
Basement	1,013 sq. ft.
Bedrooms	Three
Baths	2
Foundation	Basement, Crawlspace or Slab

Photography by Donna & Ron Kolb, Exposures Unlimited

Refined and Distinctive

Designed with your family in mind, this home boasts many features. There is a furniture alcove in the formal dining room, a high ceiling and French doors topped with arched windows in the Great room, a wood rail at the split stairs, large pantry in the kitchen and a roomy laundry room. The spacious kitchen and breakfast area encourages relaxing gatherings. The master suite offers a whirlpool tub, his and her vanities, a shower stall and a walk-in closet. Two additional bedrooms share a full bath.

Plan info

First Floor	1,036 sq. ft.
Second Floor	861 sq. ft.
Garage	420 sq. ft.
Bedrooms	Three
Baths	2 1/2
Foundation	Basement

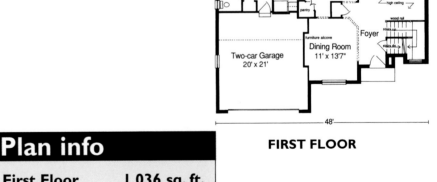

FIRST FLOOR

SECOND FLOOR

Photography by Bob Greenspan

Yesteryear Revisited

WIDTH 43'-0"
DEPTH 69'-0"

SECOND FLOOR

FIRST FLOOR

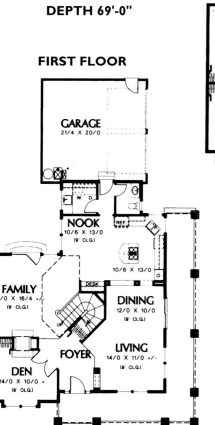

A quaint wrapping porch shelters the entrance of this home. The foyer gives access to the combined living and dining room, the secluded den or the family room. A terrific two-sided fireplace accentuates the den and family room. For ease in serving, the nook flows from the island kitchen. On the second floor, a master suite with a vaulted ceiling, two additional bedrooms and a full bath complete the plan.

Plan info

First Floor	1,371 sq. ft.
Second Floor	916 sq. ft.
Garage	427 sq. ft.
Bedrooms	Three
Baths	2 1/2
Foundation	Crawlspace

A Porch with Gazebo

A summer's breeze and a cool, refreshing drink are all you need when realxing on this great front porch on a hot afternoon. The unique gazebo area gives this home a style all its own. Inside, the breakfast area overlooks the porch. The kitchen's peninsula counter extends the work space. There is a pass-through from the kitchen into the Great room for convenience in serving, plus a built-in pantry for added storage. From the garage, you enter the home through the laundry room, which will reduce the amount of dirt tracked in. The Great room and the formal dining room are enhanced by a two-sided fireplace. The three bedrooms are on the left side of the home, with the two secondary bedrooms sharing a full bath. The master suite pampers the owner with a whirlpool tub and a walk-in closet.

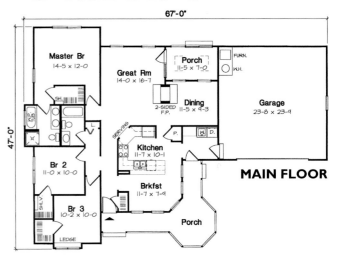

MAIN FLOOR

Plan info

Main Floor	1,452 sq. ft.
Garage	584 sq. ft.
Bedrooms	Three
Baths	2 (full)
Foundation	Crawlspace

Compact Comfort

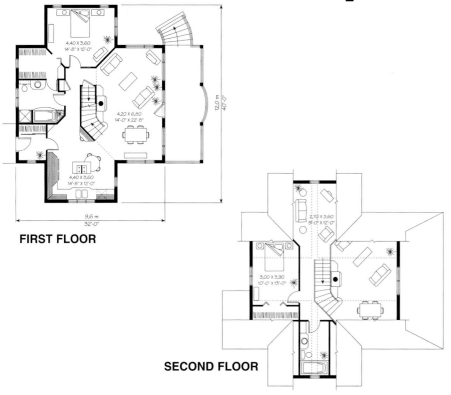

FIRST FLOOR

4,40 X 3,60
14'-8" X 12'-0"

4,20 X 6,80
14'-0" X 22'-8"

4,40 X 3,60
14'-8" X 12'-0"

12,0 m
40'-0"

9,6 m
32'-0"

SECOND FLOOR

2,70 X 3,60
9'-0" X 12'-0"

3,00 X 3,90
10'-0" X 13'-0"

Comfort, charm, the right blend of open spaces and private retreats combine for a home that is perfect for today's lifestyles. The two-story great room features a woodstove and open staircase which leads to an second floor loft. This loft space could serve as a third bedroom or be used to create a private sitting area or lounge.

Plan info

First Floor	1,024 sq. ft.
Second Floor	456 sq. ft.
Bedrooms	Two
Baths	2
Foundation	Basement

Charming Cottage

This cozy design packs a lot of living into its efficient use of space with ample storage and volume ceilings. The slope ceiling of the living room rises to the second floor balcony and loft area. This versatile space creates a sitting area outside the master bedroom, or could serve as a study or even a guest room.

Plan info

First Floor	**593 sq. ft.**
Second Floor	**383 sq. ft.**
Bedrooms	**Two**
Baths	**2**
Foundation	**Crawlspace**

FIRST FLOOR

SECOND FLOOR

Delightful, Compact Home

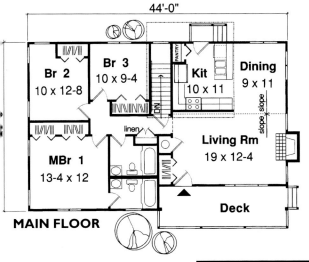

44'-0"

Br 2
10 x 12-8

Br 3
10 x 9-4

Kit
10 x 11

Dining
9 x 11

PANTRY

DN

slope slope

linen

Living Rm
19 x 12-4

MBr 1
13-4 x 12

Deck

MAIN FLOOR

W

D

**CRAWLSPACE/
SLAB OPTION**

Plan info

Main Floor	1,146 sq. ft.
Bedrooms	Three
Baths	Two
Foundation	Basement, Crawlspace or Slab

Hanging plants would create a magnificent entrance to this charming home. Enter the fireplaced living room, which is brightened by a wonderful picture window. The kitchen and dining area are separated by a counter island featuring double sinks. In the hallway, a linen closet and full bath are conveniently located between the living areas and bedrooms. The master bedroom features a private bath and double closets. The two secondary bedrooms have good-sized closets, keeping clutter to a minimum. Many windows throughout this home lighten each room, creating a warm, cozy atmosphere.

Convenient and Affordable

There's a lot of convenience packed into this affordable design. Flanking the kitchen to the right is the dining room which has a sliding glass door to the backyard; to the left is the laundry room with an entrance to the garage. The master bedroom boasts its own full bathroom. The two secondary bedrooms share a full hall bath.

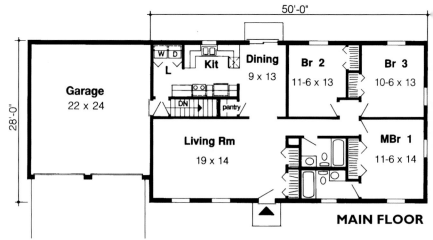

MAIN FLOOR

Plan info

Main Floor	1,400 sq. ft.
Basement	1,400 sq. ft.
Garage	528 sq. ft.
Bedrooms	Three
Baths	2 (full)
Foundation	Basement, Crawlspace or Slab

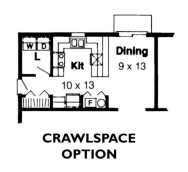

CRAWLSPACE OPTION

Classic Contemporary

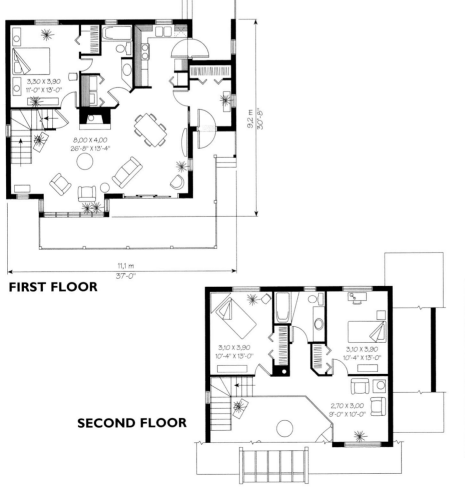

3,30 X 3,90
11'-0" X 13'-0"

8,00 X 4,00
26'-8" X 13'-4"

9,2 m
30'-8"

11,1 m
37'-0"

FIRST FLOOR

3,10 X 3,90
10'-4" X 13'-0"

3,10 X 3,90
10'-4" X 13'-0"

2,70 X 3,00
9'-0" X 10'-0"

SECOND FLOOR

Bright and spacious are the hallmarks of a truly contemporary home. This smaller home has both qualities in abundance. The main living spaces open up with greenhouse windows and volume ceilings. Glass doors provide access from the dining area to the large deck. Two second floor bedrooms share a full bath and a lovely loft with balcony that overlooks the living room and gets plenty of natural light from that large greenhouse window.

Plan info

First Floor	**946 sq. ft.**
Second Floor	**604 sq. ft.**
Bedrooms	**Three**
Baths	**2**
Foundation	**Basement**

Compact Charmer

This lovely, compact home offers tremendous curb appeal. From the gables to the covered entry and the bay window, this home presents a friendly face to the world. The living room opens to the bay windowed dining area and the thoughtfully planned kitchen beyond. Two bedrooms share a large full bath.

Plan info

Main Floor	1,068 sq. ft.
Garage	245 sq. ft.
Bedrooms	Two
Baths	1
Foundation	Basement

MAIN FLOOR

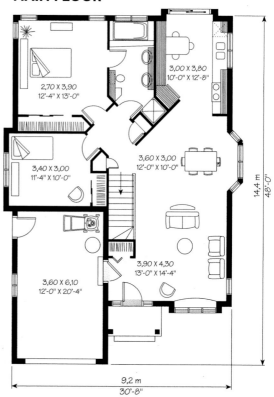

2,70 X 3,90
12'-4" X 13'-0"

3,00 X 3,80
10'-0" X 12'-8"

3,40 X 3,00
11'-4" X 10'-0"

3,60 X 3,00
12'-0" X 10'-0"

3,90 X 4,30
13'-0" X 14'-4"

3,60 X 6,10
12'-0" X 20'-4"

14,4 m
48'-0"

9,2 m
30'-8"

Photography by Laurie Solomon

Farmhouse Favorite

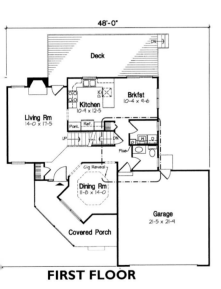

FIRST FLOOR

48'-0"

Deck

Brkfst
10-4 x 9-6

Kitchen
10-4 x 12-5

Living Rm
14-0 x 17-5

Dining Rm
11-8 x 14-0

Ctg Reveal

Garage
21-5 x 21-4

Covered Porch

SECOND FLOOR

Line of Floor Below

Br 3
12-2 x 10-1

Master Br
14-3 x 17-5

Railing

Br 2
13-11 x 11-9

**CRAWLSPACE/
SLAB OPTION**

Plan info

First Floor	**909 sq. ft.**
Second Floor	**854 sq. ft.**
Garage	**491 sq. ft.**
Bedrooms	**Three**
Baths	**2 1/2**
Foundation	**Basement, Crawlspace or Slab**

Perfect for a family with young children, all of the bedrooms are located upstairs close to each other. The covered porch offers guests a warm welcome, no matter what the weather. The U-shaped kitchen is conveniently located between the living room and breakfast area, perfect for grabbing a quick snack while watching television or for enjoying informal family meals. An optional deck in the rear provides outdoor living space. There is a convenient rear entry door to the garage.

27

Brick, Wood and Gables

A classic design and spacious interior make this home attractive and exciting to the discriminating buyer. Brick and wood trim, multiple gables and wing walls enhance the outside, while the interior offers features that are designed for entertaining guests. Sloped ceilings, a corner fireplace, windows across the rear of the Great room and a boxed window in the dining room are all visible as you enter the open foyer. The large kitchen provides plenty of counter space and includes a pantry. The breakfast area is surrounded by windows that flood the room with natural light. In the master bedroom suite, an ultra-bath with a whirlpool tub, double sink, shower and walk-in closet await.

MAIN FLOOR

WIDTH 65'-10"
DEPTH 56'-0"

Plan info

Main Floor	1,746 sq. ft.
Basement	1,560 sq. ft.
Garage	455 sq. ft.
Bedrooms	Three
Baths	2 (full)
Foundation	Basement

Two-Story Turret

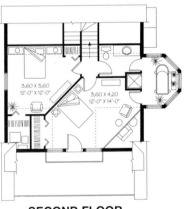

SECOND FLOOR
Two Bedroom Option

SECOND FLOOR
One Bedroom Option

FIRST FLOOR

This fanciful home is truly eye-catching with its magnificent exterior detailing, yet it remains clean, elegant and functional on the interior. The first floor features an open floor plan that makes the most of the space and allows sunlight to pour into all the rooms. On the second floor, take your choice between the one-bedroom option or the two-bedroom option — this house is ready to cater to your needs.

Plan info

First Floor	737 sq. ft.
Second Floor	587 sq. ft.
Bedrooms	One or Two
Baths	2 1/2
Foundation	Basement

Elegantly Efficient

Wonderful use of space and attention to detail combine to create a home that is both economical and elegant. This beautifully crafted floor plan provides plenty of storage and closet space, while at the same time creating rooms that seem large and spacious, all in a compact home. Note the columns that define the entrance to the living room, the vaulted ceiling in the luxurious master suite and the built-ins thoughtfully provided throughout this fine home.

Plan info

Main Floor	**1,557 sq. ft.**
Garage	**434 sq. ft.**
Bedrooms	**Three**
Baths	**2**
Foundation	**Crawlspace**

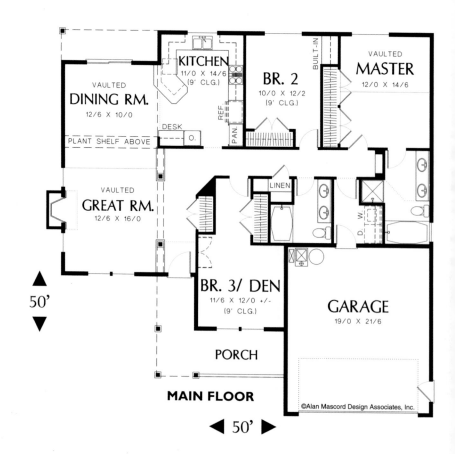

MAIN FLOOR

◄ 50' ►

©Alan Mascord Design Associates, Inc.

lan no.
4654

price code **B**

total living area: 1,554 sq. ft.

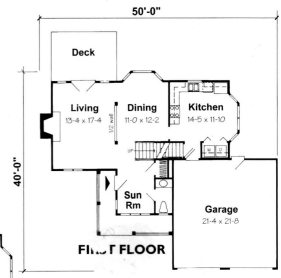

FIRST FLOOR

Deck

Living
13-4 x 17-4

Dining
11-0 x 12-2

Kitchen
14-5 x 11-10

Sun Rm

Garage
21-4 x 21-8

50'-0"

40'-0"

Plan info

First Floor	806 sq. ft.
Second Floor	748 sq. ft.
Garage	467 sq. ft.
Bedrooms	Three
Baths	2 ½
Foundation	Basement, Crawlspace or Slab

Master Br
16-0 x 11-11

Br 2
11-8 x 10-8

Br 3
111-4 x 10-7

linen

SECOND FLOOR

Plan no.
1026

price code **A**

total living area: 1,354 sq. ft.

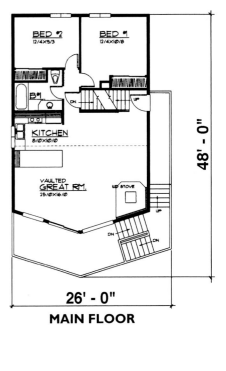

BED #2
12/4x9/3

BED #1
12/4x10/8

B#1

KITCHEN
8/0x10/10

VAULTED
GREAT RM.
25/0x16/0

UP STOVE

48' - 0"

26' - 0"

MAIN FLOOR

Plan info

First Floor	988 sq. ft.
Second Floor	366 sq. ft.
Bedrooms	Three
Baths	1(full), 1(¾)
Foundation	Basement

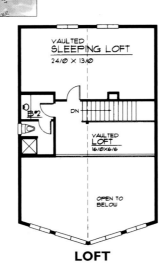

VAULTED
SLEEPING LOFT
24/0 X 13/0

B#2

VAULTED
LOFT
16/0x6/6

OPEN TO BELOW

LOFT

Plan no.
92609

price code **C**

total living area: 1,768 sq. f

Photography supplied by Studer Residential Design, Inc.

FIRST FLOOR

WIDTH 55'-4"
DEPTH 40'-4"

Plan info

First Floor	960 sq. ft.
Second Floor	808 sq. ft.
Basement	922 sq. ft.
Garage	413 sq. ft.
Bedrooms	Three
Baths	2 1/2
Foundation	Basement

SECOND FLOOR

Plan no.
34603

price code **B**

total living area: 1,560 sq. f

FIRST FLOOR

SECOND FLOOR

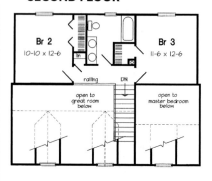

Plan info

First Floor	1,061 sq. ft.
Second Floor	499 sq. ft.
Bedrooms	Three
Baths	2 1/2
Foundation	Basement,
	Crawlspace or Slab

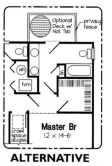

ALTERNATIVE
FOUNDATION PLAN

■ *Total living area 1,492 sq. ft.* ■ *Price Code A* ■

No. 34150

This plan features:

Two bedrooms (optional third)

Two full baths

A huge, arched window floods the front room with natural light

A homey, well-lit Office or Den

Compact, efficient use of space

An efficient Kitchen with easy access to the Dining Room

A fireplaced Living Room with a sloping ceiling and a window wall

A Master Bedroom sporting a private Master Bath with a roomy walk-in closet

This home is designed with basement, slab and crawlspace foundation options

Main floor — 1,492 sq. ft.
Basement — 1,486 sq. ft.
Garage — 462 sq. ft.

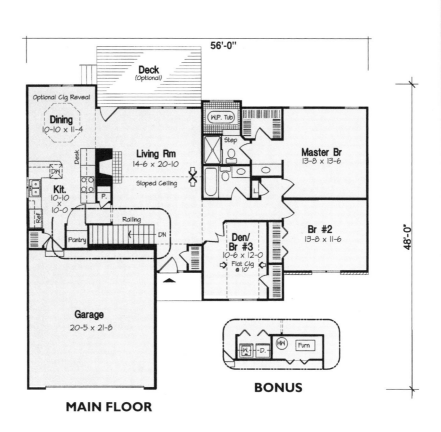

Cozy Farmhouse Ranch

■ *Total living area 1,372 sq. ft.* ■ *Price Code A* ■

SLAB/CRAWL SPACE OPTION

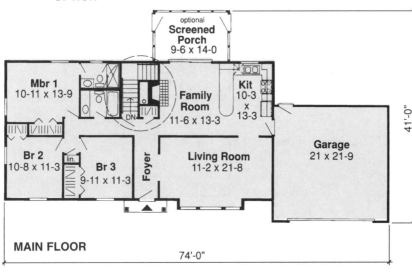

MAIN FLOOR

No. 34952

■ This plan features:

— Three bedrooms

— One full and one three-quarter baths

■ Traditional clapboard siding accented by a triple gable window and vertical siding

■ Central Foyer opens to spacious Living Room

■ U-shaped Kitchen with peninsula counter efficiently serves Family Room and Screened Porch

■ Convenient Family Room with an inviting fireplace and sliding glass door to Porch

■ This home is designed with basement, slab and crawlspace foundation options

Main floor — 1,372 sq. ft.
Porch — 150 sq. ft.
Garage — 484 sq. ft.

Total living area 1,367 sq. ft. ■ **Price Code A** ■

No. 99639

This plan features:

Three bedrooms

Two full bath

A Living Room with a high ceiling that slopes down to focus on the decorative fireplace

An efficient Kitchen that adjoins the Dining Room which views the front porch

A Dinette Area for informal eating in the Kitchen that comfortably seat six people

A Master Suite arranged with a large Dressing Area that has a walk-in closet plus two linear closets and space for a vanity

This home is designed with basement and slab foundation options

Main floor — 1,367 sq. ft.
Basement — 1,267 sq. ft.
Garage — 431 sq. ft.

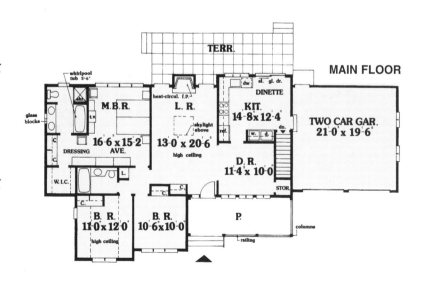

Compact and Quaint

■ Total living area 828 sq. ft. ■ Price Code A ■

No. 93422

■ **This Plan features:**

– Two bedrooms

– One full bath

■ Within its compact footprint, this classic Carpenter-style design provides all the elements of home

■ When entertaining, let the party flow from the Family Room onto the charming Covered Porch

■ Thanks to careful planning, every square inch of this home works hard

■ A large under-stairs storage area is convenient to the Kitchen

■ This home is designed with a crawlspace foundation

First floor – 660 sq. ft.
Second floor – 168 sq. ft.

FIRST FLOOR

28'

32'

Stoop

Br.#1
12x10

Kitchen
11/8x11

Dining

Porch
12x7/4

Family Room
15/4x12/7

Br.#2
11/8x11

SECOND FLOOR

Easy Living

■ Total living area 1,333 sq. ft. ■ Price Code A ■

No. 93453

■ **This plan features:**

– Three bedrooms

– Two full baths

■ The front Porch spans the width of the home

■ A fireplace warms the Family Room

■ The U-Shaped Kitchen has an island in the center

■ All the Bedrooms have ample closet space

■ The Carport has a connected Storage Space

■ This home is designed with slab and crawlspace foundation options

Main floor –1,333 sq. ft.

MAIN FLOOR

Storage
20 x 6   8' Clg

Carport
20 x 20
8' Clg

Master
15 x 13
9' Recessed Clg

10/6 x 8

Rear Porch
22 x 4

Dining
10 x 13
8' Clg

Kitchen
9/9 x 13

Family Room
17 x 14/7
9' Clg

B.R. #3
10 x 12
8' Clg

B.R. #2
10 x 11
8' Clg

Porch
40/6 x 6   8' Clg

WIDTH 55'-6"
DEPTH 64'-3"

Total living area 1,087 sq. ft. ■ Price Code A

No. 65093

This plan features:

- Two bedrooms

- One full baths

- A Foyer with coat closet and easy access to the Living Room, Kitchen and basement

- Two Bedrooms have large closets and share a full Bath

- A fully-eqquipped L-shaped Kitchen with a center work island

- A Living Room with double window treatments

- This home is designed with a basement foundation

- Main floor — 1,087 sq. ft.

MAIN FLOOR

Style and Convenience

■ *Total living area 1,373 sq. ft.* ■ *Price Code A* ■

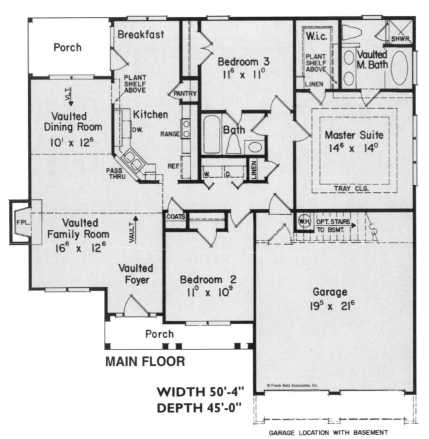

MAIN FLOOR

WIDTH 50'-4"
DEPTH 45'-0"

© Frank Betz Associates, Inc.

GARAGE LOCATION WITH BASEMENT

No. 98411

■ This plan features:

—Three bedrooms

—Two full baths

■ Large front windows, dormers and an old-fashioned Porch give pleasing style to the home

■ A vaulted ceiling tops the Foyer and the fireplaced Family Room

■ The vaulted Dining Room opens to a rear Porch

■ The efficient Kitchen enhanced a Pantry, plenty of counter space and a sunny Breakfast Room

■ A decorative tray ceiling, a five-piece, private Bath and a walk-in closet in the Master Suite

■ This home is designed with basement and crawlspace foundation options

Main floor — 1,373 sq. ft.
Basement — 1,386 sq. ft.

■ *Total living area 1,247 sq. ft.* ■ *Price Code A* ■

No. 96511

This plan features:

- Three bedrooms
- Two full baths
- The pretty front Porch opens into a large fireplaced Living Room
- The Dining Room offers access to a rear Porch
- The Kitchen features an angled serving bar which is open to the Dining Room
- The Master Suite includes a private Bath and walk-in closet
- Two additional Bedrooms include large closets
- This home is designed with slab and crawlspace foundation options

Main floor — 1,247 sq. ft.
Garage — 512 sq. ft.

MAIN FLOOR

WIDTH 43'-0"
DEPTH 60'-0"

Three-Bedroom Charmer

■ *Total living area 1,297 sq. ft.* ■ *Price Code A* ■

WIDTH 42'-0"
DEPTH 43'-0"

REAR ELEVATION

No. 97476

■ This plan features:

—Three bedrooms

—Two full, and one half baths

■ Covered Porch leads to small Foyer with coat closet

■ The Living Room includes a fireplace and front bay window

■ The efficient U-shaped Kitchen opens to the Dining Room, which has access to a rear Porch

■ The Master Bedroom features a sloped ceiling and includes a private Bath and large closet

■ This home is designed with a basement foundation

■ Alternate foundation options available at an additional charge. Please call 1-800-235-5700 for more information.

First floor — 603 sq. ft.
Second floor — 694 sq. ft.
Garage — 478 sq. ft.
Bonus — 354 sq. ft.

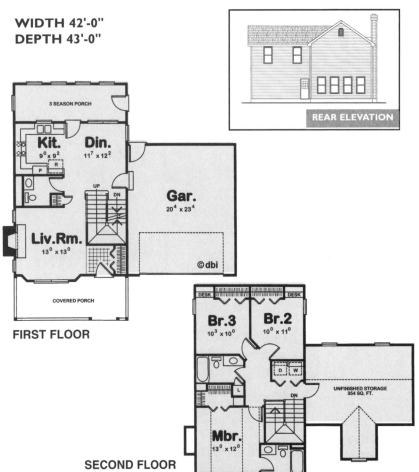

3 SEASON PORCH

Kit.
9⁰ x 9²

Din.
11⁷ x 12²

Gar.
20⁴ x 23⁴

UP
DN

©dbi

Liv.Rm.
13⁰ x 13⁰

COVERED PORCH

FIRST FLOOR

DESK **DESK**

Br.3
10³ x 10⁰

Br.2
10⁰ x 11⁰

D **W**

UNFINISHED STORAGE
354 SQ. FT.

DN

Mbr.
13⁰ x 12⁰

SECOND FLOOR

A Nest for Empty-Nesters

No. 90934

This plan features:

Two bedrooms

One full bath

This compact home features an economical design while remaining architecturally interesting

The covered Sun Deck adds outdoor living space

The Mudroom/Laundry Area inside the side door traps dirt before it can enter the house

An open layout between the Living Room with fireplace, Dining Room and Kitchen features large windows and interesting angles to define the spaces

This home is designed with a slab foundation

Main floor — 884 sq. ft.

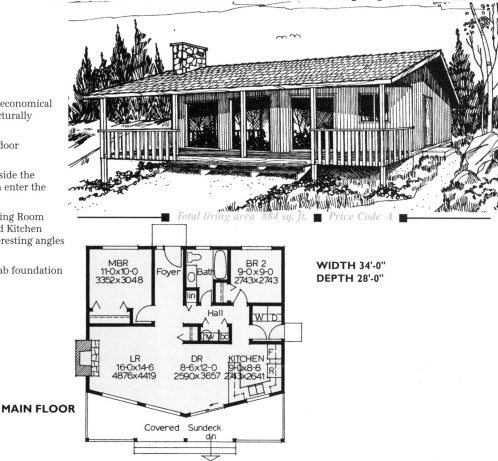

■ *Total living area 884 sq. ft.* ■ *Price Code A* ■

WIDTH 34'-0"
DEPTH 28'-0"

MAIN FLOOR

Simply Cozy

No. 98912

This plan features:

Three bedrooms

Two full baths

Quaint front Porch shelters Entry into the large Living Area, which features a massive fireplace and built-ins below a vaulted ceiling

The formal Dining Room is accented by a bay of glass with Sun Deck access

An efficient galley Kitchen at the rear of the home includes a Breakfast Area, Laundry closet and outdoor access

Secluded Master Bedroom offers a roomy walk-in closet and plush Bath with two vanities and a garden window tub

Two additional Bedrooms with ample closets share a full Bath with a skylight

This home is designed with a basement foundation

Main floor — 1,345 sq. ft.
Basement — 1,345 sq. ft.

■ *Total living area 1,345 sq. ft.* ■ *Price Code A* ■

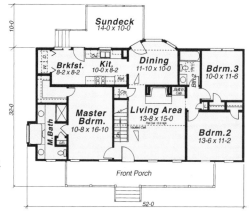

MAIN FLOOR

Soaring Ceilings Add Drama

■ *Total living area 1,387 sq. ft.* ■ *Price Code A* ■

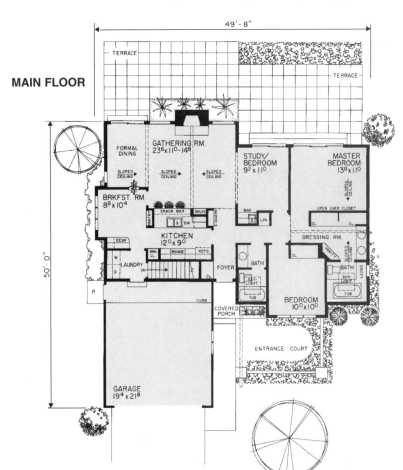

MAIN FLOOR

No. 90288

■ **This plan features:**

— Two bedrooms (with optional third bedroom)

— Two full baths

■ A sunny Master Suite with a sloping ceiling, private Terrace entry and luxurious garden Bath with an adjoining Dressing Room

■ A Gathering Room with fireplace a Study and the formal Dining Room, flow together for a more spacious feeling

■ A convenient pass-through that adds to the efficiency of the galley Kitchen and adjoining Breakfast Room

■ This home is designed with a basement foundation

Main floor — 1,387 sq. ft.
Garage — 440 sq. ft.

■ *Total living area 1,388 sq. ft.* ■ *Price Code A* ■

No. 93279

This plan features:

Three bedrooms

Two full baths

The Living Area, the Kitchen and the Dining Area form a great space around a pass-through fireplace

The Master Suite includes a walk-in closet, a double vanity and a separate shower and tub Bath

Two additional Bedrooms share a full Bath in the hall

The Patio can be accessed from the Dining Area

This home is designed with crawlspace and slab foundation options

Main floor — 1,388 sq. ft.
Garage — 400 sq. ft.

Patio
12-0 x 10-0

48-0

Dining
10-0 x 11-0

Living Area
13-8 x 17-6

Master Bdrm.
13-6 x 12-2

Brkfst. Bar

Pass Thru Fire Place

Vaulted Ceil.

Opt. Plant Shelf Above

Dw.

Kitchen
10-0 x 12-6

Ref. | Pant.

Foyer

W/H

Fum.

M. Bath

W. D.

Clo.

Stor.

Bth.2

Lnd.

Lin.

Lin.

46-0

Bdrm.3
10-0 x 10-0

Bdrm.2
11-0 x 10-8

Double Garage
19-4 x 19-4

MAIN FLOOR

© 1988, Jannis Vann & Associates, Inc.

Expansive Living Room

Total living area 1,346 sq. ft. ■ Price Code A

MAIN FLOOR

No. 98434

■ **This plan features:**

—Three bedrooms

—Two full baths

■ Vaulted ceiling crowns spacious Living Room highlighted by a fireplace

■ Built-in Pantry and direct access from the Garage adding to the conveniences of the Kitchen

■ Walk-in closet and a private five-piece Bat topped by a vaulted ceiling in the Master Bedroom Suite

■ Proximity to the full Bath in the hall from the secondary Bedrooms

■ This home is designed with basement, sla and crawlspace foundation options

Main floor — 1,346 sq. ft.
Garage — 395 sq. ft.

Cathedral Ceiling

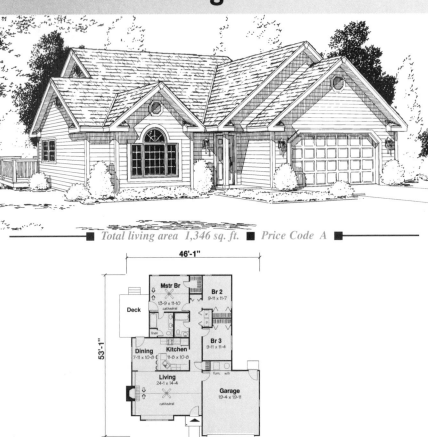

Total living area 1,346 sq. ft. ■ Price Code A

MAIN FLOOR

No. 24402

■ **This plan features:**

— Three bedrooms

— Two full baths

■ A spacious Living Room with a cathedral ceiling and elegant fireplace

■ A Dining Room that adjoins both the Livir Room and the Kitchen

■ An efficient Kitchen with double sinks, ample cabinet space and peninsula counte that doubles as an eating bar

■ A convenient hallway Laundry center

■ A Master Suite with a cathedral ceiling an a private Master Bath

■ This home is designed with slab and crawlspace foundation options

Main floor — 1,346 sq. ft.
Garage — 449 sq. ft.

Total living area 1,396 sq. ft. ■ *Price Code A*

No. 90983

■ **This plan features:**

- Three bedrooms

- One full and one three-quarter baths

■ An open floor plan shared by the sunken Living Room, Dining and Kitchen Areas

■ An unfinished daylight Basement could provide future Bedrooms, a Bathroom and Laundry facilities

■ A Master Suite with a big walk-in closet and a private Bath featuring a double shower

■ This home is designed with a basement foundation

Main floor — 1,396 sq. ft.
Basement — 1,396 sq. ft.
Garage — 389 sq. ft.

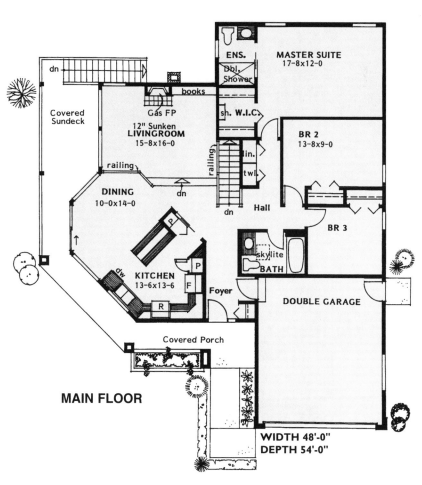

Country Charm

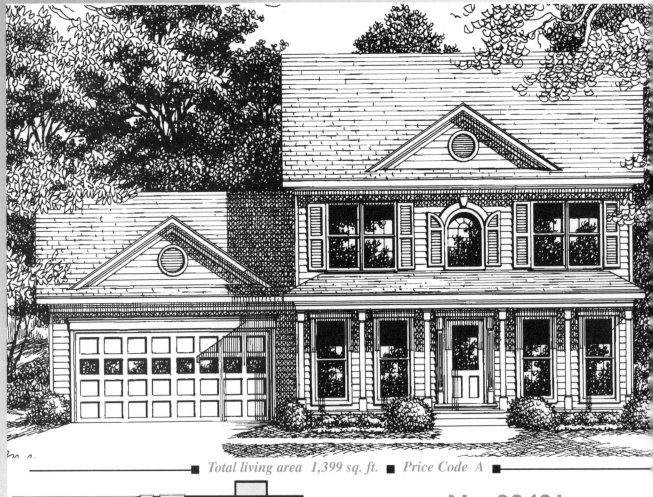

■ *Total living area 1,399 sq. ft.* ■ *Price Code A* ■

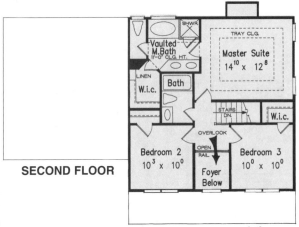

SECOND FLOOR

TRAY CLG.

Vaulted M.Bath
11'-0" CLG. HT.

SHWR

Master Suite
14¹⁰ x 12⁸

LINEN

W.i.c.

Bath

STAIRS DN.

W.i.c.

OVERLOOK

Bedroom 2
10³ x 10⁰

OPEN RAIL

Bedroom 3
10⁰ x 10⁰

Foyer Below

47'-0"

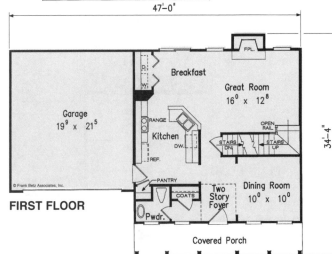

FIRST FLOOR

Garage
19⁹ x 21⁵

Breakfast

FPL.

Great Room
16⁰ x 12⁸

RANGE

Kitchen

DW.

REF.

OPEN RAIL

STAIRS DN

STAIRS UP

34'-4"

PANTRY

COATS

Two Story Foyer

Dining Room
10⁰ x 10⁰

Pwdr.

© Frank Betz Associates, Inc.

Covered Porch

No. 98481

■ **This plan features:**

— Three bedrooms

— Two full and one half baths

■ The two-story Foyer has a convenient coat closet and Powder Room

■ The angled Kitchen has views of the fireplace in the Great Room

■ Sliding doors access the backyard from the Breakfast Area

■ The Master Bedroom is crowned with a tray ceiling and has a vaulted Bath

■ Two additional Bedrooms share a full Bath

■ This home is designed with basement and crawlspace foundation options

First Floor — 729 sq. ft.
Second Floor — 670 sq. ft.
Basement — 676 sq. ft.
Garage — 440 sq. ft.

■ *Total living area 1,359 sq. ft.* ■ *Price Code A* ■

No. 20156

■ This plan features:

- Three bedrooms

- Two full baths

■ The Living Room features ten-foot ceilings and a fireplace

■ Glass windows and doors in the Dining Room overlook the Deck

■ An efficient, compact Kitchen includes a built-in Pantry and peninsula counter

■ The Master Suite features a window seat, a private Bath and a walk-in closet

■ Two additional Bedrooms share a full Bath

■ This home is designed with basement, slab and crawlspace foundation options

Main floor — 1,359 sq. ft.
Basement — 1,359 sq. ft.
Garage — 501 sq. ft.

Three Bedroom A-Frame

Total living area 1,011 sq. ft. ■ Price Code A ■

No. 90995

■ This plan features:

— Three bedrooms

— One three-quarter bath

■ A wraparound Deck provides panoramic views and access to the home through French doors

■ The spacious Living/Dining Area features a glass wall and a vaulted ceiling and opens to the Kitchen

■ A well-equipped Kitchen with a serving island opens to the Dining and Living Area

■ A Mudroom entrance includes a large closet, a Laundry Area and a built-in bench

■ Large Master Bedroom with French doors to private Sun Deck

■ This home is designed with a basement foundation

First floor — 768 sq. ft.
Second floor — 243 sq. ft.

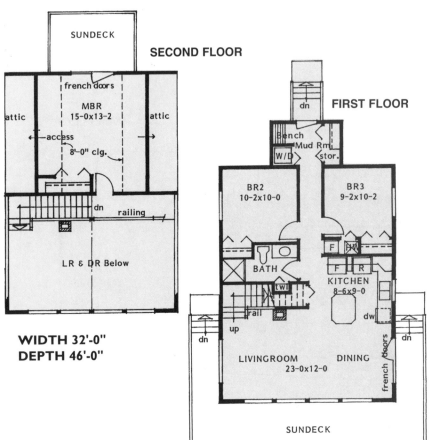

SUNDECK

SECOND FLOOR

french doors

attic

MBR
15-0x13-2

attic

access

8'-0" clg.

dn railing

LR & DR Below

WIDTH 32'-0"
DEPTH 46'-0"

dn

FIRST FLOOR

Bench
Mud Rm
W/D
stor.

BR2
10-2x10-0

BR3
9-2x10-2

F W

BATH

F R

KITCHEN
8-6x9-0

dw

rail

up

dn

french doors

dn

LIVINGROOM
23-0x12-0

DINING

SUNDECK

Lattice Trim Adds Nostalgic Charm

■ *Total living area 1,359 sq. ft.* ■ *Price Code A* ■

No. 99315

This plan features:

Three bedrooms

One full, one three quarter and one half baths

Wood and fieldstone exterior

A vaulted Living Room with balcony view and floor-to-ceiling corner window treatment

A Master Suite with private Bath and Dressing Area

A two-car Garage with access to Kitchen

This home is designed with a basement foundation

First floor — 668 sq. ft.
Second floor — 691 sq. ft.
Garage — 459 sq. ft.

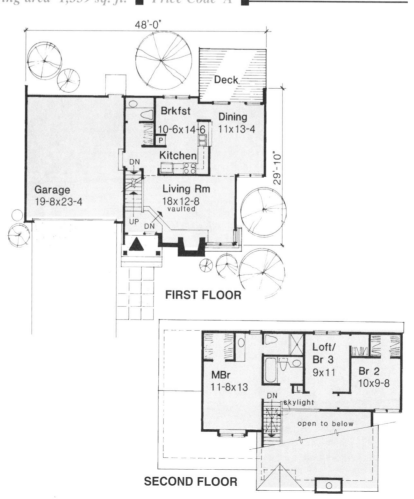

FIRST FLOOR

SECOND FLOOR

Packed with Cottage Charm

Total living area 894 sq. ft. ■ Price Code A

MAIN FLOOR

- GARAGE 19'4 x 21'4
- KIT 9'8 x 10'6
- DIN 9' x 10'
- MBR 11'6 x 14'
- LIV RM 13'6 x 15'4
- BATH
- BR 2 9'2 x 11'
- Foyer
- Covered Entry

No. 94126

■ **This plan features:**

— Two bedrooms

— One full bath

■ Classic clapboard siding adds to the Country charm

■ Compact and efficient, the Kitchen is packed with everything you need

■ The small, elegant Porch offers a quiet place to sit and enjoy your world

■ A large Master Bedroom Suite makes this home complete

■ This home is designed with a basement foundation

Main floor — 894 sq. ft.
Basement — 894 sq. ft.
Garage — 440 sq. ft.

WIDTH 51'-8"
DEPTH 32'-0"

Versatile Chalet

Total living area 1,360 sq. ft. ■ Price Code A

FIRST FLOOR

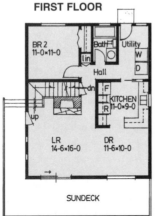

- BR 2 11'-0 x 11'-0
- Bath
- Utility
- W D
- Hall
- KITCHEN 11'-0 x 9'-0
- LR 14'-6 x 16'-0
- DR 11'-6 x 10'-0
- SUNDECK

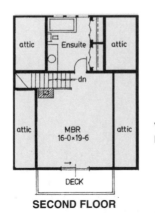

SECOND FLOOR

- attic
- Ensuite
- attic
- attic
- MBR 16'-0 x 19'-6
- attic
- DECK

No. 90847

■ **This plan features:**

— Two bedrooms

— Two full baths

■ A Sun Deck entry into a spacious Living Room/Dining Room with a fieldstone fireplace, a large window and a sliding glass door

■ A well-appointed Kitchen with extended counter space and easy access to the Dining Room and the Utility Area

■ A first floor Bedroom adjoins a full Bath

■ A spacious Master Bedroom, with a private Deck, a suite Bath and plenty of storage

■ This home is designed with a basement foundation

First floor — 864 sq. ft.
Second floor — 496 sq. ft.
Basement — 864 sq. ft.

WIDTH 27'-0"
DEPTH 32'-0"

■ *Total living area 1,401 sq. ft.* ■ *Price Code A* ■

No. 98487

■ **This plan features:**

- Three bedrooms

- Two full baths

■ The Dining Room, Family Room, and Breakfast Nook all have vaulted ceilings

■ The Family Room has a rear wall fireplace with a French door to one side

■ With an angle at one end a new twist is placed on this galley-style Kitchen

■ The Master Suite has a tray ceiling as well as a private Bath

■ This home is designed with a basement foundation

Main floor — 1,349 sq. ft.
Lower level — 871 sq. ft.
Stairs — 52 sq. ft.
Garage — 478 sq. ft.

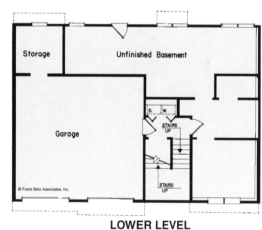

LOWER LEVEL

MAIN FLOOR

A Lovely Small Home

■ *Total living area 1,402 sq. ft.* ■ *Price Code A* ■

No. 93026

■ This plan features:

— Three bedrooms

— Two full baths

■ The fireplaced Living Room features a ten-foot ceiling and access to a rear Porch

■ The Dining Room has a distinctiv bay window

■ The Breakfast Room, located off the Kitchen, includes a Laundry closet

■ A Master Suite with ten-foot slope ceiling has his and her vanities, a combination whirlpool tub and shower plus a huge walk-in closet

■ This home is designed with slab and crawlspace foundation options

Main floor — 1,402 sq. ft.
Garage — 437 sq. ft.

WIDTH 59-10

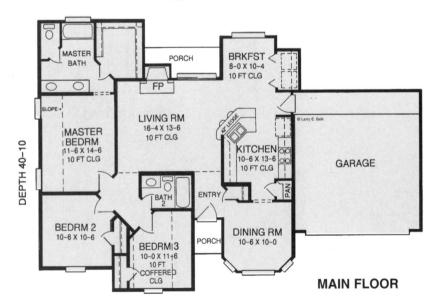

MAIN FLOOR

Great Starter or Empty-Nester

■ *Total living area 1,420 sq. ft.* ■ *Price Code A* ■

No. 91545

■ This plan features:

- Two bedrooms

- Two full baths

■ A formal Living Room or a cozy Den, the front room to the right of the Entry adapts to your needs

■ The efficient Kitchen offers ample counter and storage space

■ The formal Dining Room opens to a rear Patio

■ A corner fireplace highlights the Great Room

■ A walk-in closet and a private double vanity Bath in the Master Suite

■ An additional Bedroom that easily accesses a full Bath

■ This home is designed with a crawlspace foundation

Main floor — 1,420 sq. ft.

This plan cannot be built in Clark County, WA.

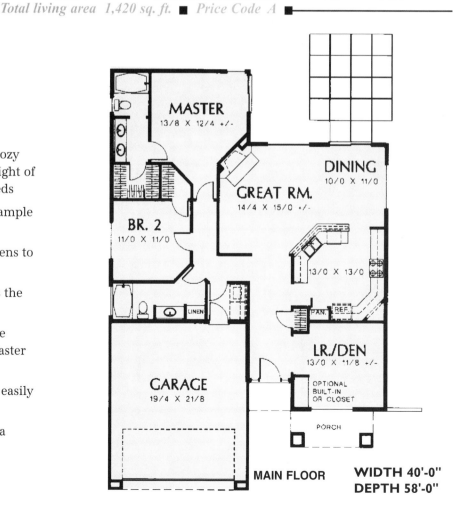

MASTER
13/8 X 12/4 +/-

DINING
10/0 X 11/0

GREAT RM.
14/4 X 15/0 +/-

BR. 2
11/0 X 11/0

13/0 X 13/0

LINEN

PAN. REF.

LR./DEN
13/0 X 11/8 +/-

GARAGE
19/4 X 21/8

OPTIONAL BUILT-IN OR CLOSET

PORCH

MAIN FLOOR   WIDTH 40'-0"
              DEPTH 58'-0"

Captivating Sun-Catcher

■ *Total living area 1,421 sq. ft.* ■ *Price Code A* ■

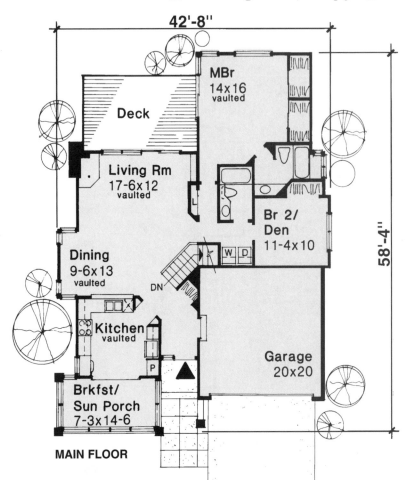

42'-8"

Deck

MBr
14 x 16
vaulted

Living Rm
17-6 x 12
vaulted

Dining
9-6 x 13
vaulted

Br 2/
Den
11-4 x 10

W D

DN

Kitchen
vaulted

P

Garage
20 x 20

Brkfst/
Sun Porch
7-3 x 14-6

58'-4"

MAIN FLOOR

No. 99303

■ **This plan features:**

— Two bedrooms

— Two full baths

■ A glass-walled Breakfast Room adjoining the vaulted ceiling Kitchen

■ A fireplaced, vaulted ceiling Living Room that flows from the Dining Room

■ A greenhouse window over the tub in the luxurious Master Bath

■ Two walk-in closets and glass sliders in the Master Bedroom

■ This home is designed with a basement foundation

Main Floor — 1,421 sq. ft.
Garage — 400 sq. ft.

No. 97600

This plan features:

Three bedrooms

Two full baths

The stucco exterior won't require a fresh coat of paint for years to come

The Laundry Room is conveniently located near the Master Bedroom

The Foyer opens to the Family Room, which features a vaulted ceiling and fireplace

This home is designed with basement and crawlspace foundation options

ain floor — 1,361 sq. ft.
asement — 1,359 sq. ft.
arage — 530 sq. ft.

Total living area 1,361 sq. ft. ■ *Price Code A*

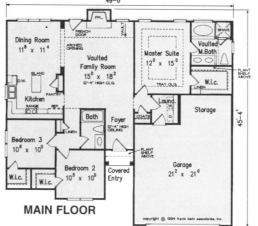

MAIN FLOOR

OPT. BASEMENT STAIR LOCATION

This plan.

No. 90433

This plan features:

Two bedrooms

One full and one half baths

A Screened Porch for enjoyment of your outdoor surroundings

A combination Living and Dining Area with cozy fireplace for added warmth

An efficiently laid out Kitchen with a built-in Pantry

Two large Bedrooms located at the rear of the home

This home is designed with slab and crawlspace foundation options

ain floor — 928 sq. ft.
reened porch — 230 sq. ft.
orage — 14 sq. ft.

Total living area 928 sq. ft. ■ *Price Code A*

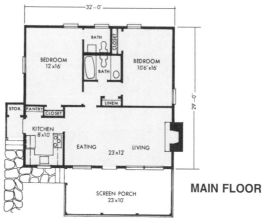

MAIN FLOOR

Comfort and Style

■ *Total living area 1,423 sq. ft.* ■ *Price Code A* ■

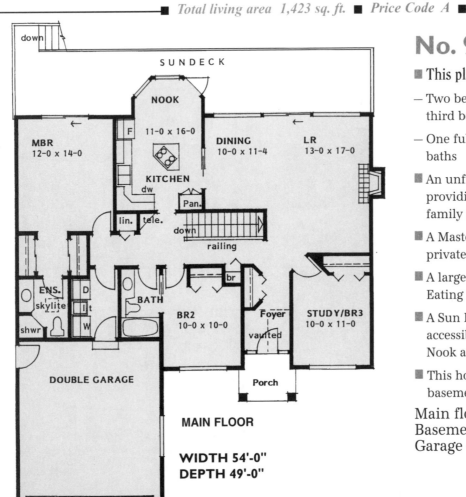

MAIN FLOOR

WIDTH 54'-0"
DEPTH 49'-0"

No. 90990

■ **This plan features:**

— Two bedrooms with possible third bedroom/den

— One full and one three-quarter baths

■ An unfinished daylight basement providing possible space for family recreation

■ A Master Suite complete with private Bath and skylight

■ A large Kitchen including an Eating Nook

■ A Sun Deck that is easily accessible from the Master Suite, Nook and the Living/Dining Area

■ This home is designed with a basement foundation

Main floor — 1,423 sq. ft.
Basement — 1,423 sq. ft.
Garage — 399 sq. ft.

Total living area 1,425 sq. ft. ■ **Price Code A** ■

No. 92056

■ This plan features:

- Three bedrooms

- One full and one three-quarter bath

■ Outstanding Living Room with a cathedral ceiling and boxed window

■ Combination Kitchen and Dining Room with a raised peninsula counter/snack bar

■ Wood rear Deck expanding living space to the outdoors

■ Secluded Master Bedroom Suite with private three-quarter Bath

■ Two additional Bedrooms with ample closet space

■ This home is designed with a basement foundation

Main floor — 1,425 sq. ft.
Basement — 1,425 sq. ft.

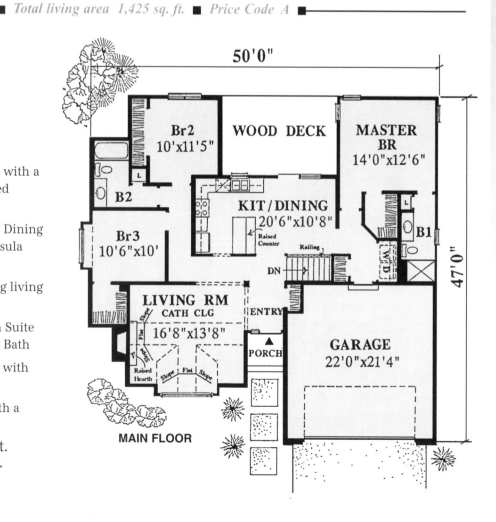

MAIN FLOOR

Open Layout

Total living area 1,363 sq. ft. ■ Price Code A

MAIN FLOOR

47'-0"

35'-4"

© Frank Betz Associates, Inc

FPL.

FRENCH DOOR

Vaulted Breakfast

Vaulted M. Bath

SHWR

TRAY CLG.

W.i.c.

Master Suite
12⁰ x 15⁸

Vaulted Great Room
13⁹ x 19⁵

Kitchen
RANGE

PASS THRU

D.W. REF

PAN.

LINEN
PLANT SHELF ABOVE

W.i.c.

DRIVE UNDER

Bath

Vaulted Foyer

D. W. COATS

Bedroom 2
10⁰ x 10⁰

LIN

Bedroom 3
11⁸ x 10⁰

Covered Porch

Dining Room
11' x 10⁰

No. 97224

■ **This plan features:**

— Three bedrooms

— Two full baths

■ Open layout with vaulted ceilings in Foyer, Great Room and Breakfast Area

■ Kitchen with pass-through and Pantry efficiently serves bright Breakfast Area, Great Room and formal Dining Room

■ Luxurious Master Suite offers a tray ceiling, two walk-in closets and a double vanity Bath with vaulted ceiling

■ Two secondary Bedrooms share a full Bath and Laundry and closets

■ This home is designed with a basement foundation

Main floor — 1,363 sq. ft.
Basement — 715 sq. ft.
Garage — 677 sq. ft.

Luxury Style on a Small Budget

Total living area 988 sq. ft. ■ Price Code A

No. 24302

■ **This plan features:**

— Three bedrooms

— Two full baths

■ Multiple gables, arched windows and a unique exterior setting this delightful Ranch apart in any neighborhood

■ Living and Dining Rooms flowing together to create a very roomy feeling

■ Sliding doors leading from the Dining Room to a covered Patio

■ A Master Bedroom with a private Bath

■ This home is designed with basement and crawlspace foundation options

Main floor — 988 sq. ft.
Basement — 988 sq. ft.
Garage — 280 sq. ft

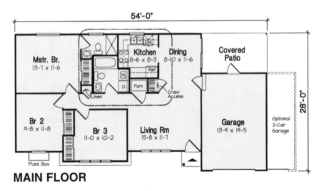

54'-0"

28'-0"

Mstr. Br.
13-7 x 11-6

Kitchen
8-6 x 8-3

Dining
8-10 x 11-6

Covered Patio

Linen

Crawl Access

Furn

Garage
13-4 x 14-5

Optional 2-Car Garage

Br 2
9-8 x 11-8

Br 3
11-0 x 10-2

Living Rm
15-8 x 11-7

Plant Box

MAIN FLOOR

Kitchen
8-6 x 8-3

Ref.

Flue

DN

OPTIONAL BASEMENT PLAN

■ *Total living area 1,312 sq. ft.* ■ *Price Code A* ■

No. 24700

This plan features:

Three bedrooms

Two full baths

The long, elegant Living Room features a beamed ceiling and fireplace

The Dining Room offers access to a rear Deck

The open Kitchen contains a convenient serving and eating counter

The generous Master Suite features a bump-out window, plenty of closet space and a private Bath

This home is designed with basement, slab and crawlspace foundation options

Main floor — 1,312 sq. ft.
Basement — 1,293 sq. ft.
Garage — 459 sq. ft.
Porch — 84 sq. ft.

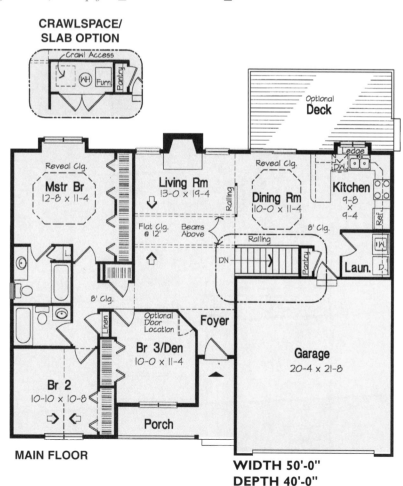

CRAWLSPACE/
SLAB OPTION

MAIN FLOOR

WIDTH 50'-0"
DEPTH 40'-0"

Comfy and Cozy

■ *Total living area 1,311 sq. ft.* ■ *Price Code A* ■

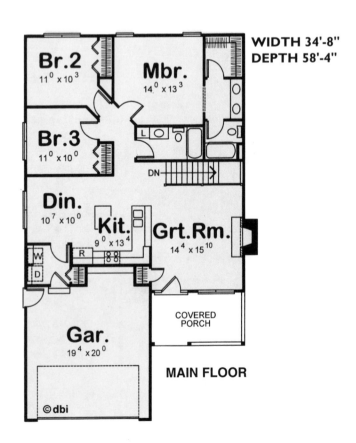

Br.2
11⁰ x 10³

Mbr.
14⁰ x 13³

Br.3
11⁰ x 10⁰

DN

Din.
10⁷ x 10⁰

Kit.
9⁰ x 13⁴

Grt.Rm.
14⁴ x 15¹⁰

W
D
R

Gar.
19⁴ x 20⁰

COVERED
PORCH

MAIN FLOOR

©dbi

WIDTH 34'-8"
DEPTH 58'-4"

No. 68096

■ This plan features:

— Three or four bedrooms

— Two full baths

■ Covered Porch opens into fireplaced Great Room

■ The L-Shaped Kitchen features a center island and is open to the Dining Room

■ A Laundry/Mudroom buffers the house from the Garage and features a coat closet

■ This home is designed with slab and crawlspace foundation options

■ Alternate foundation options available at an additional charge. Please call 1-800-235-5700 for additional information.

Main floor — 1,868 sq. ft.
Garage — 439 sq. ft.

■ *Total living area 1,429 sq. ft.* ■ *Price Code A* ■

No. 98415

This plan features:

- Three bedrooms

- Two full baths

- A tray ceiling gives a decorative touch to the Master Bedroom

- A full Bath is located between the secondary Bedrooms

- A corner fireplace and a vaulted ceiling highlight the heart of the home, the Family Room

- A wetbar, serving bar to the Family Room, and a built-in Pantry add convenience to the Kitchen

- This home is designed with basement, slab and crawlspace foundation options

Main floor — 1,429 sq. ft.
Basement — 1,472 sq. ft.
Garage — 438 sq. ft.

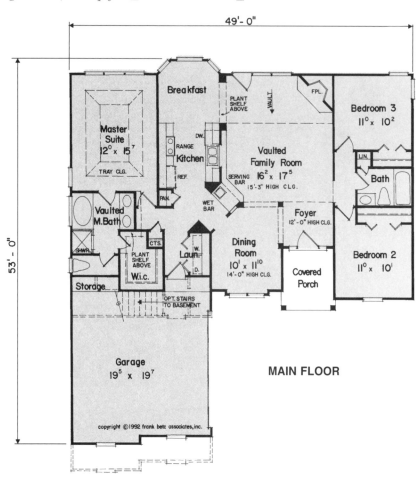

MAIN FLOOR

Small Yet Stylish

■ *Total living area 1,431 sq. ft.* ■ *Price Code A* ■

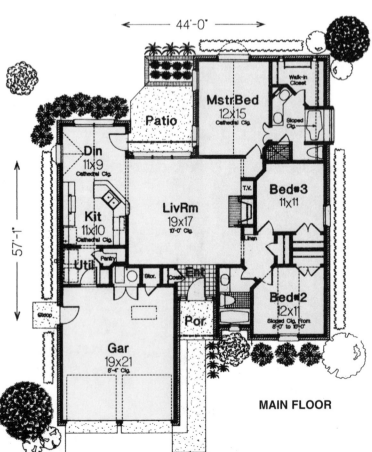

MAIN FLOOR

No. 98549

■ This plan features:

— Three bedrooms

— Two full baths

■ The Living Room is topped by a ten-foot ceiling and highlighted by a fireplace and a built-in entertainment center

■ The Kitchen and the Dining Room are open to each other and topped by cathedral ceilings

■ A walk-in Pantry is located in the Utility Room for added storage

■ A walk-in closet and a five-piece Bath enhance the Master Suite

■ This home is designed with a slab foundation

Main floor — 1,431 sq. ft.
Garage — 410 sq. ft.

Arches and Angles

No. 99321

This plan features:

Three bedrooms

Two full baths

A half-round transom window with quarter-round detail and a vaulted ceiling in the Great Room

A cozy corner fireplace which brings warmth to the Great Room

A vaulted ceiling in the Kitchen/Breakfast Area

A Master Suite with a walk-in closet and a private Master Bath

Two additional Bedrooms which share a full Bath

This home is designed with a basement foundation

Main floor — 1,368 sq. ft.

Basement — 1,368 sq. ft.

Garage — 412 sq. ft.

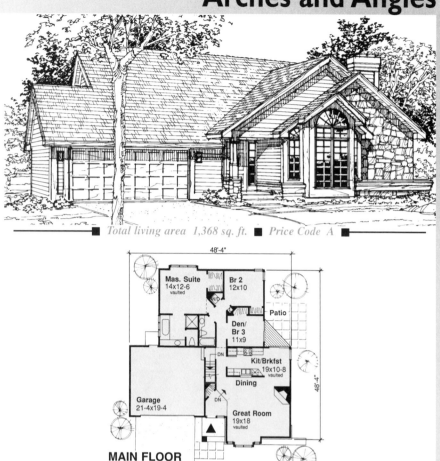

Total living area 1,368 sq. ft. ■ *Price Code A*

MAIN FLOOR

Contemporary Styling

No. 94311

This plan features:

Three bedrooms

One full and one three-quarter baths

Perfect plan for a mountainside or lot with a view

Front Deck gives far-reaching view of surrounding vistas

Cozy fireplace in the Living Room, illuminated by sunlight during the day through wall of windows

Galley Kitchen with access to the rear Deck

Two first floor Bedrooms sharing a full Bath

Loft overlooking the Living Room

Master Bedroom Suite with private Deck, a private Master Bath and a walk-in closet

This home is designed with a crawlspace foundation

First floor — 810 sq. ft.

Second floor — 560 sq. ft.

Total living area 1,370 sq. ft. ■ *Price Code A*

FIRST FLOOR

SECOND FLOOR

Striking Style

■ *Total living area 1,432 sq. ft.* ■ *Price Code A* ■

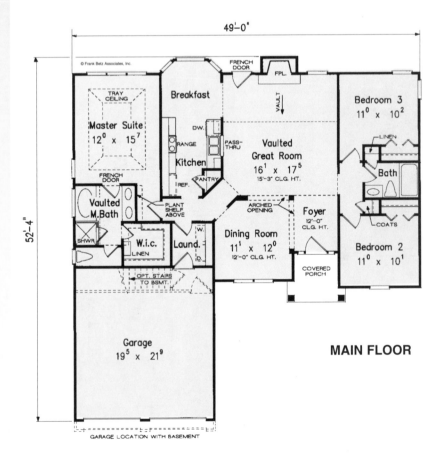

MAIN FLOOR

No. 97274

■ This plan features:

— Three bedrooms

— Two full baths

■ Windows and exterior detailing create a striking elevation

■ From the covered front Porch enter the Foyer which has a twelve-foot ceiling

■ The Dining Room has a front window wall and arched opening

■ The secondary Bedrooms are located in their own wing and share a Bath

■ The Master Suite features a tray ceiling, a walk-in closet and a private Bath

■ This home is designed with basement and crawlspace foundation options

Main floor — 1,432 sq. ft.
Basement — 1,454 sq. ft.
Garage — 440 sq. ft.

Perfect for a Woodland Setting

No. 35007

This plan features:

Two bedrooms

One full bath

A Living Room and Dining Room/Kitchen located to the front of the house

A sloped ceiling helping to create the cozy feeling of the home

A built-in entertainment center in the Living Room adding convenience

An L-shaped Kitchen that includes a double sink and Dining Area

A full Bath easily accessible from either Bedroom

A Loft and Balcony that overlooks the Living Room and the Dining Area

Storage on either side of the Loft

This home is designed with basement, slab and crawlspace foundation options

First floor — 763 sq. ft.

Second floor — 264 sq. ft.

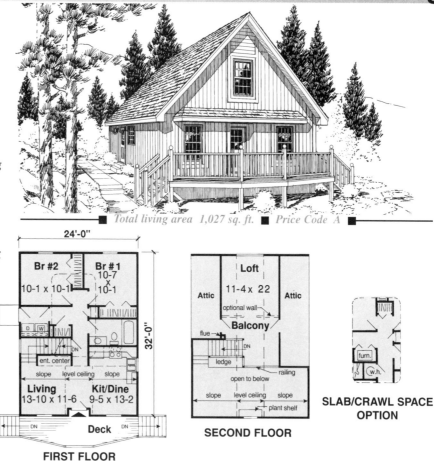

■ *Total living area 1,027 sq. ft.* ■ *Price Code A* ■

FIRST FLOOR

24'-0"

Br #2
10-1 x 10-1

Br #1
10-7 x 10-1

32'-0"

ent. center

Living
13-10 x 11-6

Kit/Dine
9-5 x 13-2

Deck

SECOND FLOOR

Loft
11-4 x 22

Attic

Attic

optional wall

Balcony

flue

ledge

railing

open to below

slope   level ceiling   slope

plant shelf

SLAB/CRAWL SPACE OPTION

furn.

w.h.

Private Master Suite

No. 92523

This plan features:

Three bedrooms

Two full baths

A spacious Den enhanced by a vaulted ceiling and fireplace

A well-equipped Kitchen with windowed double sink

A secluded Master Suite with decorative ceiling, private Master Bath and walk-in closet

Two additional Bedrooms sharing full Bath

This home is designed with slab and crawlspace foundation options

Main floor — 1,293 sq. ft.

Garage — 433 sq. ft.

■ *Total living area 1,293 sq. ft.* ■ *Price Code A* ■

MAIN FLOOR

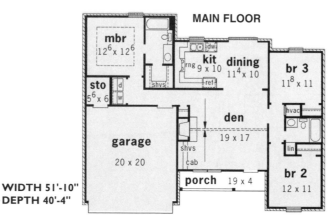

mbr
12⁶ x 12⁶

sto
5⁶ x 6

kit
9 x 10

dining
11⁴ x 10

br 3
11⁸ x 11

garage
20 x 20

den
19 x 17

porch
19 x 4

br 2
12 x 11

WIDTH 51'-10"
DEPTH 40'-4"

Delightful Doll House

■ **This plan features:**

– Three bedrooms

– Two full baths

■ A sloped ceiling in the Living Room which also has a focal point fireplace

■ An efficient Kitchen with a peninsula counter and a built-in Pantry

■ A decorative ceiling and sliding glass door to the deck in the Dining Room

■ A Master Suite with a decorative ceiling, ample closet space and a private full Bath

■ Two additional Bedrooms that share a full Bath

■ This home is designed with basement, slab and crawlspace foundation options

Main floor — 1,307 sq. ft.
Basement — 1,298 sq. ft.
Garage — 462 sq. ft.

■ Total living area 1,307 sq. ft. ■ Price Code A ■

MAIN FLOOR

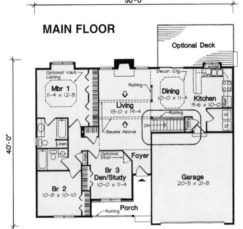

SLAB/CRAWLSPACE OPTION

Contemporary Simplicity

■ **This plan features:**

– Two bedrooms

– One full and one three-quarter baths

■ A tile Entrance leading into a two-story, beamed Living Room with a circular, center fireplace

■ An efficient, U-shaped Kitchen, with plenty of counter and storage space opens into the Dining Area with sliding glass doors to an optional Deck

■ Two Bedrooms, one with a private shower, provide ample closet space

■ A second floor Loft overlooking the Living Area

■ This home is designed with a crawlspace foundation

Main floor — 866 sq. ft.
Loft — 172 sq. ft.

■ Total living area 1,038 sq. ft. ■ Price Code A ■

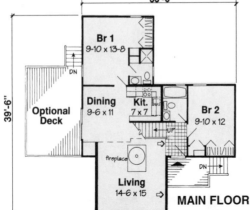

MAIN FLOOR

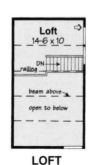

LOFT

Charming Country Home

Total living area 1,434 sq. ft. ■ Price Code A

No. 24711

This plan features:

Three bedrooms

Two full baths

Cozy fireplace below a vaulted ceiling and dormer window in Living Room

Country Kitchen with a peninsula counter/snack bar, built-in Pantry and access to Laundry and Screened Areaway and Garage beyond

Two first floor Bedrooms share a full Bath and Laundry

Private second floor Master Suite offers a dormer window, walk-in closet and private Bath

This home is designed with basement, slab and crawlspace foundation options

First floor — 1,018 sq. ft.
Second floor — 416 sq. ft.
Basement — 1,008 sq. ft.
Garage — 624 sq. ft.

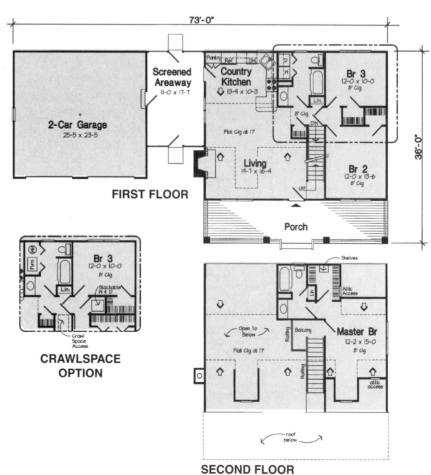

Covered Porch Shelters Entry

■ *Total living area 1,436 sq. ft.* ■ *Price Code A* ■

Bedroom 2
10² x 10⁰

Bedroom 3
10² x 10⁰

LINEN

RADIUS WDW

Vaulted M.Bath

SHOWER

Bath

LINEN

STAIRS DN.

Optional Bonus Room
19⁸ x 12⁵

Master Suite
13⁹ x 12⁰

W.i.c.

FIRST FLOOR

← 45'- 10" →

FRENCH DOOR

Breakfast

Dining Room
10³ x 10⁰

D.W.

Kitchen

RANGE

REF.

PASSTHRU

PANTRY

Garage
19⁵ x 23⁵

35'- 6"

Family Room
13⁹ x 18⁸

FPL.

Pdr.

STAIRS DN.

COATS

Foyer

STAIRS UP

SECOND FLOOR

© Frank Betz Associates, Inc.

Porch

No. 98422

■ **This plan features:**

— Three bedrooms

— Two full and one half baths

■ An easy flow into the Dining Room enhances the interaction of the Living Spaces on the first floor

■ Breakfast Room which has a French door that accesses the rear yard

■ Decorative ceiling treatment highlights the Master Bedroom while a vaulted ceiling tops the Master Bath

■ This home is designed with basement and crawlspace foundation options

First floor — 719 sq. ft.
Second floor — 717 sq. ft.
Bonus room — 290 sq. ft.
Basement — 719 sq. ft.
Garage — 480 sq. ft.

■ *Total living area 1,438 sq. ft.* ■ *Price Code A* ■

No. 96509

This plan features:

- Three bedrooms

- Two full baths

- Quaint front Porch is perfect for sitting and relaxing

- Great Room opening into Dining Area and Kitchen

- Corner Deck in rear of home accessed from Kitchen and Master Suite

- Master Suite with a private Bath, walk-in closet and built-in shelves

- Two large secondary Bedrooms in the front of the home share a full Bath

- This home is designed with slab and crawlspace foundation options

Main floor — 1,438 sq. ft.
Garage — 486 sq. ft.

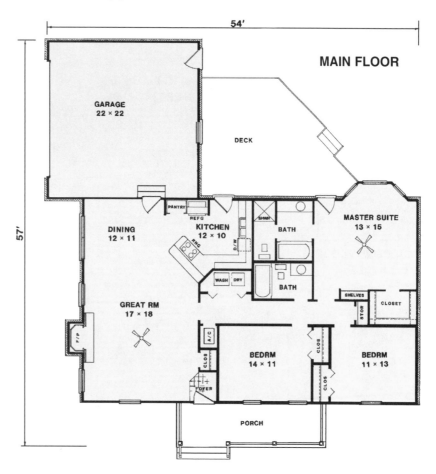

Warm and Welcoming

Total living area 1,470 sq. ft. ■ Price Code A

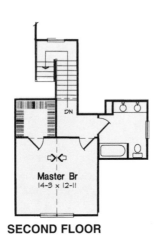

SECOND FLOOR

Master Br
14-3 x 12-11

DN

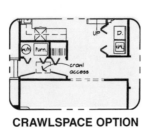

CRAWLSPACE OPTION

UP

crawl access

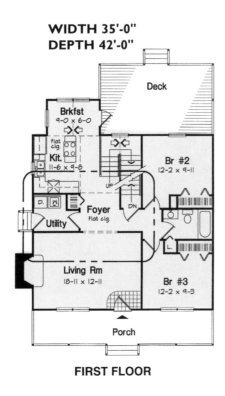

WIDTH 35'-0"
DEPTH 42'-0"

Deck

Brkfst
9-0 x 6-0

Kit.
11-6 x 9-8

flat clg.

Br #2
12-2 x 9-11

UP

DN

Foyer
flat clg.

Utility

Living Rm
18-11 x 12-11

Br #3
12-2 x 9-3

Porch

FIRST FLOOR

No. 24706

■ **This plan features:**

— Three bedrooms

— Two full baths

■ The railed front Porch offers guests a warm welcome and shelter from bad weather

■ The Living Room includes a focal point fireplace

■ The efficient Kitchen can serve the bright Breakfast Area and the Deck

■ Privacy is assured with the Master Suite upstairs

■ This home is designed with basement, slab and crawlspace foundation options

First floor — 1,035 sq. ft.
Second floor — 435 sq. ft.
Basement — 1,018 sq. ft.
Porch — 192 sq. ft.

No. 34005

This plan features:

Three bedrooms

Two full baths

Large slope ceiling Living Room with fireplace provides a great family gathering area

The Dining Room and the Master Bedroom feature decorative ceilings

The efficient Kitchen includes a plant shelf and offers access to a rear patio

A Laundry closet is conveniently located near the Bedrooms

This home is designed with basement and crawlspace foundation options

Main floor — 1,441 sq. ft.

Garage — 672 sq. ft.

Total living area 1,441 sq. ft. ■ *Price Code D* ■

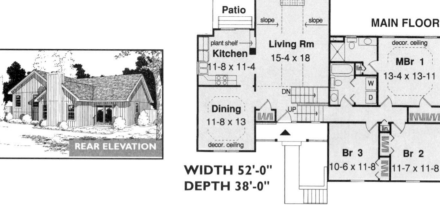

REAR ELEVATION

MAIN FLOOR

Patio

plant shelf → **Kitchen** 11-8 x 11-4

slope   slope

Living Rm 15-4 x 18

decor. ceiling **MBr 1** 13-4 x 13-11

DN

UP

Dining 11-8 x 13

decor. ceiling

Br 3 10-6 x 11-8

Br 2 11-7 x 11-8

WIDTH 52'-0"
DEPTH 38'-0"

No. 97730

This plan features:

Three bedrooms

Two full baths

The Great Room, Dining Room and Kitchen share an open space

The Master Bedroom has a full Bath and a door to the rear Deck

The two secondary Bedrooms share a full Bath

This home is designed with a basement foundation

Main floor — 1,315 sq. ft.

Basement — 1,315 sq. ft.

Total living area 1,315 sq. ft. ■ *Price Code A* ■

Deck

Master Bedroom 12'-4" x 13'-0"

Great Room 18'-8" x 17'-4"

Bedroom 11'-4" x 10'-8"

Bath

Dining

Bath

Kitchen 13'-4" x 9'-11"

Foyer

Bedroom 12'-4" x 10'-10"

Laun.

Porch

28'-0"

47'-0"

MAIN FLOOR

71

Stylish Smaller Home

Total living area 1,448 sq. ft. ■ *Price Code A* ■

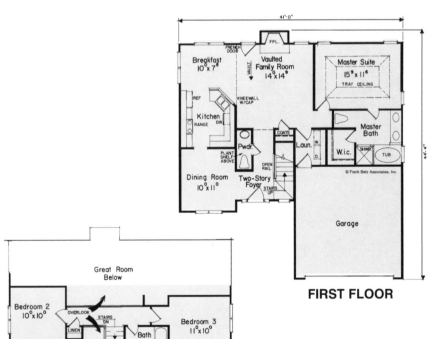

FIRST FLOOR

SECOND FLOOR

No. 97201

■ **This plan features:**

— Three bedrooms

— Two full and one half baths

■ Two-story Foyer leads into the Family Room with a vaulted ceiling

■ A cozy atmosphere is created by fireplace in the Family Room

■ Breakfast Room adjoins the Family Room and the Kitchen

■ A tray ceiling and a private Master Bath in the Master Suite

■ Two additional Bedrooms with ample closet space share the full Bath in the hall

■ This home is designed with basement, slab and crawlspace foundation options

First floor — 1,049 sq. ft.
Second floor — 399 sq. ft.
Basement — 1,051 sq. ft.
Garage — 400 sq. ft.

■ *Total living area 1,317 sq. ft.* ■ *Price Code A* ■

No. 98506

This plan features:

Three bedrooms

Two full baths

The Kitchen has a center-island workspace, a Dining Area and is convenient to the Utility Room

The Great Room has a cathedral ceiling, a fireplace and access to the Patio through a French door

The Master Bedroom has a cathedral ceiling, a walk-in closet and a five-piece Bath

Two additional Bedrooms share a full Bath

This home is designed with slab and crawlspace foundation options

ain Floor – 1,317 sq. ft.
arage – 462 sq. ft.
eck – 69 sq. ft.
orch – 105 sq. ft.

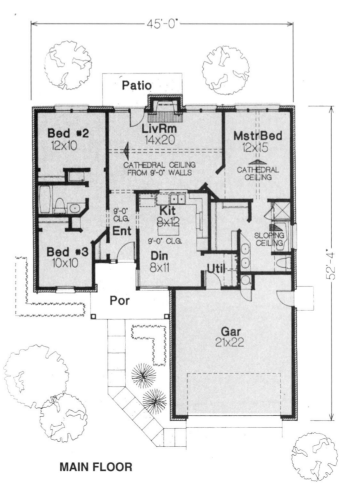

MAIN FLOOR

Home Sweet Home

■ *Total living area 1,112 sq. ft.* ■ *Price Code A* ■

No. 24723

■ This plan features:

— Three bedrooms

— Two full baths

■ Large Living Room, highlighted by a fireplace and built-in entertainment center, adjoins the Dining Room

■ Skylights, a ceiling fan and room defining columns accent the Dining Room

■ A serving bar to the Dining Room and ample counter and cabinet space in the Kitchen

■ Decorative ceiling treatment over the Master Bedroom and a private Master Bath

■ This home is designed with slab and crawlspace foundation options

Main floor — 1,112 sq. ft.

Garage — 563 sq. ft.

MAIN FLOOR

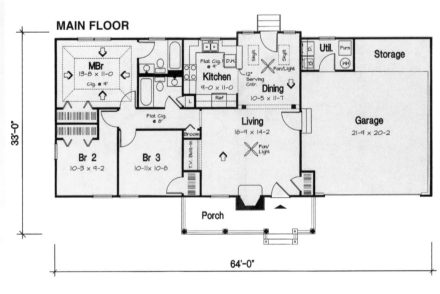

■ *Total living area 1,453 sq. ft.* ■ *Price Code A* ■

No. 94914

This plan features:

Three bedrooms

Two full baths

Cozy front Porch invites sitting, and shelters Entry

Fabulous Great Room accented by a focal point fireplace and transom windows

Efficient Kitchen with an island workspace, built-in Pantry and bright Breakfast Area

Two additional Bedrooms share a full Bath and Laundry Facilities

This home is designed with a basement foundation

Alternate foundation options available at an additional charge. Please call 1-800-235-5700 for additional information.

Main floor — 1,453 sq. ft.
Basement — 1,453 sq. ft.
Garage — 481 sq. ft.

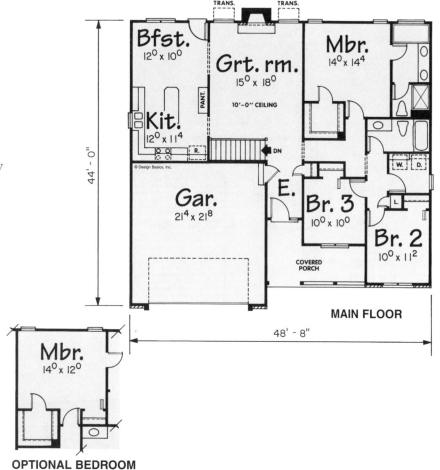

MAIN FLOOR

OPTIONAL BEDROOM

No Wasted Space

■ Total living area 1,454 sq. ft. ■ Price Code A ■

No. 90412

■ This plan features:

— Three bedrooms

— Two full baths

■ A centrally located Great Room with a cathedral ceiling, exposed wood beams, and large areas of fixed glass

■ The Living and Dining Areas separated by a massive stone fireplace

■ A secluded Master Suite with a walk-in closet and private Master Bath

■ An efficient Kitchen with a convenient Laundry Area

■ This home is designed with basement, slab and crawlspace foundation options

Main floor — 1,454 sq. ft.

MAIN FLOOR

67'-0"

34'-10"

CARPORT
20'-0"x20'-0"

STORAGE   STORAGE

KITCHEN
15'-2"x8'-8"

W D

LIN.   P.

BATH

CL.

M. BEDROOM
15'-2"x13'-6"

DINING
15'-0"x12'-0"

CATHEDRAL CEILING

LIVING
15'-0"x21'-10"

BEDROOM
15'-2"x11'-0"

BATH

CL.

BEDROOM
12'-8"x11'-0"

CL.

DECK

For First Time Buyers

No. 93048

This plan features:

- Three bedrooms
- Two full baths
- An efficiently designed Kitchen with a corner sink, ample counter space and a peninsula counter
- A sunny Breakfast Room with a convenient hide-away Laundry Center
- An expansive Family Room that includes a corner fireplace and direct access to the Patio
- A private Master Suite with a walk-in closet and a double vanity Bath
- Two additional Bedrooms, both with walk-in closets, that share a full Bath
- This home is designed with slab and crawlspace foundation options

Main floor — 1,310 sq. ft.
Garage — 449 sq. ft.

■ *Total living area 1,310 sq. ft.* ■ *Price Code A* ■

WIDTH 49-10

MAIN FLOOR

© Larry E. Belk

Cottage Ambiance

No. 32122

This plan features:

- Two bedrooms
- One full bath
- Covered Entry mimics twin gables of activity and sleeping areas of home
- High ceilings and gable windows keep interior light and airy
- Spacious Living Area with window alcove opens to Screened Porch and Kitchen with washer/dryer and Pantry
- Two Bedrooms share a full Bath and easy access to courtyard and Deck beyond
- This home is designed with basement and crawlspace foundation options

Main floor — 1,112 sq. ft.
Basement — 484 sq. ft.
Porch —152 sq. ft.

Photography supplied by The Meredith Corporation

■ *Total living area 1,112 sq. ft.* ■ *Price Code A* ■

WIDTH 47'
DEPTH 45'-6"

MAIN FLOOR

77

Split-Level Living

■ *Total living area 1,325 sq. ft.* ■ *Price Code A* ■

LOWER FLOOR

Fut.Bth.

Future Closet

W/H Furn.

W. D.

Double Garage
22-0 x 26-0

Future Playroom
15-0 x 22-8

Stor.

Sundeck
14-0 x 10-0

© 1989, Jannis Vann & Associates, Inc.

Dw.

Dining
10-0 x 9-6

M.Bath

Master Bdrm.
14-0 x 14-0

Kit.
8-0 x 9-6

Ref.

Bth.2

Opt. Plant Shelf Above

Living Area
14-8 x 15-6

Flat Ceil. Line 12-0 High

36-0

Vaulted Ceil.

Cls.

Lin.

Entry

Bdrm.3
9-4 x 11-6

Bdrm.2
10-4 x 9-6

MAIN FLOOR

45-0

No. 93265

■ **This plan features:**

— Three bedrooms

— Two full baths

■ A split-level Entry leads to the main floor and to the Garage and Bonus room on the lower floor

■ The Dining Area accesses the Sundeck through sliding doors

■ Future expansion is available on the lower floor

■ This home is designed with a basement foundation

Main floor — 1,269 sq. ft.
Lower floor — 382 sq. ft.
Garage — 598 sq. ft.

Simple, Clean Lines

■ *Total living area 1,322 sq. ft.* ■ *Price Code A* ■

No. 93072

This plan features:

- Three bedrooms

- One full and one three-quarter baths

- The cozy Kitchen with a Pantry and cooking island has an area for a table

- Ten-foot ceilings are found in all the main Living Areas

- A well-proportioned Living Room has a fireplace

- The Bedrooms are grouped for convenience and have ample closets

- A two-car Garage is tucked away in the rear

- This home is designed with slab and crawlspace foundation options

Main floor — 1,322 sq. ft.
Garage — 528 sq. ft.
Porch — 72 sq. ft.

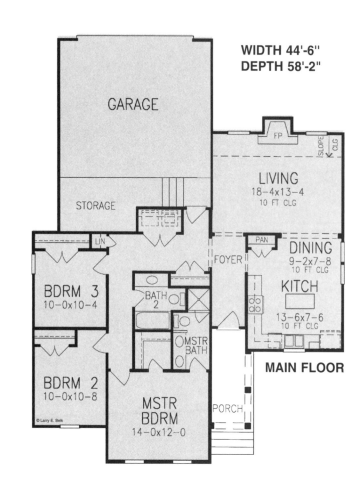

WIDTH 44'-6"
DEPTH 58'-2"

MAIN FLOOR

Country-Style Front Porch

■ Total living area 1,458 sq. ft. ■ Price Code A ■

No. 96516

■ **This plan features:**

— Three bedrooms

— Two full baths

■ A 10-foot-high ceiling accents the Great Room, which also features fireplace and access to a rear Porch

■ The Master Suite sits secluded in its own wing of the house

■ The Dining Room is open to the efficient Kitchen which includes serving bar

■ This home is designed with slab and crawlspace foundation options

Main floor — 1,458 sq. ft.
Garage — 452 sq. ft.

MAIN FLOOR

Cozy Yet Roomy

No. 98444

This plan features:

- Three bedrooms
- Two full and one half baths
- A warm and cozy fireplace highlights the Great Room
- The Dining Room and the Kitchen are adjoined, creating a comfortable Living Area
- The Master Bedroom has a tray ceiling, and a vaulted ceiling tops the Master Bath
- This home is designed with basement, slab and crawlspace foundation options

First floor — 628 sq. ft.
Second floor — 660 sq. ft.
Basement — 628 sq. ft.
Garage — 424 sq. ft.

■ *Total living area 1,288 sq. ft.* ■ *Price Code A* ■

WIDTH 42'-10"
DEPTH 39'-0"

Vaulted M.Bath · W.i.c. · Bath · Bedroom 2 11⁷ x 10⁰

Master Suite 13⁰ x 13⁵ · TRAY CEILING · PLANT SHELF ABOVE · OPEN RAIL · STAIRS DN. · LINEN · Bedroom 3 9¹⁰ X 10²

SECOND FLOOR

FRENCH DOOR · Pwdr. · Dining Room 10⁶ x 10⁰ · W. D. · COATS · PANTRY · Great Room 13⁰ x 18⁰ · OPEN RAIL · STAIRS UP · STAIRS DN · REF. · Kitchen · RANGE · DW.

Covered Porch

Garage 19⁸ X 19⁹

FIRST FLOOR

© Frank Betz Associates

L-Shaped Kitchen

No. 97731

This plan features:

- Three bedrooms
- Two full baths
- The Kitchen, Dining Area and Great Room open to each other
- The Great Room has vaulted ceilings and a fireplace
- The Master Bedroom has a tray ceiling and a private Bath
- The L-shaped Kitchen is conveniently located near the Laundry Room
- This home is designed with a basement foundation

Main floor — 1,315 sq. ft.
Basement — 1,315 sq. ft.
Garage — 488 sq. ft.
Porch — 75 sq. ft.

■ *Total living area 1,315 sq. ft.* ■ *Price Code A* ■

MAIN FLOOR

Deck

Master Bedroom 12'-4" x 13'-0" · Great Room 18'-8" x 17'-4" · Bedroom 11'-4" x 10'-8" · Bath

Bath · Dining · Kitchen 13'-4" x 9'-11" · Foyer · Bedroom 12'-4" x 10'-10"

Laun. · Porch

Garage 20'-0" x 26'-2"

54'-8"

50'-0"

Perfect Simplicity

■ *Total living area 1,040 sq. ft.* ■ *Price Code A* ■

FIRST FLOOR

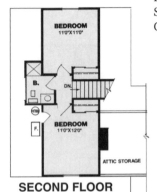

SECOND FLOOR

No. 94317

■ **This plan features:**

— Four bedrooms

— One full and one three-quarter baths

■ A Country cottage feeling is created by th[e] elevation using a front Porch dormer window and stone chimney

■ The main Living Areas — the Living Roo[m] and the Kitchen, are in an open format creating a spacious Living Area

■ The kitchen includes a Pantry closet and L-shaped counter space

■ This home is designed with slab and crawlspace foundation options

First floor — 660 sq. ft.
Second floor — 380 sq. ft.
Garage — 314 sq. ft.

A Comfortable, Informal Design

■ *Total living area 1,300 sq. ft.* ■ *Price Code A* ■

MAIN FLOOR

No. 94801

■ **This plan features:**

— Three bedrooms

— Two full baths

■ Warm, Country front Porch with wood details

■ Spacious Activity Room enhanced by a pr[e] fab fireplace

■ Open and efficient Kitchen/Dining Area highlighted by bay window, adjacent to Laundry and Garage Entry

■ Corner Master Bedroom offers a pamperi[ng] Bath topped by a vaulted ceiling and featuring a garden tub and double vanity

■ Two additional Bedrooms with ample closets, share a full Bath

■ This home is designed with slab and crawlspace foundation options

Main floor — 1,300 sq. ft.
Garage — 576 sq. ft.

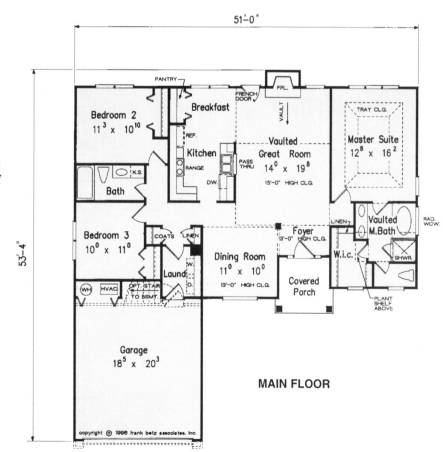

Total living area 1,459 sq. ft. ■ *Price Code A* ■

No. 97601

This plan features:

Three bedrooms

Two full baths

High ceilings enhance the main Living Space

An arched window in the Dining Room compliments the design of the Porch

The large Pantry increases the Kitchen storage space

A tray ceiling beautifies the Master Bedroom

A rear wall fireplace warms the Great Room

This home is designed with basement and crawlspace foundation options

Main floor — 1,459 sq. ft.
Basement — 1,466 sq. ft.
Garage — 390 sq. ft.

MAIN FLOOR

copyright © 1996 frank betz associates, inc.

Soaring Great Room

■ *Total living area 1,194 sq. ft.* ■ *Price Code A* ■

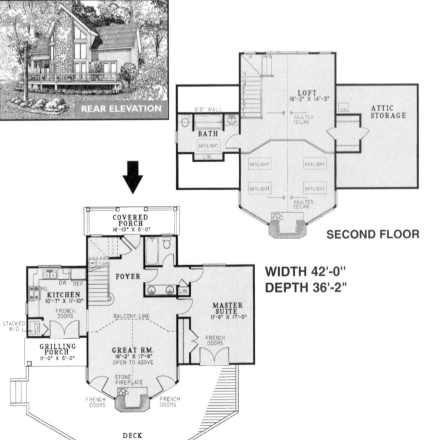

REAR ELEVATION

SECOND FLOOR

WIDTH 42'-0"
DEPTH 36'-2"

FIRST FLOOR

No. 61004

■ This plan features:

— Two bedrooms

— Two full baths

■ The incredible Great Room features a large fireplace, French doors, windows galore, and a soaring vaulted ceiling with skylights

■ The Kitchen opens through French doors to a Grilling Porch

■ The Master Bedroom has private access to the first floor Bath and French doors opening onto a large Deck

■ This home is designed with a slab foundation

Main floor — 862 sq. ft.
Second — 332 sq. ft.

■ *Total living area 1,461 sq. ft.* ■ *Price Code A* ■

No. 97137

This plan features:

Three bedrooms

Two full baths

An inviting front Porch leads into a tiled Entry and Great Room with focal point fireplace

Open layout of Great Room, Dining Area, Wood Deck and Kitchen easily accommodates a busy family

Master Bedroom set in a quiet corner, offers a huge walk-in closet and double vanity Bath

Two additional Bedrooms, one an optional Den, share a full Bath

This home is designed with a basement foundation

Main floor — 1,461 sq. ft.
Basement — 1,461 sq. ft.
Garage — 458 sq. ft.

Rustic Exterior

■ *Total living area 1,466 sq. ft.* ■ *Price Code A* ■

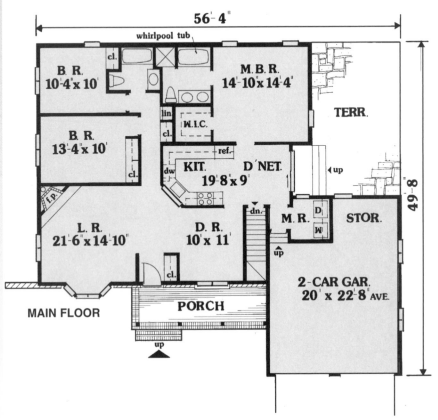

MAIN FLOOR

No. 99662

■ This plan features:

— Three bedrooms

— Two full baths

■ The covered front Porch shelters the Entry

■ A bay window and corner fireplace accent the Living Room

■ The Terrace expands the living space outdoors

■ Extra storage space is found in the rear of the Garage

■ The Master Bedroom features a walk-in closet and a full Bath

■ A secondary Bedroom can be used as a Study

■ This home is designed with basement and slab foundation options

Main floor — 1,466 sq. ft.
Basement — 1,466 sq. ft.
Garage — 477 sq. ft.

Economical Vacation Home

No. 99238

This plan features:

Three bedrooms

Two full baths

A large rectangular Living Room with a fireplace at one end and plenty of room for separate activities at the other end

A galley-style Kitchen with adjoining Dining Area

A second floor Master Bedroom with a children's dormitory across the hall

A second floor Deck outside the Master Bedroom

This home is designed with a basement foundation

First floor — 784 sq. ft.

Second floor — 504 sq. ft.

■ *Total living area 1,288 sq. ft.* ■ *Price Code A* ■

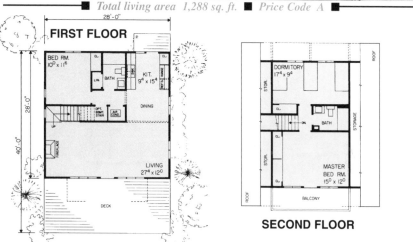

FIRST FLOOR

28'-0"

BED RM.
10⁰ x 11⁶

BATH

KIT.
9⁴ x 15⁴

DINING

40'-0"

28'-0"

OPT. BSMT. STAIR

AIR COND.

UP

FIREPLACE

LIVING
27⁴ x 12⁰

DECK

DORMITORY
17⁴ x 9⁴

STOR.

BATH

STORAGE

STOR.

ROOF

MASTER BED RM.
15⁰ x 12⁰

ROOF

BALCONY

SECOND FLOOR

Quaint Starter Home

No. 92400

This plan features:

Three bedrooms

Two full baths

A vaulted ceiling giving an airy feeling to the Dining and Living Rooms

A streamlined Kitchen with a comfortable work area, a double sink and ample cabinet space

A cozy fireplace in the Living Room

A Master Suite with a large closet, French doors leading to the Patio and a private Bath

Two additional Bedrooms sharing a full Bath

This home is designed with basement and slab foundation options

Main floor — 1,050 sq. ft.

Garage — 261 sq. ft.

■ *Total living area 1,050 sq. ft.* ■ *Price Code A* ■

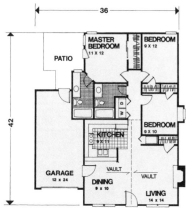

36

42

MASTER BEDROOM
11 X 12

BEDROOM
9 X 12

PATIO

W D

BEDROOM
9 X 10

KITCHEN
9 X 11

GARAGE
12 x 24

DINING
9 X 10

VAULT

VAULT

LIVING
14 X 14

MAIN FLOOR

Magical Ceilings

■ *Total living area 1,467 sq. ft.* ■ *Price Code A* ■

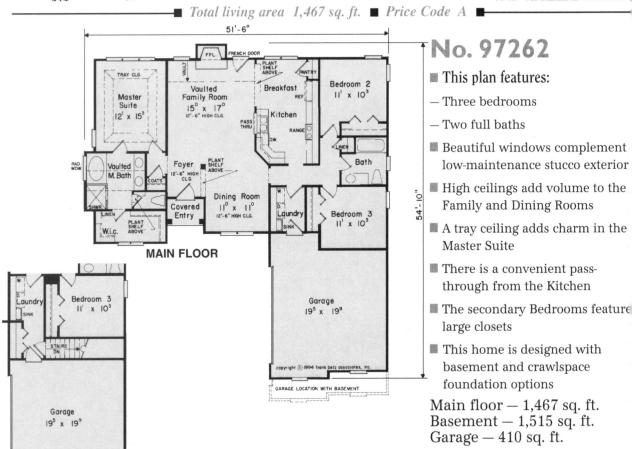

MAIN FLOOR

OPT. BASEMENT STAIR LOCATION

No. 97262

■ This plan features:

— Three bedrooms

— Two full baths

■ Beautiful windows complement low-maintenance stucco exterior

■ High ceilings add volume to the Family and Dining Rooms

■ A tray ceiling adds charm in the Master Suite

■ There is a convenient pass-through from the Kitchen

■ The secondary Bedrooms feature large closets

■ This home is designed with basement and crawlspace foundation options

Main floor — 1,467 sq. ft.
Basement — 1,515 sq. ft.
Garage — 410 sq. ft.

■ *Total living area 1,354 sq. ft.* ■ *Price Code A* ■

No. 97272

This plan features:

Three bedrooms

Two full baths

Foyer opens into high ceilinged Great Room featuing fireplace flanked by tall windows

From the Garage, enter into a convenient Laundry/Mud Room that opens to the efficient Kitchen with sunny Breakfast Area

The Master Suite features a tray ceiling and Sitting Room

Two additional Bedrooms share a full Bath

This home is designed with basement and crawlspace foundation options

ain floor — 1,354 sq. ft.

asement — 1,390 sq. ft.

arage — 434 sq. ft.

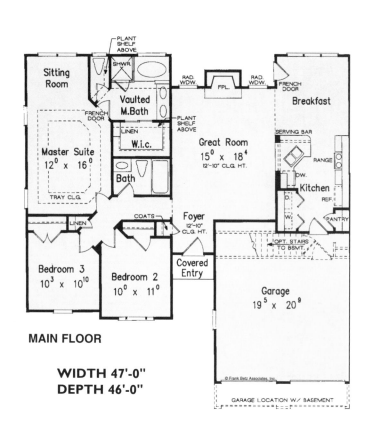

MAIN FLOOR

WIDTH 47'-0"
DEPTH 46'-0"

Exterior Charm

Total living area 1,093 sq. ft. ■ **Price Code A**

FIRST FLOOR

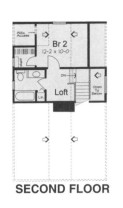

SECOND FLOOR

No. 24740

■ **This plan features:**

— Two bedrooms

— One full and one three-quarter baths

■ Skylights brighten the soaring Great Room and covered Porch

■ The second floor Bedroom enjoys a near Bath and a Loft overlooking the Great Room

■ The Master Suite is on the first floor

■ This home is designed with a crawlspace foundation

First floor — 792 sq. ft.
Second floor — 301 sq. ft.
Basement — 301 sq. ft.

Traditional & Contemporary

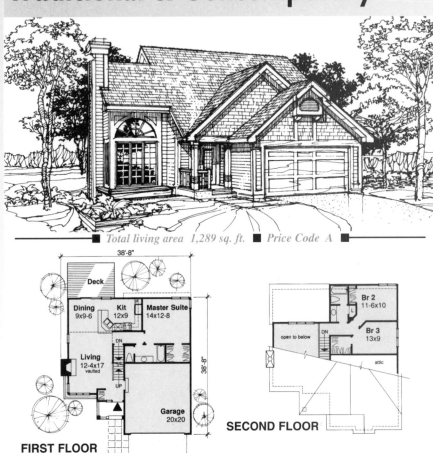

Total living area 1,289 sq. ft. ■ **Price Code A**

FIRST FLOOR

SECOND FLOOR

No. 99327

■ **This plan features:**

— Three bedrooms

— Two full baths

■ A vaulted ceiling in the Entry

■ A formal Living Room with a fireplace and half-round transom

■ A Dining Room with sliders to the Deck and easy access to the Kitchen

■ A main floor Master Suite with corner windows, a closet and private Bath access

■ Two additional Bedrooms that share a full hall Bath

■ This home is designed with a basement foundation

First floor — 858 sq. ft.
Second floor — 431 sq. ft.
Basement — 858 sq. ft.
Garage — 400 sq. ft.

■ *Total living area 1,470 sq. ft.* ■ *Price Code A* ■

No. 92633

This plan features:

Three bedrooms

One full and one half baths/alternate plan offers one full and one three-quarter baths

Sloped ceilings, low walls and open spaces

Glass doors to the rear Deck make outdoor entertaining fun and convenient

A two Bath option with a comfortable Master Bedroom with a large closet and a private Bath

A lower level with a fireplace, half Bath, two-car Garage and a Laundry Room

This home is designed with a basement foundation

Main floor — 1,042 sq. ft.
Lower floor — 428 sq. ft.
Garage — 986 sq. ft.

ALTERNATE BEDROOM PLAN

Bath

Master Bedroom
13'7" x 10'6"

Bath

Bedroom
9'3" x 8'5"

Bedroom
10'8" x 9'5"

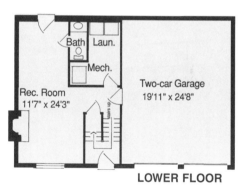

LOWER FLOOR

Bath   Laun.

Mech.

Rec. Room
11'7" x 24'3"

Two-car Garage
19'11" x 24'8"

stairs up

ALTERNATE LIVING ROOM/ KITCHEN PLAN

Deck

Living Room
17'2" x 13'11"

Kitchen
12' x 12'1"

MAIN FLOOR

40'

Deck

Dining Room
9'7" x 10'10"

Kitchen

Master Bedroom
14'0" x 10'6"

Bath

Hall

plant shelf

Living Room
12'0" x 15'3"

Bedroom
9'7" x 8'5"

Bedroom
10'6" x 10'10"

stairs up
stairs dn

Porch

27'

Brick Details Add Style

■ *Total living area 1,472 sq. ft.* ■ *Price Code A* ■

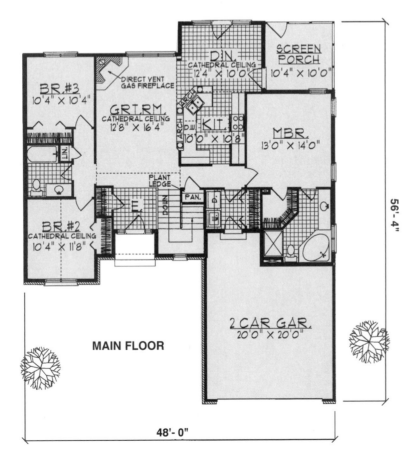

MAIN FLOOR

No. 93165

■ **This plan features:**

— Three bedrooms

— Two full baths

■ Keystone entrance leads into tile Entry with plant ledge and close

■ Expansive Great Room features cathedral ceiling over triple window and a corner gas firepla

■ Hub Kitchen accented by arches and columns serves Great Room and Dining Area

■ Dining Area features large windows, access to rear yard and Screened Porch

■ Private Master Bedroom include a walk-in closet and plush Bath

■ This home is designed with a basement foundation

Main floor — 1,472 sq. ft.
Basement — 1,472 sq. ft.
Garage — 424 sq. ft.

* This plan is not to be built within a 20 mile radius of Iowa City, IA.

For Established Neighborhood

No. 93222

This plan features:

Three bedrooms

Two full baths

A covered Entrance sheltering and welcoming visitors

An expansive Living Room enhanced by natural light streaming in from the large front window

A bayed formal Dining Room with direct access to the Sun Deck and the Living Room for entertainment ease

An efficient, galley Kitchen, convenient to both formal and informal eating areas, and equipped with a double sink and adequate counter and storage space

An informal Breakfast Room with direct access to the Sun Deck

A large Master Suite equipped with a walk-in closet and a full private Bath

Two additional Bedrooms that share a full in the hall Bath

This home is designed with a basement foundation

ain floor — 1,276 sq. ft.

nished staircase — 16 sq. ft.

asement — 392 sq. ft.

arage — 728 sq. ft.

■ *Total living area 1,292 sq. ft.* ■ *Price Code A* ■

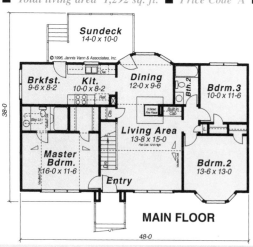

MAIN FLOOR

Double Decks

No. 91002

This plan features:

Two bedrooms

One full and one three-quarter baths

Abundant windows, indoor planters and three Decks uniting every room with the outdoors

An efficient Kitchen with direct access to the Nook and the formal Dining Room

A wood stove warming the spacious Family Room

A secluded Master Suite with private Deck, Den and Master Bath

This home is designed with a crawlspace foundation

rst floor — 808 sq. ft.

cond floor — 288 sq. ft.

■ *Total living area 1,096 sq. ft.* ■ *Price Code A* ■

WIDTH 24'-0"
DEPTH 32'-0"

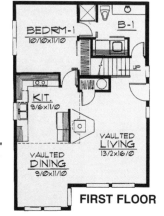

FIRST FLOOR

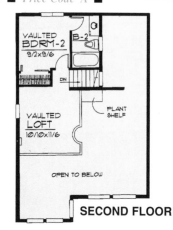

SECOND FLOOR

93

Lakeside or Mountain Retreat

■ *Total living area 1,472 sq. ft.* ■ *Price Code A* ■

No. 90479

■ This plan features:

— Three bedrooms

— Two full baths

■ The large Screened Porch allows for peaceful evening entertaining or relaxation

■ The Living/Dining Room has a cathedral ceiling and a fireplace

■ The U-shaped see-through Kitchen has a breakfast counter

■ The Master Bedroom has a walk-in closet and a private Bath

■ Two additional Bedrooms share a full Bath

■ There is a Porch located in the rear of the home off the Utility Room

■ This home is designed with slab and crawlspace foundation options

Main floor — 1,472 sq. ft.
Porch — 320 sq. ft.

Main Floor Plan

PORCH

BEDROOM
14-0 x 11-6

BATH

BEDROOM
13-0 x 11-6

BATH

WALK-IN CLOSET

FREEZ. CAB.

WH

PANT

CLOSET

LINEN

LINEN

UTILITY
9-8 x 11-4

KITCHEN
11-0 x 11-2

LIVING / DINING
24-2 x 13-6
CATHEDRAL CEILING

BEDROOM
15-8 x 16-0

W D

CAB.

MAIN FLOOR

SCREENED PORCH
26-0 x 10-0

WOOD DECK
16-0 x 8-0

36'-0"

62'-0"

Comfortable Three Bedroom

No. 35008

This plan features:

Three bedrooms

One full bath

A welcoming front Porch sheltering the entrance

A simple and practical floor plan with lovely extras

An efficient, galley Kitchen equipped with a breakfast bar for informal eating

A formal Dining Room with a sloped ceiling

A sloped ceiling and a built-in entertainment center in the Living Room

A full Bath close to the Bedrooms

A Loft area overlooking the Living Room and the Dining Room

This home is designed with basement, slab and crawlspace foundation options

First floor — 955 sq. ft.

Second floor — 336 sq. ft.

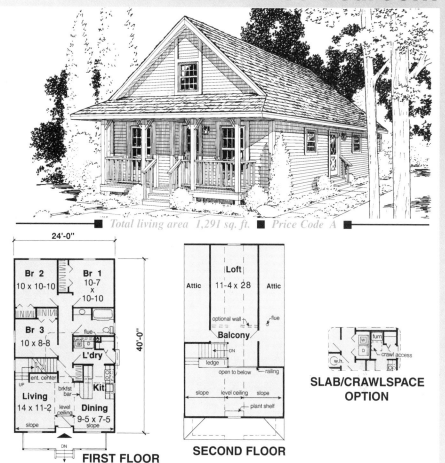

Total living area 1,291 sq. ft. ■ *Price Code A*

FIRST FLOOR

24'-0"

40'-0"

Br 2 10 x 10-10

Br 1 10-7 x 10-10

Br 3 10 x 8-8

L'dry

Kit

brkfst bar

ent. center

Living 14 x 11-2

Dining 9-5 x 7-5

SECOND FLOOR

Loft 11-4 x 28

Attic

Attic

Balcony

ledge

open to below

railing

slope

level ceiling

slope

plant shelf

SLAB/CRAWLSPACE OPTION

Cozy Bungalow

No. 93070

This plan features:

Three bedrooms

One full and one three-quarter baths

Simple and classic, the exterior is reminiscent of a less complicated time

This compact design has ten-foot ceilings adding a spacious feeling

The Kitchen flows into the Dining Area and includes a forty-two-inch breakfast bar

The two-car Garage is tucked in the rear

The Master Suite has a private three-quarter Bath and a walk-in closet

Two additional Bedrooms share the full Bath

This home is designed with slab and crawlspace foundation options

Main floor — 1,322 sq. ft.

Garage — 528 sq. ft.

Total living area 1,322 sq. ft. ■ *Price Code A*

Width 44'-6"

MAIN FLOOR

© Larry E. Belk

GARAGE

STORAGE

Depth 58'-2"

BDRM 3 10-0x10-4

BATH

LIVING 18-4x13-4 10 FT CLG

BDRM 2 10-0x10-8

MSTR BDRM 14-0x12-0

FOYER

KITCH 13-4x5-4

DINING 13-4x5-6

PORCH

Form and Function

■ *Total living area 1,471 sq. ft.* ■ *Price Code A* ■

No. 65000

■ **This plan features:**

– Three bedrooms

– Two full baths

■ The Living Room features an angled fireplace that can be equally enjoyed from the open Dining Area

■ The L-shaped Kitchen offers efficiency and a center-island workspace and serving area

■ Three Bedrooms — one on the fi floor, two on the second — offer ample closet space

■ A large Screened Porch at the front of the home adds addition living and entertaining space

■ This home is designed with a basement foundation

First floor — 895 sq. ft.
Second floor — 576 sq. ft.
Basement — 895 sq. ft.

WIDTH 26'-3"
DEPTH 36'-6"

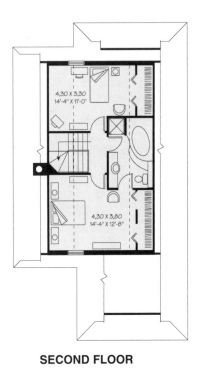

SECOND FLOOR

FIRST FLOOR

Private Master Suite

No. 92503

This plan features:

Three bedrooms

Two full baths

A spacious Living Room enhanced by a vaulted ceiling and fireplace

A well-equipped Kitchen with windowed double sink

A secluded Master Suite with decorative ceiling, private Master Bath and walk-in closet

Two additional Bedrooms sharing full Bath

This home is designed with slab and crawlspace foundation options

Main floor — 1,271 sq. ft.

Garage — 506 sq. ft.

■ *Total living area 1,271 sq. ft.* ■ *Price Code A* ■

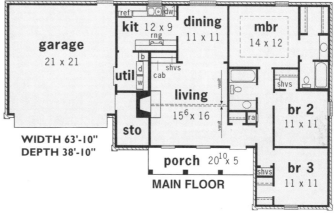

WIDTH 63'-10"
DEPTH 38'-10"

MAIN FLOOR

Modern 'Savoir Faire'

No. 99504

This plan features:

Three bedrooms

Two full baths

Spacious Country Kitchen has a built-in Pantry

Great Room crowned in a vaulted ceiling and decorated by a fireplace, has convenient access to the Kitchen

Master Bedroom highlighted by a private, full Bath and a walk-in closet

Two additional Bedrooms sharing a full Bath

This home is designed with slab and crawlspace foundation options

Main floor — 1,127 sq. ft.

Garage — 257 sq. ft.

■ *Total living area 1,127 sq. ft.* ■ *Price Code A* ■

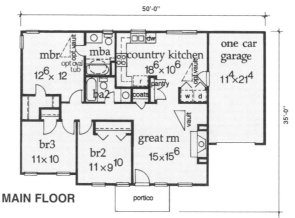

MAIN FLOOR

Easy Living

■ *Total living area 1,474 sq. ft.* ■ *Price Code A* ■

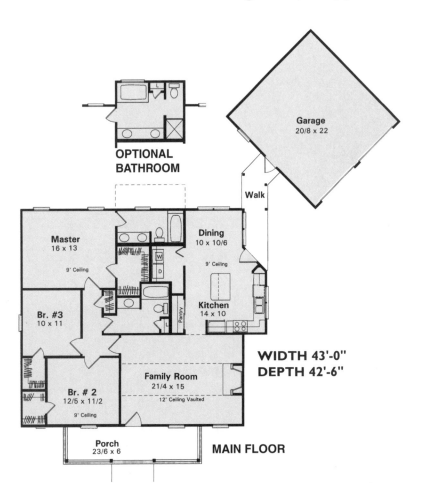

OPTIONAL BATHROOM

Garage
20/8 x 22

Walk

Master
16 x 13

9' Ceiling

Dining
10 x 10/6

9' Ceiling

W
D

Br. #3
10 x 11

Pantry

Kitchen
14 x 10

WIDTH 43'-0"
DEPTH 42'-6"

Br. # 2
12/5 x 11/2

9' Ceiling

Family Room
21/4 x 15

12' Ceiling Vaulted

Porch
23/6 x 6

MAIN FLOOR

No. 93447

■ **This plan features:**

— Three bedrooms

— Two full baths

■ The Family Room is enlarged by vaulted ceiling and also has a fireplace

■ The Kitchen is L-shaped and includes a center island

■ The Dining Room is open to the Kitchen for maximum convenience

■ A covered walkway leads to the two-car Garage

■ The Master Bedroom has a priva Bath, which has two building options

■ This home is designed with slab and crawlspace foundation options

Main floor — 1,474 sq. ft.
Garage — 454 sq. ft.

Modern Cottage with Vintage Appeal

■ *Total living area 1,311 sq. ft.* ■ *Price Code A* ■

No. 65173

This plan features:

Two bedrooms

One full and one three-quarter baths

Long Living Room opens to large Eat-in-Kitchen with efficient L-shaped counter

Open staircase and balcony add drama and interest to the Living Room space

First floor Bath includes Laundry closet

Two second floor Bedrooms share a full Bath

This home is designed with a basement foundation

First floor — 713 sq. ft.
Second floor — 598 sq. ft.
Basement — 713 sq. ft.
Second floor — 158 sq. ft.

FIRST FLOOR

SECOND FLOOR

Vaulted Ceilings

■ *Total living area 1,198 sq. ft.* ■ *Price Code A* ■

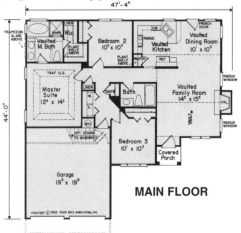

MAIN FLOOR

No. 97256

■ **This plan features:**

— Three bedrooms

— Two full baths

■ The Family Room of this home is topped by a vaulted ceiling and flows into the Dining Area

■ A vaulted ceiling also tops the Dining Area and the efficient L-shaped Kitchen

■ The Master Suite has been designed with tray ceiling over the Bedroom and a vaulted ceiling over the Master Bath

■ The two additional Bedrooms share a full Bath in the hall

■ The Laundry center is located in the hall next to the Garage entrance

■ This home is designed with basement and crawlspace foundation options

Main floor — 1,198 sq. ft.
Basement — 1,216 sq ft.
Garage — 410 sq. ft.

Efficient and Compact

■ *Total living area 1,253 sq. ft.* ■ *Price Code A* ■

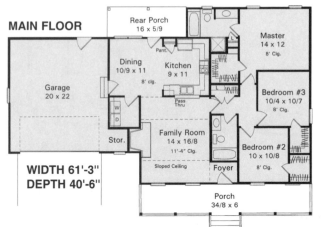

No. 93449

■ **This plan features:**

— Three bedrooms

— Two full baths

■ The covered front Porch adds style to the exterior

■ A sloped ceiling and fireplace are in the Family Room

■ The U-shaped Kitchen opens to the Dining Room

■ The Laundry Room is conveniently located

■ The Bedrooms have walk-in closets

■ The two-car Garage features extra storage space

■ This home is designed with slab and crawlspace foundation options

Main floor — 1,253 sq. ft.
Garage — 486 sq. ft.
Porch — 208 sq. ft.

Formal Balance

■ *Total living area 1,476 sq. ft.* ■ *Price Code A* ■

No. 90689

This plan features:

Three bedrooms

Two full baths

A cathedral ceiling in the Living Room with a heat-circulating fireplace as the focal point

A bow window in the Dining Room that adds elegance as well as natural light

A well-equipped Kitchen that serves both the Dinette and the formal Dining Room efficiently

A Master Bedroom with three closets and a private Master Bath with sliding glass doors to the Master Deck with a hot tub

This home is designed with basement and slab foundation options

Main floor — 1,476 sq. ft.
Basement — 1,361 sq. ft.
Garage — 548 sq. ft.

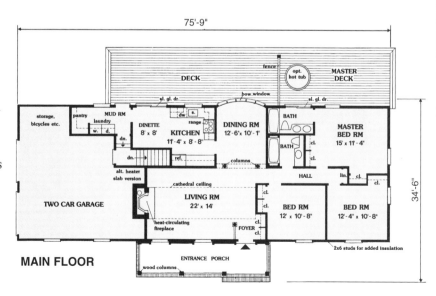

Charm and Style

■ Total living area 1,450 sq. ft. ■ Price Code A ■

FIRST FLOOR

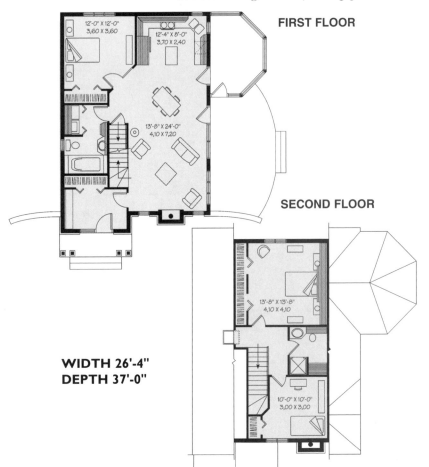

12'-0" X 12'-0"
3,60 X 3,60

12'-4" X 8'-0"
3,70 X 2,40

13'-8" X 24'-0"
4,10 X 7,20

SECOND FLOOR

13'-8" X 13'-8"
4,10 X 4,10

10'-0" X 10'-0"
3,00 X 3,00

WIDTH 26'-4"
DEPTH 37'-0"

No. 65179

■ **This plan features:**

— Three bedrooms

— One full and one three-quarter baths

■ Entry features large coat closet and provides storm break between the outdoors and your home

■ Large main Living Space include Living and Dining Area — with access to Patio and Screened Porch — open to efficient U-shaped Kitchen

■ First floor Bath includes Laundr closet

■ This home is designed with a basement foundation

First floor — 918 sq. ft.
Second room — 532 sq. ft.
Basement — 918 sq. ft.

Decorative Ceilings

No. 92559

This plan features:

Three bedrooms

Two full baths

The Den has a vaulted ceiling and a fireplace

The galley Kitchen is open to the Dining Area and is near the Utility Room

The Master Suite has a tray ceiling, a walk-in closet and a Bath

Two additional Bedrooms share a full Bath

This home has a two-car Garage with extra storage space

This home is designed with slab and crawlspace foundation options

Main floor — 1,265 sq. ft.

Garage — 523 sq. ft.

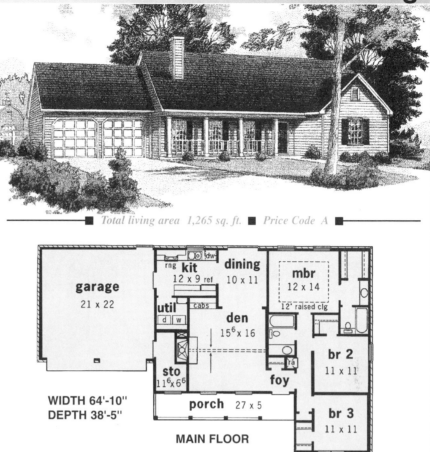

■ *Total living area 1,265 sq. ft.* ■ *Price Code A* ■

garage 21 x 22

rng kit 12 x 9 ref

dining 10 x 11

mbr 12 x 14
12' raised clg

util
d w

cabs

den 15⁶ x 16

br 2 11 x 11

sto 11⁶ x 6⁶

foy

WIDTH 64'-10"
DEPTH 38'-5"

porch 27 x 5

br 3 11 x 11

MAIN FLOOR

Traditional Brick Home

No. 93019

This plan features:

Three bedrooms

Two full baths

A traditional brick elevation that is accented with quoins

A Family Room that vaults to a 10-foot ceiling, giving a larger feel to the room

A Breakfast Room with a sunny bay window

An efficient, compact Kitchen that is entered through an arched opening

A Master Suite with a large walk-in closet, double vanity and a built-in linen cabinet

Two additional Bedrooms that share a full Bath

This home is designed with slab and crawlspace foundation options

Main floor — 1,136 sq. ft.

Garage — 434 sq. ft.

■ *Total living area 1,136 sq. ft.* ■ *Price Code A* ■

8 FT CLG

BRKFST 10-6 X 10-0

KITCHEN 8-0 X 8-0

MASTER BEDRM 11-0 X 14-0

BATH 2

FAMILY ROOM 12-0 X 17-8

STORAGE

MASTER BATH

BEDRM 3 10-6 X 11-6

ENTRY

2 CAR GARAGE

DEPTH 35-6

BEDRM 2 11-0 X 10-0

PORCH

© Larry E. Belk

MAIN FLOOR

WIDTH 48-10

Spacious Feeling

■ *Total living area 1,481 sq. ft.* ■ *Price Code A* ■

No. 96508

■ **This plan features:**

— Three bedrooms

— Two full baths

■ There is a definite feeling of spaciousness in the Living Room

■ An angled serving bar in the Kitchen is accessible from the Dining Room

■ The secondary Bedrooms have their own wing and share a full Bath

■ The Master Suite has a tray ceili and dual walk-in closets

■ The Master Bath contains a whirlpool tub

■ This home is designed with slab and crawlspace foundation options

Main floor — 1,481 sq. ft.
Garage — 477 sq. ft.
Porch — 40 sq. ft.

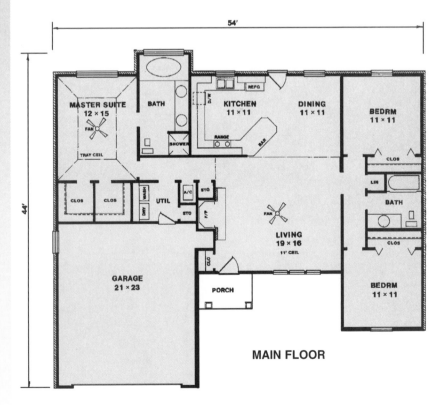

MAIN FLOOR

High Impact in a Small Package

Photography supplied by Meredith Corporation

■ *Total living area 1,220 sq. ft.* ■ *Price Code A* ■

No. 19491

This plan features:

- Three bedrooms

- Two full baths

- A sheltered Porch leading into a bright two-story Living Room with skylights and windows above and a warm, hearth-fireplace below

- An efficient U-shaped Kitchen serves Dining Room with convenient pass-through, and adjoins Deck and Garage

- A secluded Master Suite on second floor with a private Deck, a room-sized closet and full Bath

- Two additional Bedrooms located on the first floor, adjacent to a full Bath with Laundry Center

- This home is designed with a crawlspace foundation

First floor — 920 sq. ft.
Second floor — 300 sq. ft.
Garage — 583 sq. ft.

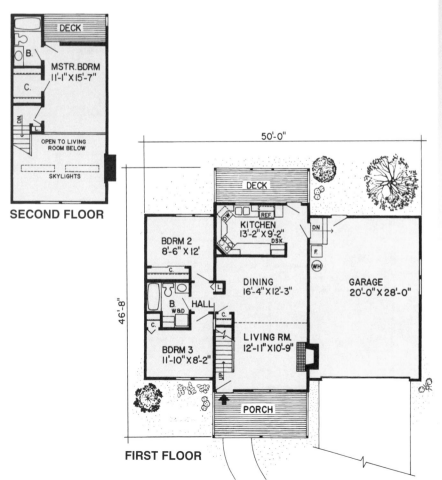

Welcoming Master Retreat

■ *Total living area 1,486 sq. ft.* ■ *Price Code A* ■

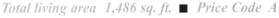

MAIN FLOOR

OPTION

No. 34154

■ **This plan features:**

— Three bedrooms

— Two full baths

■ Foyer opens into a huge Living Room with a fireplace below a sloped ceiling and Deck access

■ Efficient Kitchen with a Pantry, serving counter, Dining Area, Laundry closet and Garage entry

■ Corner Master Bedroom offers a walk-in closet and pampering Bath with a raised tub

■ Two more Bedrooms, one with a Den option, share a full Bath

■ This home is designed with basement, slab and crawlspace foundation options

Main floor — 1,486 sq. ft.
Garage — 462 sq. ft.

■ *Total living area 1,487 sq. ft.* ■ *Price Code A* ■

No. 26112

This plan features:

- Two bedrooms, with possible third bedroom/den

- One full and one half baths

- A solar design with south-facing glass doors and windows, plus an air-lock entry

- R-26 insulation used for floors and sloping ceilings

- A Deck rimming the front of the home

- A Dining Room separated from the Living Room by a half wall

- An efficient Kitchen with an eating bar

- This home is designed with a basement foundation

First floor — 911 sq. ft.

Second floor — 576 sq. ft.

Basement — 911 sq. ft.

Two Choices for Courtyard Home

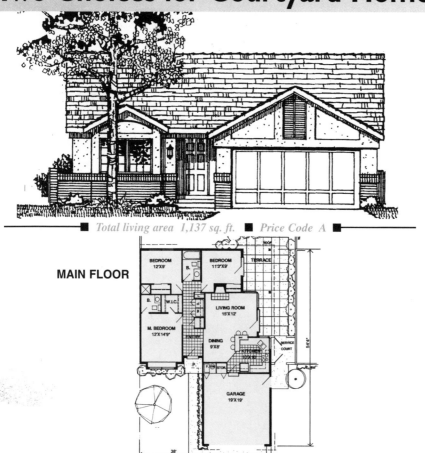

MAIN FLOOR

Total living area 1,137 sq. ft. ■ Price Code A

No. 94302

■ **This plan features:**

— Three bedrooms

— One full and one three-quarter baths

■ A tiled Entry leading to an open Dining/Living Room Area with hearth fireplace and a wall of windows with an atrium door to Terrace

■ An efficient Kitchen with a corner window and eating bar adjoins Dining Area, Garage and Terrace

■ A Master Bedroom with walk-in closet and private Bath featuring either recessed, decorative window or atrium door to Terrace

■ Two additional Bedrooms with ample closets near full Bath

■ This home is designed with a crawlspace foundation

Main floor — 1,137 sq. ft.
Garage — 390 sq. ft.

Spectacular Traditional

Total living area 1,237 sq. ft. ■ Price Code A

No. 92502

■ **This plan features:**

— Three bedrooms

— Two full baths

■ The use of gable roofs and the blend of stucco and brick to form a spectacular exterior

■ A high, vaulted ceiling and a cozy fireplace with built-in cabinets in the Den

■ An efficient, U-shaped Kitchen with an adjacent Dining Area

■ A Master Bedroom, with a raised ceiling, that includes a private Bath and a walk-in closet

■ Two family Bedrooms share a full Bath

■ This home is designed with slab and crawlspace foundation options

Main floor — 1,237 sq. ft.
Garage — 436 sq. ft.

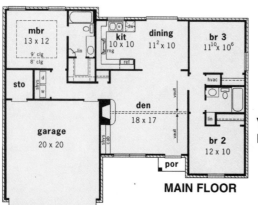

WIDTH 50'-0"
DEPTH 38'-0"

MAIN FLOOR

Total living area 1,432 sq. ft. ■ **Price Code A** ■

This plan.

No. 65181

This plan features:

Three bedrooms

One full and one three-quarter baths

This plan features a beautiful cottage look

A covered Porch leads to the Entry with ample closet

U-shaped Kitchen with angled breakfast bar opens to Dining Room

Three second floor Bedrooms share a large Bath with separate shower

This home is designed with a basement foundation

First floor — 756 sq. ft.
Second floor — 676 sq. ft.
Basement — 657 sq. ft.
Porch — 148 sq. ft.

FIRST FLOOR

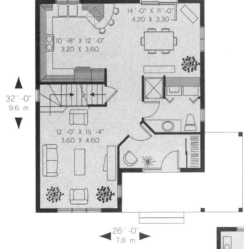

32'-0"
9.6 m

14'-0" X 11'-0"
4.20 X 3.30

10'-8" X 12'-0"
3.20 X 3.60

12'-0" X 15'-4"
3.60 X 4.60

26'-0"
7.8 m

SECOND FLOOR

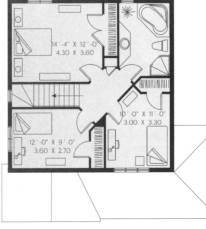

14'-4" X 12'-0"
4.30 X 3.60

10'-0" X 11'-0"
3.00 X 3.30

12'-0" X 9'-0"
3.60 X 2.70

Flexible Den

■ *Total living area 1,488 sq. ft.* ■ *Price Code A* ■

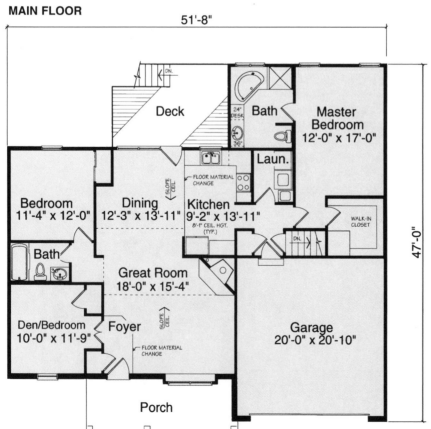

MAIN FLOOR

51'-8"

Deck

Bath

Master Bedroom
12'-0" x 17'-0"

24" DESK

36"

FLOOR MATERIAL CHANGE

Laun.

Bedroom
11'-4" x 12'-0"

Dining
12'-3" x 13'-11"

Kitchen
9'-2" x 13'-11"
8'-1" CEIL. HGT. (TYP.)

SLOPE CEIL.

WALK-IN CLOSET

Bath

47'-0"

Great Room
18'-0" x 15'-4"

SLOPE CEIL.

DN.

Den/Bedroom
10'-0" x 11'-9"

Foyer

FLOOR MATERIAL CHANGE

Garage
20'-0" x 20'-10"

Porch

No. 97724

■ **This plan features:**

— Three bedrooms

— Two full and baths

■ The Foyer opens to the Great Room, which includes a sloped ceiling and a corner fireplace

■ The Kitchen is just steps away from a French door leading to the rear Deck

■ The Den could be used as a Bedroom

■ This home is designed with a basement foundation

Main floor — 1,488 sq. ft.
Basement — 1,488 sq. ft.
Main floor — 417 sq. ft.

No. 92052

This plan features:

Three bedrooms

Two full and one half baths

At 36' feet wide this home still has a double Garage, Great Room and a large Dining Area

The Great Room is topped by a cathedral ceiling and flows into the Dining Area

The Dining Area has direct access to the rear Patio

Three nice-sized Bedrooms and two full Baths are on the second floor

The Master Bedroom is highlighted by a cathedral ceiling and a wardrobe closet

Secondary Bedrooms share the full Bath in the hall

This home is designed with a basement foundation

First floor — 615 sq. ft.

Second floor — 574 sq. ft.

Basement — 615 sq. ft.

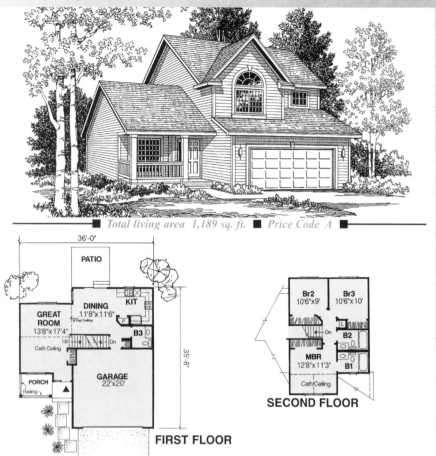

■ *Total living area 1,189 sq. ft.* ■ *Price Code A* ■

FIRST FLOOR

SECOND FLOOR

Inviting Porch

No. 90682

This plan features:

Three bedrooms

Two full baths

A large and spacious Living Room that adjoins the Dining Room for ease in entertaining

A private bedroom wing offering a quiet atmosphere

A Master Bedroom with his and her closets and a private Bath

An efficient Kitchen with a walk-in Pantry

This home is designed with basement and slab foundation options

Main floor — 1,103 sq. ft.

Laundry/mudroom — 83 sq. ft.

Garage — 490 sq. ft.

■ *Total living area 1,243 sq. ft.* ■ *Price Code A* ■

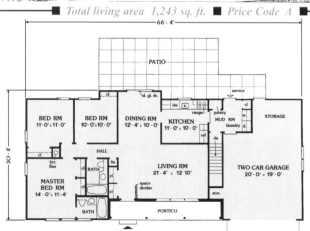

MAIN FLOOR

That Old Fashioned Feeling

Total living area 1,492 sq. ft. ■ *Price Code A* ■

SECOND FLOOR

FIRST FLOOR

No. 97250

■ **This plan features:**

— Three bedrooms

— Two full and one half baths

■ A wrapping front Porch

■ Decorative columns define the Great Room

■ The U-shaped Kitchen includes a built-in Pantry

■ The Master Suite is topped by a vaulted ceiling

■ Two additional spacious Bedrooms share the full Bath

■ This home is designed with basement, slab and crawlspace foundation options

First floor — 757 sq. ft.
Second floor — 735 sq. ft.
Basement — 757 sq. ft.
Garage — 447 sq. ft.

■ *Total living area 1,280 sq. ft.* ■ *Price Code A* ■

No. 98747

This plan features:

- Three bedrooms

- Two full baths

- Front Entry leading to generous Living Room with a vaulted ceiling

- Large two-car Garage with access through Utility Room

- Roomy secondary Bedrooms share the full Bath in the hall

- Kitchen highlighted by a built-in Pantry and a garden window

- Vaulted ceiling adds volume to the Dining Room

- Master Suite in an isolated location enhanced by abundant closet space, separate vanity and linen storage

- This home is designed with a crawlspace foundation

Main floor — 1,280 sq. ft.

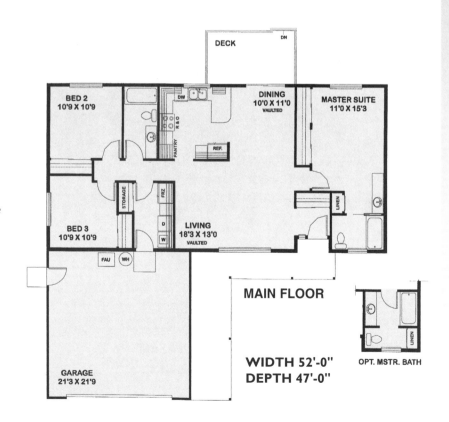

MAIN FLOOR

WIDTH 52'-0"
DEPTH 47'-0"

OPT. MSTR. BATH

Compact and Charming

■ Total living area 1,206 sq. ft. ■ Price Code A ■

No. 90951

■ **This plan features:**

— Three bedrooms

— One full and two half baths

■ Covered Porch shelters guests entering central Foyer

■ Spacious Living Room with cozy fireplace and elegant bay window

■ Formal Dining Room with view of rear yard adjoins Living Room

■ Efficient, U-shaped Kitchen highlighted by bright eating Nook

■ Handy first floor Laundry Room, half Bath and Garage entrance

■ Master Bedroom with private half Bath

■ Two additional Bedrooms share a full Bath

■ This home is designed with a basement foundation

First floor — 670 sq. ft.
Second floor — 536 sq. ft.

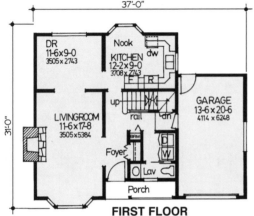

FIRST FLOOR

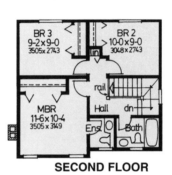

SECOND FLOOR

Charming Three-Bedroom

■ Total living area 1,222 sq. ft. ■ Price Code A ■

No. 97259

■ **This plan features:**

— Three bedrooms

— Two full baths

■ Covered Porch leads into Foyer with plant shelves and Vaulted Family Room beyond

■ Efficient Kitchen with Pantry, Laundry and pass-through opens to bright Breakfast Area

■ Private Master Suite offers a vaulted ceiling, walk-in closet and vaulted Master Bath

■ Two secondary Bedrooms with spacious closets share a full Bath in the hall

■ This home is designed with basement and crawlspace foundation options

Main floor — 1,222 sq. ft.
Basement — 1,218 sq. ft.
Garage — 410 sq. ft.

MAIN FLOOR

OPT. BASEMENT STAIR LOCATION

■ *Total living area 1,493 sq. ft.* ■ *Price Code A* ■

No. 94135

This plan features:

Three bedrooms

Two full and one half baths

Columns define the entrance from the Great Room to the Dining Room and also support an overhead plant shelf

First floor Master Bedroom includes a large closet and private Bath

Entry from Garage includes Laundry closet and Powder Room

Two secondary Bedrooms share a balcony that overlooks the Great Room

This home is designed with a basement foundation

First floor — 973 sq. ft.

Second floor — 520 sq. ft.

Basement — 973 sq. ft.

Garage — 462 sq. ft.

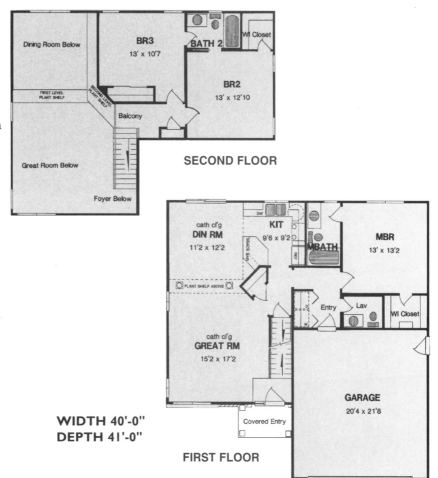

SECOND FLOOR

FIRST FLOOR

WIDTH 40'-0"
DEPTH 41'-0"

Traditional Country Cape

■ *Total living area 1,494 sq. ft.* ■ *Price Code A* ■

SECOND FLOOR

FIRST FLOOR

No. 99022

■ **This plan features:**

— Three bedrooms

— Two full and one half baths

■ Entry area with a coat closet

■ An ample Living Room includes
  fireplace

■ The Dining Room offers a view of
  the rear yard

■ A U-shaped Kitchen has a
  double sink, ample cabinet and
  counter space and a side door to
  the outside

■ A first floor Master Suite with a
  private Master Bath

■ Two additional second floor
  Bedrooms that share a full, double
  vanitied Bath with a separate
  shower

■ This home is designed with a
  basement foundation

First floor — 913 sq. ft.
Second floor — 581 sq. ft.

■ *Total living area 1,208 sq. ft.* ■ *Price Code A* ■

No. 98915

This plan features:

Three bedrooms

Two full baths

Porch shelters Entry into Living Area with an inviting fireplace topped by a vaulted ceiling

Convenient Dining Area opens to Living Room, Kitchen and Sun Deck

Efficient, U-shaped Kitchen serves Dining Area and Sun Deck beyond

Pampering Master Bedroom with a vaulted ceiling, two closets and a double vanity Bath

Two additional Bedrooms share a full Bath and convenient Laundry center

This home is designed with a basement foundation

Main floor — 1,208 sq. ft.
Basement — 728 sq. ft.
Garage — 480 sq. ft.

MAIN FLOOR

Sundeck
10-0 x 10-0

M. Bath

Bedroom 2

Kitchen
8-0 x 10-0

Dining
10-4 x 10-0

Bath 2

W. D.

Opt. Plant Shelf
Open To Bdrm.

Vaulted Ceil.

Ref.

Master Bedroom
11-6 x 14-6

Cls.

Down

Family Room
18-4 x 13-0

Vaulted Ceil.

Bedroom 3
11-0 x 10-0

Entry

© 1989, Jannis vann & Associates, Inc.

48-0

2-4

10-0

29-0

Contemporary Classic

Total living area 1,498 sq. ft. ■ Price Code A

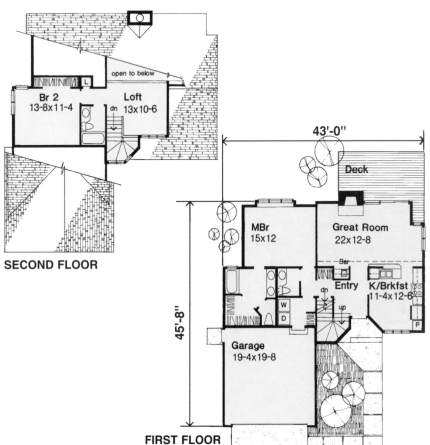

SECOND FLOOR

FIRST FLOOR

No. 99314

■ This plan features:

— Two bedrooms

— Two and a half baths

■ A well-appointed Kitchen with an angular Nook

■ A two-story Great Room accentuated by a massive fireplace and glass sliders to the rear Deck

■ A bump-out window seat and private Bath with double vanities in the Master Suite

■ This home is designed with a basement foundation

First floor — 1,044 sq. ft.
Second floor — 454 sq. ft.
Basement — 1,044 sq. ft.
Garage — 380 sq. ft.

Empty Nest Delight

No. 82026

This plan features:

Three bedrooms

Two full baths

Covered Porch leads to Foyer with coat closet

Large Great Room features a corner fireplace and access to a rear Porch

The Kitchen offers plenty of counter space and a serving bar open to the Great Room, and adjoins a sunny Breakfat Room

The Master Bedroom has a spacious Bath featuring a Spa tub surrounded by his and hers walk-in closets

This home is designed with slab and crawlspace foundation options

Main Floor — 1,485 sq. ft.

Garage — 415 sq. ft.

Porch — 180 sq. ft.

REAR ELEVATION

MAIN FLOOR

■ *Total living area 1,485 sq. ft.* ■ *Price Code A* ■

Mountain Retreat

No. 34625

This plan features:

Two bedrooms

Two full baths

A Deck entrance through double sliding glass doors into a spacious Living Room with a cozy fireplace and a sloped ceiling

An efficient, U-shaped Kitchen with an open counter to the Living Room and a view

A Master Bedroom with a double closet, full Bath and a Laundry Room

An upper level with a Bedroom and a Loft sharing a full Bath

This home is designed with basement, slab and crawlspace foundation options

First floor — 780 sq. ft

Second floor — 451 sq. ft.

Basement — 780 sq. ft.

■ *Total living area 1,231 sq. ft.* ■ *Price Code A* ■

SECOND FLOOR

FIRST FLOOR

SLAB/CRAWL SPACE OPTION

Uncomplicated Living Space

■ *Total living area 1,212 sq. ft.* ■ *Price Code A* ■

MAIN FLOOR

No. 94913

■ **This plan features:**

— Two bedrooms

— One full and one three-quarter bath

■ Recessed Entrance below keystone arch adds distinctive detail to elevation

■ Spacious Great Room highlighted by a large fireplace between transom windows and built-in shelves

■ Breakfast Area with access to rear yard easily served by snack bar counter in step saving Kitchen

■ Laundry Room and Garage Entry convenient to Kitchen

■ Master Bedroom complemented by a large walk-in closet and a double vanity Bath

■ The second Bedroom next to a full Bath and linen closet

■ This home is designed with a basement foundation

■ Alternate foundation options available at an additional charge. Please call 1-800-235-5700 for additional information.

Main floor — 1,212 sq. ft.
Basement — 1,212 sq. ft.
Garage — 448 sq. ft.

Designed for Narrow Lots

■ *Total living area 1,250 sq. ft.* ■ *Price Code A* ■

SECOND FLOOR

FIRST FLOOR

No. 91091

■ **This plan features:**

— Three bedrooms

— Two full baths

■ An efficient floor plan makes the most from narrow or infill building lots

■ A trellis compliments the covered Porch and provides a relaxing retreat

■ Open floor plan allows maximum use of space in this home

■ Living and Dining Areas are open to efficient galley Kitchen with ample counter space

■ First floor Master Bedroom is a secluded hideaway with a vaulted ceiling

■ Two second floor Bedrooms share a full Bath and each have ample closet space

■ This home is designed with a crawlspace foundation

First floor — 842 sq. ft.
Second floor — 408 sq. ft.

■ *Total living area 1,475 sq. ft.* ■ *Price Code A* ■

No. 93416

This plan features:

Three bedrooms

Two full baths

Down-sized Country plan for home builder on a budget

Great front Porch made for relaxing and welcoming neighbors opens into large Living Room with corner fireplace

The L-shaped Kitchen includes a center island and oversized Laundry closet

The Dining Room opens to a rear Deck

A covered walk joins the home to the Garage

This home is designed with slab and crawlspace foundation options

Main floor — 1,475 sq. ft.
Garage — 455 sq. ft.
Porch — 234 sq. ft.

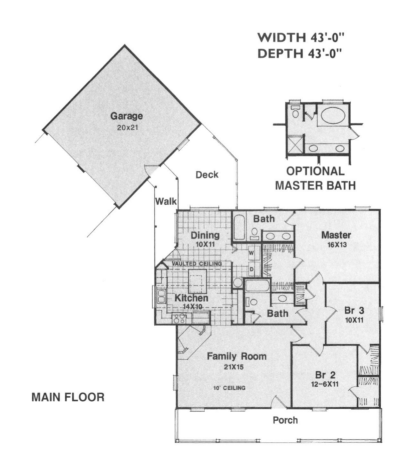

WIDTH 43'-0"
DEPTH 43'-0"

OPTIONAL MASTER BATH

MAIN FLOOR

Quaint and Cozy Ranch

■ Total living area 1,185 sq. ft. ■ Price Code A ■

MAIN FLOOR

OPTIONAL BASEMENT

No. 98461

■ **This plan features:**

— Three bedrooms

— Two full baths

■ A Great Room includes a vaulted ceiling and cozy fireplace with windows to either side

■ A galley Kitchen is efficiently arranged flowing into the Eating Area

■ A Covered Porch expands living space outdoors

■ A Master Suite with a tray ceiling over the Bedroom and a vaulted ceiling over the private Bath

■ Two secondary Bedrooms share the full Bath in the hall

■ This home is designed with basement and crawlspace foundation options

Main floor – 1,185 sq. ft.
Basement – 1,185 sq. ft.
Garage – 425 sq. ft.

Vaulted Ceiling

■ Total living area 1,246 sq. ft. ■ Price Code A ■

FIRST FLOOR

SECOND FLOOR

No. 90353

■ **This plan features:**

— Three bedrooms

— Two full baths

■ A vaulted ceiling in the Living Room and the Dining Room, with a clerestory above

■ A Master Bedroom with a walk-in closet and full Bath

■ An efficient Kitchen with a corner double sink and peninsula counter

■ A Dining Room with sliding doors to the Deck

■ A Living Room with a fireplace that adds warmth to open areas

■ Two additional Bedrooms that share a full Bathroom

■ This home is designed with a basement foundation

First floor — 846 sq. ft.
Second floor — 400 sq. ft.

Simplicity and Efficiency

1,501-2,000 sq. ft. HOME PLANS

■ *Total living area 1,701 sq. ft.* ■ *Price Code B* ■

No. 93404

This plan features:

Three bedrooms

Two full and one half baths

A well-appointed Kitchen that serves the formal Dining Room and the informal Breakfast Area with equal ease

A wood Deck, accessed from the Breakfast Area, that increases the living space in the warmer months

A wood stove in the Family Room that adds to the cozy feeling

This home is designed with a basement foundation

First floor — 878 sq. ft.
Second floor — 823 sq. ft.
Basement — 878 sq. ft.
Garage — 427 sq. ft.
Bonus room — 257 sq. ft.

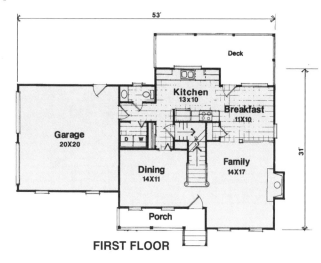

FIRST FLOOR

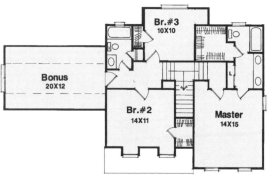

SECOND FLOOR

High Ceilings and Arched Windows

No. 98441

■ **This plan features:**

— Three bedrooms

— Two full baths

■ Natural illumination streaming into the Dining Room and Sitting Area of the Master Suite through large, arched windows

■ Kitchen with convenient pass-through to the Great Room and a serving bar for the Breakfast Room

■ Great Room topped by a vaulted ceiling accented by a fireplace and a French door

■ Decorative columns accenting the entrance of the Dining Room

■ Tray ceiling over the Master Suite and a vaulted ceiling over the Sitting Room and the Master Bath

■ This home is designed with basement and crawlspace foundation options

Main floor — 1,502 sq. ft.
Basement — 1,555 sq. ft.
Garage — 448 sq. ft.

Total living area 1,502 sq. ft. ■ Price Code B

MAIN FLOOR

© Frank Betz Associates, Inc.

Timeless Two-Story

No. 99155

■ **This plan features:**

— Three bedrooms

— Two full and one half baths

■ This plan has functionality without sacrificing style

■ The Dining Room runs the width of the home with a corner fireplace for added coziness

■ The Kitchen/Dining Area is arranged for convenience and efficiency

■ The Bedrooms are all located on the second floor

■ This home is designed with a basement foundation

First floor — 786 sq. ft.
Second floor — 723 sq. ft.
Basement — 786 sq. ft.
Garage — 406 sq. ft.

Total living area 1,509 sq. ft. ■ Price Code B

FIRST FLOOR

SECOND FLOOR

WIDTH 40'-0"
DEPTH 40'-0"

A-Frame for Year-Round Living

■ *Total living area 1,702 sq. ft.* ■ *Price Code B* ■

No. 90930

This plan features:

Three bedrooms

One full and one three-quarter baths

A vaulted ceiling in the Living Room with a massive fireplace

A wrap-around Sun Deck that gives you a lot of outdoor Living Space

A luxurious Master Suite complete with a walk-in closet, full Bath and private Deck

Two additional Bedrooms that share a full Bath

This home is designed with a basement foundation

Main floor — 1,238 sq. ft.
Loft — 464 sq. ft.
Basement — 1,175 sq. ft.

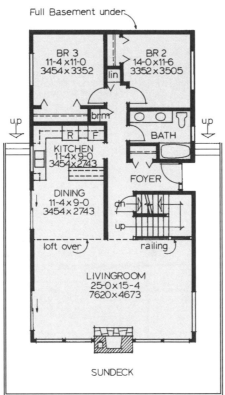

Full Basement under

BR 3
11-4 x 11-0
3454 x 3352

BR 2
14-0 x 11-6
3352 x 3505

lin

BATH

up

up

R F

KITCHEN
11-4 x 9-0
3454 x 2743

FOYER

DINING
11-4 x 9-0
3454 x 2743

dn

loft over

railing

up

LIVINGROOM
25-0 x 15-4
7620 x 4673

SUNDECK

MAIN FLOOR

WIDTH 34'-0"
DEPTH 56'-0"

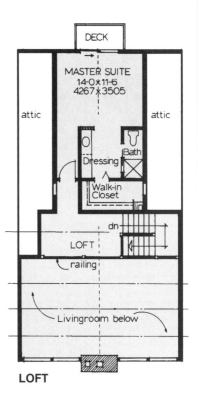

DECK

MASTER SUITE
14-0 x 11-6
4267 x 3505

attic

attic

Bath

Dressing

Walk-in
Closet

lin

dn

LOFT

railing

Livingroom below

LOFT

Enchanting Elevation

■ *Total living area 1,704 sq. ft.* ■ *Price Code B* ■

SECOND FLOOR

Bath

Master Bedroom
15'2" x 14'6"

Bedroom
10'1" x 11'6"

walk-in closet

Bath

Bedroom
13'6" x 10'0"

No. 92695

■ **This plan features:**

— Three bedrooms

— One full, one three-quarter and one half baths

■ The large Foyer showcases interesting angled entries to the rooms beyond

■ The Dining Room has a tray ceiling and is directly connected to the Kitchen

■ The Kitchen is well equipped and features a serving bar

■ The Breakfast Nook has an access door to the rear yard and stairs to the second floor

■ This home is designed with a basement foundation

First floor — 906 sq. ft.
Second floor — 798 sq. ft.
Basement — 906 sq. ft.
Garage — 437 sq. ft.

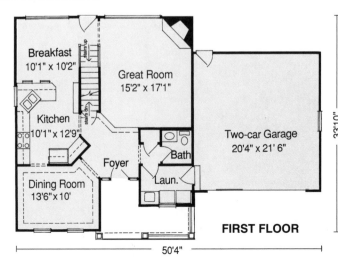

Breakfast
10'1" x 10'2"

Great Room
15'2" x 17'1"

Kitchen
10'1" x 12'9"

Foyer

Bath

Laun.

Two-car Garage
20'4" x 21' 6"

Dining Room
13'6" x 10'

33'10"

50'4"

FIRST FLOOR

Efficient Country Cottage

No. 97456

This plan features:

- Three bedrooms
- Two full baths
- Cottage styling adds tremendous curb appeal
- The Dining Room has a decorative ceiling
- The Kitchen, Breakfast Area and Great Room open to each other
- The Great Room has a cathedral ceilings, a fireplace and direct access to the Deck
- The Master Bedroom has a cathedral ceiling, walk-in closet and five-piece Bath
- Two additional Bedrooms share a full Bath
- This home is designed with a basement foundation
- Alternate foundation options available at an additional charge. Please call 1-800-235-5700 for more information.

Main floor — 1,758 sq. ft.
Garage — 494 sq. ft.

■ Total living area 1,758 sq. ft. ■ Price Code C ■

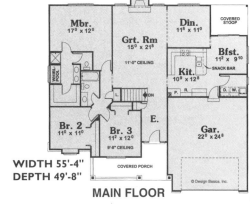

WIDTH 55'-4"
DEPTH 49'-8"

MAIN FLOOR

Arched Windows

No. 97757

This plan features:

- Three bedrooms
- Two full baths
- Multi-paned bay window, dormers, covered Porch and a variety of building materials provide warm appeal for this plan
- Foyer opens to formal Dining Room and a large Great Room with fireplace, cathedral ceiling and a wall of windows
- Kitchen convenient to Dining Room, Breakfast Alcove, Utility, Garage and Deck
- Master Bedroom wing features Deck access and a plush Master Bath
- Two secondary Bedrooms with ample closets, share another full Bath
- This home is designed with a basement foundation

Main floor — 1,755 sq. ft.
Garage — 796 sq. ft.

■ Total living area 1,755 sq. ft. ■ Price Code B ■

MAIN FLOOR

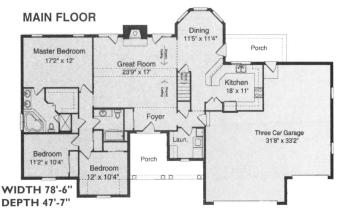

WIDTH 78'-6"
DEPTH 47'-7"

Open-Plan Living

■ *Total living area 1,792 sq. ft.* ■ *Price Code C* ■

REAR ELEVATION

No. 20198

■ This plan features:

—Three bedrooms

—Two full baths

■ Today's comforts with cost-effective construction

■ The Living Room features a fabulous beamed ceiling and fireplace with stone hearth

■ The efficient Kitchen is open to the Dining Room, which has access to a rear Deck

■ The Master Bedroom includes a private Bath and large closet

■ A Pantry and Laundry Room located near the Dining Room enhance the efficiency of this plan

■ This home is designed with a basement foundation

Main floor — 1,792 sq. ft.
Basment — 818 sq. ft.
Garage — 857 sq. ft.

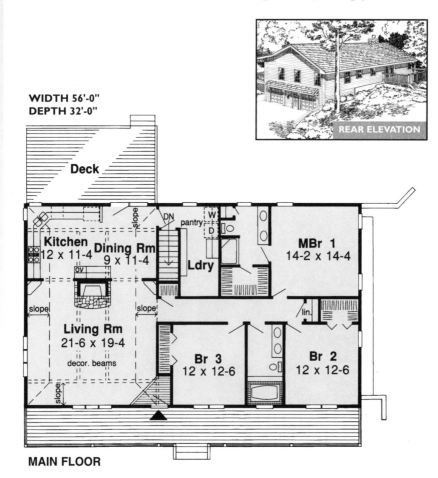

WIDTH 56'-0"
DEPTH 32'-0"

Deck

Kitchen
12 x 11-4

Dining Rm
9 x 11-4

DN

pantry

Ldry

W
D

MBr 1
14-2 x 14-4

ov

slope

slope

Living Rm
21-6 x 19-4

decor. beams

slope

lin.

Br 3
12 x 12-6

Br 2
12 x 12-6

MAIN FLOOR

■ *Total living area   1,707 sq. ft.* ■ *Price Code B* ■

No. 91514

This plan features:

Three bedrooms

Two full and one half baths

An outstanding two-story Great Room with an unusual floor-to-ceiling corner front window and cozy hearth fireplace

A formal Dining Room opening from the Great Room makes entertaining easy

An efficient Kitchen with a work island, Pantry, a corner sink opening to the Great Room, and a bright, bay window eating Nook

A quiet, Master Suite with a vaulted ceiling and a plush Bath with a double vanity, Spa tub and walk-in closet

This home is designed with a crawlspace foundation

First floor — 1,230 sq. ft.
Second floor — 477 sq. ft.
Bonus — 195 sq. ft.

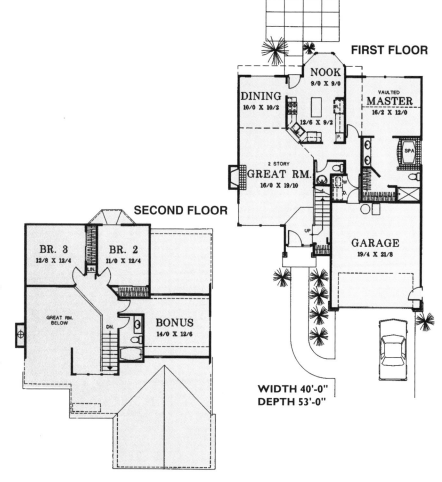

FIRST FLOOR

NOOK
9/0 X 9/0

DINING
10/0 X 10/2

VAULTED
MASTER
16/2 X 12/0

12/6 X 9/2

2 STORY
GREAT RM.
16/0 X 19/10

SPA

SECOND FLOOR

BR. 3
12/8 X 12/4

BR. 2
11/0 X 12/4

LIN.

GREAT RM.
BELOW

DN.

BONUS
14/0 X 12/6

UP

GARAGE
19/4 X 21/8

WIDTH 40'-0"
DEPTH 53'-0"

Cozy Three Bedroom

■ *Total living area 1,515 sq. ft.* ■ *Price Code B* ■

No. 96522

■ **This plan features:**

— Three bedrooms

— Two full baths

■ The triple-arched front Porch add[?] to the curb appeal of the home

■ The expansive Great Room is accented by a cozy gas fireplace

■ The efficient Kitchen includes a[?] eating bar that separates it from the Great Room

■ The Master Bedroom is highlighted by a walk-in closet and a whirlpool Bath

■ Two secondary Bedrooms share use of a full Bath

■ This home is designed with slab and crawlspace foundation options

Main floor — 1,515 sq. ft.
Garage — 528 sq. ft.
Porch — 225 sq. ft.

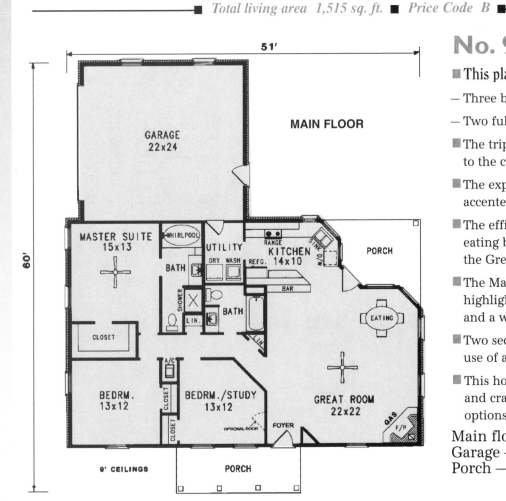

MAIN FLOOR

51'

60'

GARAGE
22x24

MASTER SUITE
15x13

WHIRLPOOL

UTILITY

RANGE
KITCHEN
14x10

SINK D/W

PORCH

BATH

DRY   WASH   REFG.

SHOWER

BAR

BATH

LIN.

EATING

CLOSET

A/C

BEDRM.
13x12

CLOSET

CLOSET

BEDRM./STUDY
13x12

GREAT ROOM
22x22

GAS
F/P

OPTIONAL DOOR

FOYER

9' CEILINGS

PORCH

Second-Floor Balcony

■ *Total living area 1,765 sq. ft.* ■ *Price Code C* ■

No. 98931

This plan features:

Three bedrooms

Two full and one half baths

The Living Room soars two full stories with pleasing architectural details like dormer windows and an overhead plant shelf

The Master Bath has a sloped ceiling over a garden tub

The open Breakfast Nook offers views of the Sun Deck and backyard

This home is designed with a basement foundation

First floor — 1,210 sq. ft.
Second floor — 555 sq. ft.
Garage — 612 sq. ft
Porch — 144 sq. ft.

WIDTH 43'-4"
DEPTH 37'-0"

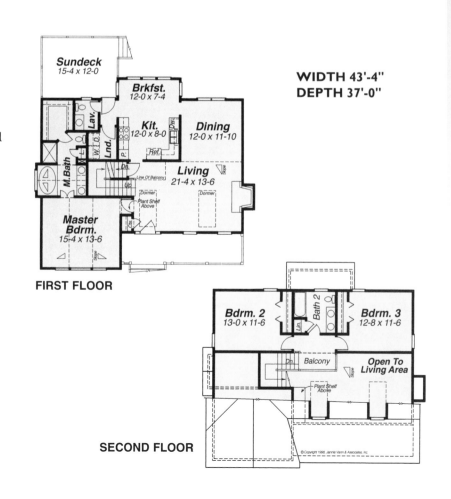

Elegant Dining Room

■ *Total living area 1,710 sq. ft.* ■ *Price Code B* ■

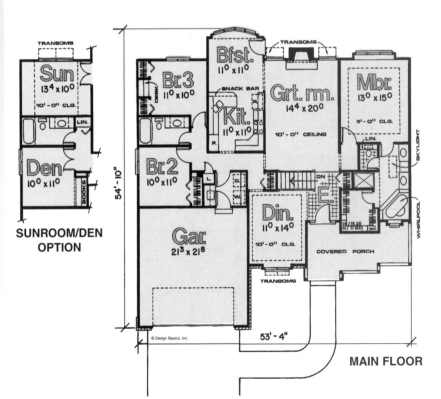

SUNROOM/DEN OPTION

Sun 13⁴ x 10⁰
10'-0" CLG.

Den 10⁰ x 11⁰
BOOKS

Br.3 11⁰ x 10⁰

Bfst. 11⁰ x 11⁰

SNACK BAR

Kit. 11⁰ x 11⁰

Grt. rm. 14⁴ x 20⁰
10'-0" CEILING

Mbr. 13⁰ x 15⁰
9'-0" CLG.

LIN.

Br.2 10⁰ x 11⁰

Din. 11⁰ x 14⁰
10'-0" CLG.

Gar. 21³ x 21⁸

COVERED PORCH

WHIRLPOOL

SKYLIGHT

TRANSOMS

54'-10"

53'-4"

© Design Basics, Inc.

MAIN FLOOR

No. 94922

■ **This plan features:**

— Three bedrooms

— Two full baths

■ Formal Dining Room off Entry features a double transom window crowned by a decorative ceiling

■ Volume Great Room with raised hearth fireplace framed by transom windows

■ Well-designed Kitchen with built-in Pantry, peninsula snack bar and bright Breakfast Area

■ This home is designed with a basement foundation

■ Alternate foundation options available at an additional charge. Please call 1-800-235-5700 for additional information.

Main floor — 1,710 sq. ft.
Basement — 1,710 sq. ft.
Garage — 480 sq. ft.

Attractive Gables and Arches

No. 94917

This plan features:

- Three bedrooms
- Two full baths
- Entry opens to formal Dining Room with arched window
- Angles and transom windows add interest to the Great Room
- Bright Hearth area expands Breakfast/Kitchen area and shares three-sided fireplace
- Kitchen offers an angled snack bar and a large Pantry
- This home comes with a slab foundation.
- Alternate foundation options available at an additional charge, call 1.800.235.5700 for more information.

Main floor — 1,782 sq. ft.
Basement — 1,782 sq. ft.
Garage — 466 sq. ft.

■ *Total living area 1,782 sq. ft.* ■ *Price Code C* ■

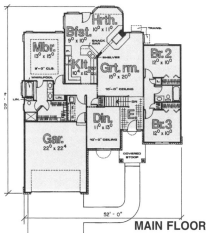

MAIN FLOOR

Country Flair

No. 10785

This plan features:

- Three bedrooms
- Two full and one half baths
- This charming home features a lovely wrap-around Porch
- The open Foyer includes a coat closet and Powder Room
- The Dining Room features a beautiful bay window
- The large Living Room and the Master Bedroom open through sliders onto a rear Deck
- This home is designed with basement, slab and crawlspace foundation options

First floor — 1,269 sq. ft.
Second floor — 638 sq. ft.
Basement — 1,269 sq. ft.

■ *Total living area 1,907 sq. ft.* ■ *Price Code C* ■

WIDTH 47'-0"
DEPTH 39'-0"

FIRST FLOOR

CRAWLSPACE/SLAB OPTION

SECOND FLOOR

133

Compact Comfort

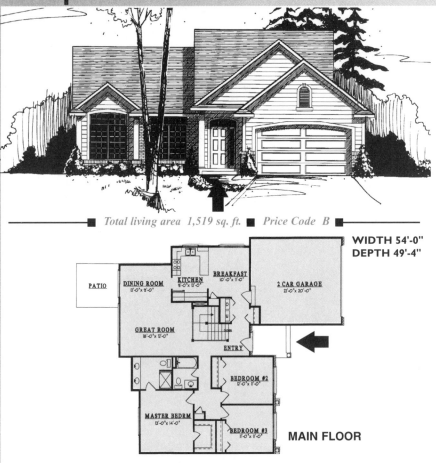

■ Total living area 1,519 sq. ft. ■ Price Code B ■

WIDTH 54'-0"
DEPTH 49'-4"

MAIN FLOOR

No. 93129

■ **This plan features:**

— Three bedrooms

— One full and one three-quarter baths

■ An open-rail staircase in the Entry leads t[...]
the basement

■ Sliding doors from the Dining Room to th[...]
Patio

■ A Master Suite with walk-in closet and du[...]
vanities in the
three-quarter Bath

■ This home is designed with a basement
foundation

Main floor — 1,519 sq. ft.

Duplex For a Sloping Lot

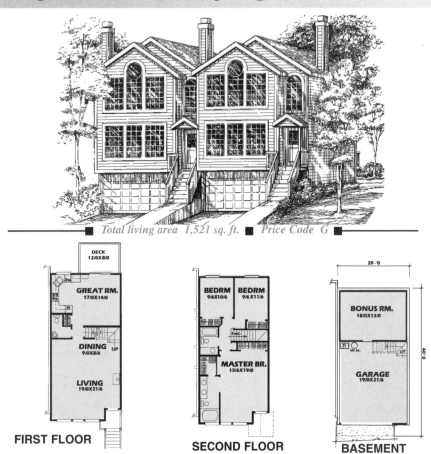

■ Total living area 1,521 sq. ft. ■ Price Code G ■

FIRST FLOOR   **SECOND FLOOR**   **BASEMENT**

No. 91323

■ **This plan features:**

— Three bedrooms

— Two full and one half baths

■ Multiple windows front and back provide[...]
lots of natural light

■ Expansive Living/Dining Area with cozy
fireplace for easy entertaining

■ U-shaped Kitchen opens to Great Room a[...]
Deck beyond for expanded living space

■ Large Master Bedroom offers a wonderful
view, two closets and a double-vanity Bat[...]
with a window tub

■ Two additional Bedrooms with ample
closets share a full Bath

■ Bonus Room behind Garage for many use[...]

■ This home is designed with a basement
foundation

First floor — 788 sq. ft.
Second floor — 733 sq. ft.

■ *Total living area 1,715 sq. ft.* ■ *Price Code B* ■

No. 98456

This plan features:

Three bedrooms

Two full baths

A covered Entry gives way to a 14-foot high ceiling in the Foyer

An arched opening greets you in the Great Room that also has a vaulted ceiling and a fireplace

The Dining Room is brightened by triple windows with transoms above

The Kitchen is a gourmet's delight and is open to the Breakfast Nook

The Master Suite is sweet with a tray ceiling, vaulted Sitting Area and private Bath

This home is designed with basement, slab and crawlspace foundation options

Main floor — 1,715 sq. ft.
Basement — 1,715 sq. ft.
Garage — 450 sq. ft.

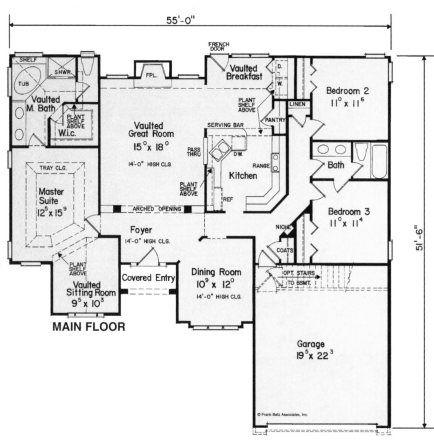

Upper-Level Bedrooms

■ *Total living area 1,719 sq. ft.* ■ *Price Code B* ■

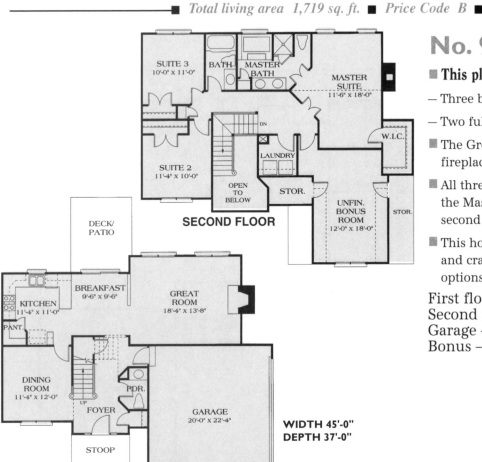

SECOND FLOOR

SUITE 3
10'-0" x 11'-0"

BATH

MASTER BATH

MASTER SUITE
11'-6" x 18'-0"

W.I.C.

SUITE 2
11'-4" x 10'-0"

LAUNDRY

OPEN TO BELOW

STOR.

UNFIN. BONUS ROOM
12'-0" x 18'-0"

STOR.

DN

FIRST FLOOR

DECK/ PATIO

BREAKFAST
9'-6" x 9'-6"

GREAT ROOM
18'-4" x 13'-8"

KITCHEN
11'-4" x 11'-0"

PANT.

DINING ROOM
11'-4" x 12'-0"

PDR.

FOYER

UP

GARAGE
20'-0" x 22'-4"

STOOP

WIDTH 45'-0"
DEPTH 37'-0"

No. 96900

■ **This plan features:**

— Three bedrooms

— Two full and one half baths

■ The Great Room features a fireplace and wide backyard view

■ All three Bedrooms, including the Master Suite, are on the second floor

■ This home is designed with slab and crawlspace foundation options

First floor — 844 sq. ft.
Second floor — 875 sq. ft.
Garage — 466 sq. ft.
Bonus — 242 sq. ft.

Cozy Front Porch

■ *Total living area 1,728 sq. ft.* ■ *Price Code B* ■

No. 97434

This plan features:

Four bedrooms

Two full and one half baths

Terrific Great Room with 12-foot ceiling and fireplace

Kitchen/Breakfast Room with ample counter and storage

Laundry Room doubling as a Mudroom, eliminating tracked-in dirt

The Master Bedroom includes a private double vanity Bath and a walk-in closet

This home is designed with a basement foundation

Alternate foundation options available at an additional charge. Please call 1-800-235-5700 for additional information.

First floor — 845 sq. ft.
Second floor — 883 sq. ft.
Garage — 454 sq. ft.

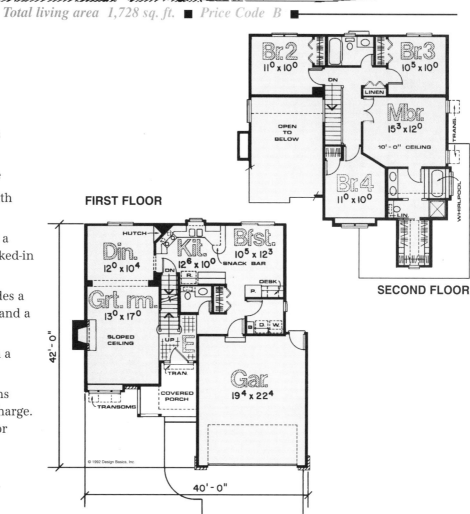

FIRST FLOOR

SECOND FLOOR

Lovely Covered Porches

■ Total living area 1,768 sq. ft. ■ Price Code C ■

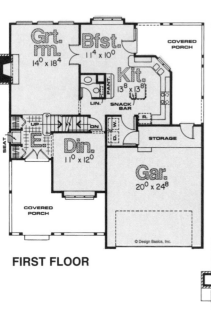

WIDTH 40'-8"
DEPTH 46'-0"

FIRST FLOOR

SECOND FLOOR

No. 94907

■ This plan features:

— Three bedrooms

— Two full one half baths

■ Large covered Porch leads to tile Entry with generous closet space

■ Great Room features a fireplace and French doors opening into the sunny Breakfast Room

■ Master Bedroom with cathedral ceiling includes his and hers closets and Dressing Area

■ This home is designed with a basement foundation

■ Alternate foundation options available at an additional charge. Please call 1-800-235-5700 for additional information.

First floor — 905 sq. ft.
Second floor — 863 sq. ft.
Basement — 905 sq. ft.
Garage — 487 sq. ft.

Brick Abounds

No. 98522

This plan features:

Three bedrooms

Two full baths

The covered front Porch opens into the Entry that has a 10-foot ceiling and a coat closet

The large Living Room is distinguished by a fireplace and a front window wall

The Dining Room features a 10-foot ceiling and access to the rear covered Patio

The Kitchen is angled and has a Pantry and a cooktop island

The Master Bedroom is located in the rear for privacy and boasts a triangular walk-in closet, plus a private Bath

Two more Bedrooms each have large closets and share a full Bath

This home has a two-car Garage that is accessed through the Utility Room

This home is designed with a slab foundation

Main floor — 1,528 sq. ft.

Garage — 440 sq. ft.

Total living area 1,528 sq. ft. ■ *Price Code B* ■

MAIN FLOOR

Four-Bedroom Design

No. 90358

This plan features:

Three bedrooms

Two full baths

A vaulted ceiling in the Great Room and a fireplace

An efficient Kitchen with a peninsula counter and double sink

A Family Room with easy access to the wood Deck

A Master Bedroom with private Bath entrance

Convenient Laundry facilities outside the Master Bedroom

Two additional Bedrooms upstairs with walk-in closets and the use of the full Bath

This home is designed with a basement foundation

First floor — 1,062 sq. ft.

Second floor — 469 sq. ft.

Total living area 1,531 sq. ft. ■ *Price Code B* ■

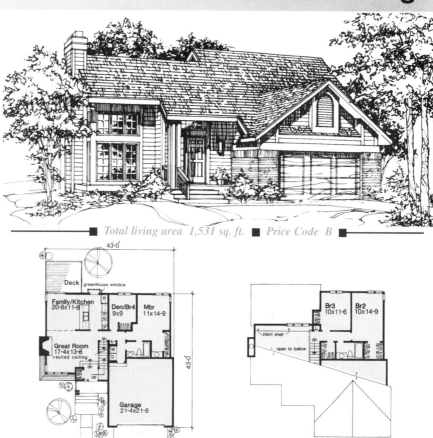

FIRST FLOOR

SECOND FLOOR

139

Cozy Front Porch

Photography by John Ehren

■ Total living area 1,735 sq. ft. ■ Price Code B ■

SECOND FLOOR

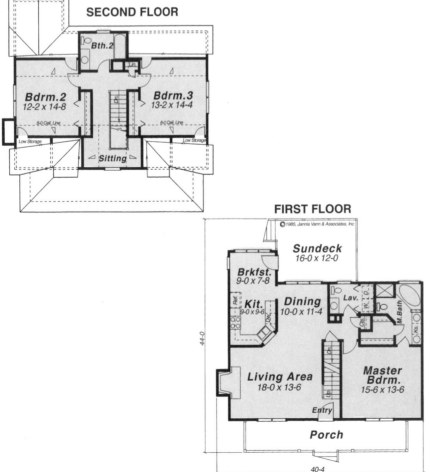

Bth.2

Bdrm.2
12-2 x 14-8

Bdrm.3
13-2 x 14-4

Low Storage

Low Storage

Sitting

FIRST FLOOR

© 1985, Jannis Vann & Associates, Inc.

Sundeck
16-0 x 12-0

Brkfst.
9-0 x 7-8

Kit.
9-0 x 9-6

Dining
10-0 x 11-4

Lav.

M.Bath

Living Area
18-0 x 13-6

Master
Bdrm.
15-6 x 13-6

Entry

Porch

44-0

40-4

No. 93269

■ This plan features:

— Three bedrooms

— Two full and one half bath

■ A Living Room enhanced by a large fireplace

■ A formal Dining Room that is open to the Living Room, giving more spacious feel to the rooms

■ An efficient Kitchen that include ample counter and cabinet space as well as double sinks and pass-through window to Living Area

■ A sunny Breakfast Area with vaulted ceiling and a door to the Sun Deck

■ This home is designed with a basement foundation

First floor — 1,045 sq. ft.
Second floor — 690 sq. ft.
Basement — 465 sq. ft.
Garage — 580 sq. ft.

■ *Total living area* 1,737 sq. ft. ■ *Price Code* B ■

No. 90406

This plan features:

Three bedrooms

Three full baths

A large front Parlor with a raised-hearth fireplace

A Dining Room with a sunny bay window

An efficient galley Kitchen serving the formal Dining Room and informal Breakfast Room

A beautiful Master Suite with two closets, an oversized tub and double vanity, plus a private Sitting Room with a bayed window and vaulted ceiling

This home is designed with basement, slab and crawlspace foundation options

First floor — 954 sq. ft.
Second floor — 783 sq. ft.

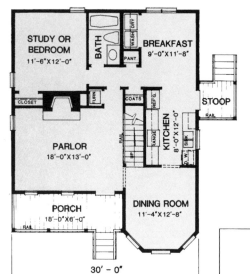

FIRST FLOOR

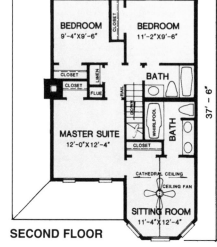

SECOND FLOOR

Bonus Room

Total living area 1,531 sq. ft. ■ *Price Code B* ■

FIRST FLOOR

SECOND FLOOR

No. 97612

■ **This plan features:**

— Three bedrooms

— Two full and one half baths

■ A Balcony overlooks the two-story Family Room

■ French door access to the rear yard from the vaulted Family Room

■ All Bedrooms are isolated for privacy

■ This home is designed with basement and crawlspace foundation options

First floor — 1,067 sq. ft.
Second floor — 464 sq. ft.
Bonus — 207 sq. ft.
Basement — 1,067 sq. ft.
Garage — 398 sq. ft

Abundance of Closet Space

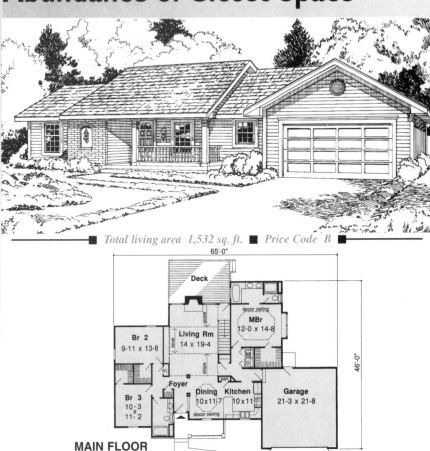

Total living area 1,532 sq. ft. ■ *Price Code B* ■

MAIN FLOOR

No. 20204

■ **This plan features:**

— Three bedrooms

— Two full baths

■ Roomy walk-in closets in all the Bedrooms

■ A Master Bedroom with decorative ceiling and a private full Bath

■ A fireplaced Living Room with sloped ceilings and sliders to the Deck

■ An efficient Kitchen, with plenty of cupboard space and a Pantry

■ This home is designed with a basement foundation

Main floor —1,532 sq. ft.
Garage — 484 sq. ft.

142

■ *Total living area 1,743 sq. ft.* ■ *Price Code B* ■

No. 97233

This plan features:

- Three bedrooms
- Two full baths
- Arched windows, keystones and shutters highlight the exterior
- The Great Room and the Breakfast Nook feature vaulted ceilings
- There is direct access from the Dining Room to the Kitchen
- The Kitchen has a space-saving Pantry and plenty of counter space
- The Master Suite is enormous and features a glass-walled Sitting Area
- A walk-in closet, a dual vanity and a whirlpool tub highlights the Master Bath
- This home is designed with a basement foundation

Main Floor — 1,743 sq. ft.
Basement — 998 sq. ft.
Garage — 763 sq. ft.

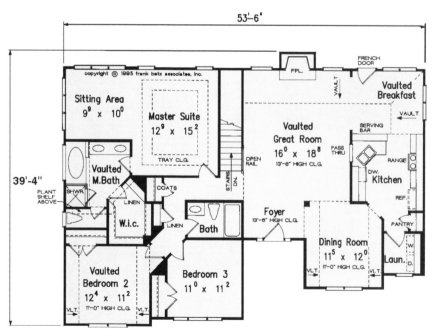

MAIN FLOOR

Enchanting Elevation

© Donald A. Gardner Architects, Inc.

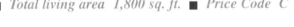

■ *Total living area 1,800 sq. ft.* ■ *Price Code C* ■

No. 97610

■ **This plan features:**

— Three bedrooms

— Two full and one half baths

■ Palladian windows and gables provide dramatic curb appeal

■ Vaulted and volume ceilings add to the feeling of spaciousness throughout this lovely home

■ The large, well-planned Kitchen open to a sunny Breakfast Room which includes a Laundry closet and access to a rear Porch

■ The secluded first floor Master Suite gets plenty of natural light

■ This home is designed with basement and crawlspace foundation options

First floor — 1,378 sq. ft.
Second floor — 422 sq. ft.
Basement — 1,378 sq. ft.
Bonus — 244 sq. ft.

SECOND FLOOR

WIDTH 48'-0"
DEPTH 45'-10"

FIRST FLOOR

■ *Total living area 1,537 sq. ft.* ■ *Price Code B* ■

No. 99167

This plan features:

Three bedrooms

Two full baths

The vaulted ceiling and open layout of the Living Room add drama to the home

The Garage Storage alcove provides room for sports or lawn equipment

One of the secondary Bedrooms has a more than 10-foot-high ceiling

This home is designed with a basement foundation

Main floor — 1,537 sq. ft.

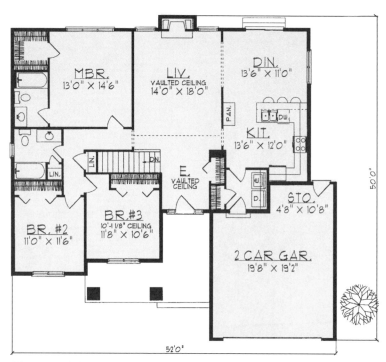

MAIN FLOOR

Triple-Arched Porch

■ *Total living area 1,744 sq. ft.* ■ *Price Code B* ■

No. 98474

■ **This plan features:**

— Four bedrooms

— Three full baths

■ A triple-arched front Porch, segmented arched window, keystones and shutters accent th exterior

■ The Family Room, Breakfast Room and Kitchen have an open layout

■ The Master Suite is topped by a tray ceiling while there is a vaulted ceiling over the Bath

■ An optional Bonus Room offers expansion for future needs

■ This home is designed with basement and crawlspace foundation options

First floor — 972 sq. ft.
Second floor — 772 sq. ft.
Bonus room — 358 sq. ft.
Basement — 972 sq. ft.
Garage — 520 sq. ft.

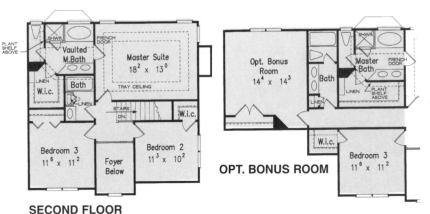

SECOND FLOOR

OPT. BONUS ROOM

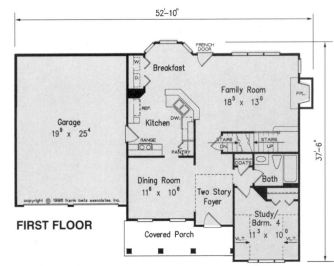

FIRST FLOOR

■ *Total living area 1,539 sq. ft.* ■ *Price Code B* ■

No. 24721

This plan features:

- Three bedrooms

- Two full baths

- Tiled Foyer leading into the Living Room

- Sloped ceiling tops the Living Room, which is also accented by a fireplace

- Built-in shelves on either side of the arched opening between the Living Room and the Dining Room

- Master Suite crowned with a decorative ceiling, and contains a private whirlpool Bath

- This home is designed with basement, crawlspace and slab foundation options

Main floor — 1,539 sq. ft.
Basement — 1,530 sq. ft.
Garage — 460 sq. ft.

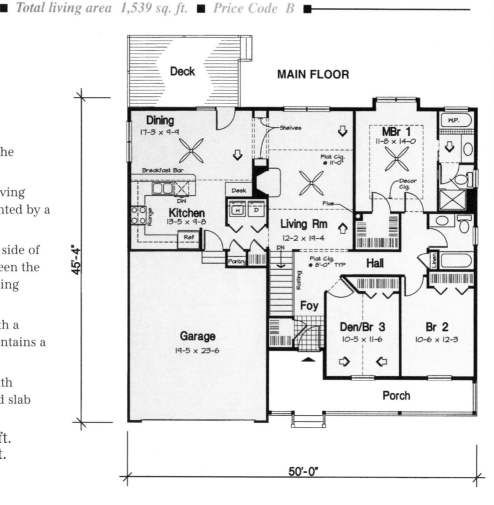

Outdoor-Lovers' Delight

■ *Total living area 1,540 sq. ft.* ■ *Price Code B* ■

No. 10748

■ **This plan features:**

– Three bedrooms

– Two full baths

■ A roomy Kitchen and Dining Room

■ A massive Living Room with a fireplace and access to the wraparound porch through double French doors

■ An elegant Master Suite and two additional spacious Bedrooms closely located to the Laundry Area

■ This home is designed with a crawlspace and slab foundation options

Main floor — 1,540 sq. ft.
Porch — 530 sq. ft.

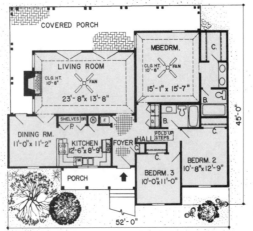

MAIN FLOOR

Hip Roof Ranch

■ *Total living area 1,540 sq. ft.* ■ *Price Code B* ■

No. 93161

■ **This plan features:**

– Three bedrooms

– Two full baths

■ Cozy front Porch leads into Entry with vaulted ceiling and sidelights

■ Open Living Room enhanced by a cathedral ceiling, a wall of windows and corner fireplace

■ Large and efficient Kitchen with an extended counter to serve a bright Dining Area that access the Screened Porch

■ Convenient Utility Area with access to Garage and Storage Area

■ Spacious Master Bedroom with a walk-in closet and private Bath

■ Two additional Bedrooms with ample closets share a full Bath

■ This home is designed with a basement foundation

Main floor — 1,540 sq. ft.
Basement — 1,540 sq. ft.

MAIN FLOOR

■ *Total living area 1,746 sq. ft.* ■ *Price Code B* ■

No. 92655

This plan features:

Three bedrooms

Two full baths

Front Porch accesses open Foyer, and spacious Dining Room and Great Room with sloped ceilings

Corner fireplace, windows and atrium door to Patio enhance Great Room

Convenient Kitchen with a Pantry, peninsula serving counter for bright Breakfast Area and nearby Laundry/Garage Entry

Luxurious Bath, walk-in closet and backyard view offered in Master Bedroom

This home is designed with a basement foundation

Main floor — 1,746 sq. ft.
Garage — 480 sq. ft.
Basement — 1,697 sq. ft.
Porch — 111 sq. ft.

WIDTH 65'-10"
DEPTH 56'-0"

MAIN FLOOR

Southern Hospitality

■ *Total living area   1,830 sq. ft.* ■ *Price Code C* ■

No. 92220

■ **This plan features:**

— Three bedrooms

— Two full baths

■ Welcoming covered Veranda catches breezes

■ Easy-care tiled Entry leads into Great Room with fieldstone fireplace, cathedral ceiling and atrium door to another covered Veranda

■ A bright Kitchen/Dining Room includes a stovetop island/ snack bar, built-in Pantry and desk, and access to the rear Veranda

■ This home is designed with basement, slab and crawlspace foundation options

Main floor — 1,830 sq. ft.
Garage — 759 sq. ft.
Porch — 390 sq. ft.

MAIN FLOOR

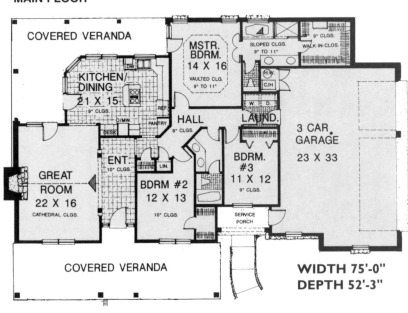

WIDTH 75'-0"
DEPTH 52'-3"

Fabulous Foyer

■ *Total living area 1,749 sq. ft.* ■ *Price Code B* ■

No. 99912

This plan features:

Three bedrooms

Three full baths

The main Living Area is located on the main floor

The Living Room looks over the two-story Foyer

Open to the Family Room and Nook, the Kitchen has a cooktop island

A covered Deck is accessed by sliding doors from the Family Room and Master Bedroom

Two additional Bedrooms share a full Bath

This home is designed with a basement foundation

Main floor — 1,749 sq. ft.

Basement — 1,433 sq. ft.

Garage — 446 sq. ft.

Deck — 294 sq. ft.

Porch — 115 sq. ft.

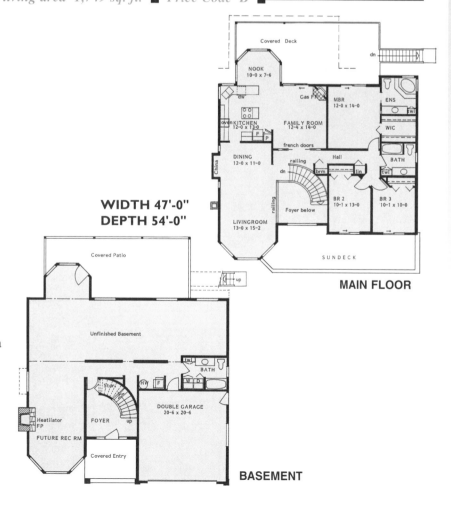

WIDTH 47'-0"
DEPTH 54'-0"

MAIN FLOOR

BASEMENT

Grace with an Elegant Front Porch

Total living area 1,750 sq. ft. ■ *Price Code B* ■

No. 98462

■ **This plan features:**

— Three bedrooms

— Two full and one half baths

■ The two-story Foyer accesses the Dining Room, Living Room and Family Room with ease

■ The Kitchen opens to the Breakfast Area which flows into the Family Room

■ The Master Suite with a private Bath is topped by a vaulted ceilin

■ The front secondary Bedroom is highlighted by a window seat

■ This home is designed with basement, slab and crawlspace foundation options

First floor — 926 sq. ft.
Second floor — 824 sq. ft.
Bonus room — 282 sq. ft.
Basement — 926 sq. ft.
Garage — 440 sq. ft.

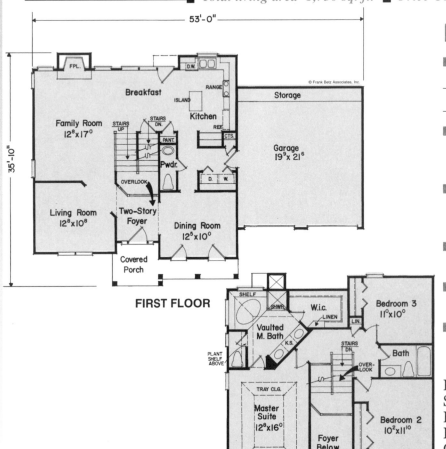

© Frank Betz Associates, Inc.

FIRST FLOOR

SECOND FLOOR

Country Charmer

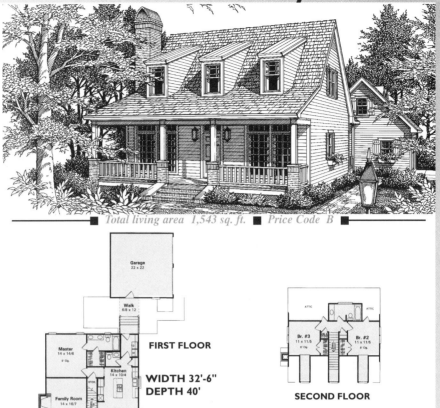

No. 93412

This plan features:

Three bedrooms

Two full and one half baths

The Family Room has a nine-foot ceiling and a fireplace

The Kitchen has a center-island cooktop and is open to the Dining Room

The Master Suite has a walk-in closet and a private Bath

Two additional Bedrooms share a full Bath

This home has a detached two-car Garage

This home is designed with crawlspace and slab foundation options

First Floor — 1,040 sq. ft.

Second Floor — 503 sq. ft.

Garage — 484 sq. ft.

Porch — 260 sq. ft.

■ Total living area 1,543 sq. ft. ■ Price Code B ■

FIRST FLOOR

WIDTH 32'-6"
DEPTH 40'

SECOND FLOOR

Economical and Appealing

No. 97113

This plan features:

Three bedrooms

Two full baths

Entry with tray ceiling leads to Great Room features corner fireplace

Well-planned Kitchen opens to Dining Room with access to rear yeard

Secluded Master Bedroom includes large walk-in closet and private Bath

Mudroom/Laundry Room entrance from Garage is both convenient and practical

Two additional Bedrooms share a full Bath

Two additional Bedrooms with ample closets, share a full Bath in the hall

This home is designed with a basement foundation

Main floor — 1,416 sq. ft.

Garage — 478 sq. ft.

■ Total living area 1,416 sq. ft. ■ Price Code A ■

WIDTH 48'-0"
DEPTH 55'-5"

MAIN FLOOR

Perfect Plan for Busy Family

■ *Total living area 1,756 sq. ft.* ■ *Price Code C* ■

No. 93191

■ This plan features:

— Three bedrooms

— Two full baths

■ Covered Entry opens to vaulted Foyer and Family Room

■ Spacious Family Room with a vaulted ceiling, central fireplace and expansive backyard views

■ Angular and efficient Kitchen with an eating bar, built-in desk, Dining Area with outdoor access and nearby Laundry and Garage Entry

■ Secluded Master Bedroom with a large walk-in closet and double vanity Bath

■ This home is designed with a basement foundation

Main floor — 1,756 sq. ft.
Basement — 1,756 sq. ft.

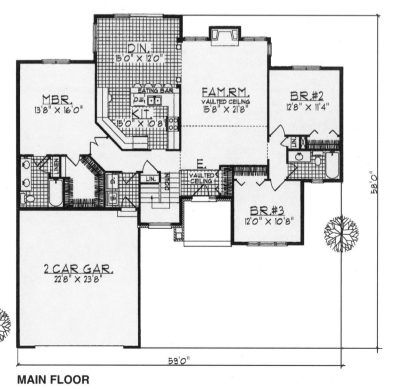

MAIN FLOOR

Curving Entry

■ *Total living area 1,759 sq. ft.* ■ *Price Code C* ■

No. 93457

This plan features:

Three bedrooms

Two full and one half baths

The Entry and custom staircase with curved landing and open Loft make a lasting first impression

Convenience and efficiency highlight the Kitchen with Laundry Room, half Bath and access to the Garage

The Dining Area and Master Bedroom open to the rear Porch through French doors

This home is designed with a basement foundation

First floor — 1,128 sq. ft.
Second floor — 631 sq. ft.
Bonus — 130 sq. ft.
Garage — 473 sq. ft.
Porch — 51 sq. ft.

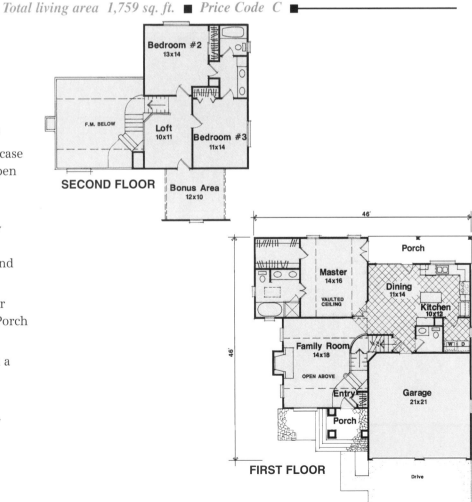

Let There Be Light

■ *Total living area 1,832 sq. ft.* ■ *Price Code C* ■

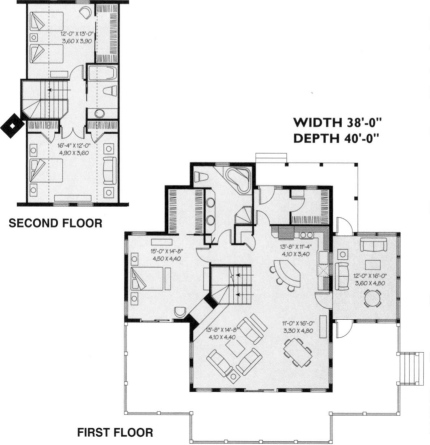

SECOND FLOOR

12'-0" X 13'-0"
3,60 X 3,90

16'-4" X 12'-0"
4,90 X 3,60

FIRST FLOOR

15'-0" X 14'-8"
4,50 X 4,40

13'-8" X 11'-4"
4,10 X 3,40

12'-0" X 16'-0"
3,60 X 4,80

13'-8" X 14'-8"
4,10 X 4,40

11'-0" X 16'-0"
3,30 X 4,80

WIDTH 38'-0"
DEPTH 40'-0"

No. 65380

■ This plan features:

— Three bedrooms

— Two full baths

■ Lots of tall windows allow natural light to flood this charming home

■ The Living and Dining Areas are open to the well-planned Kitchen which features a rounded serving bar open to the main Living Area

■ The large first floor Master Bedroom includes a walk-in closet and close proximity to a full Bath with garden tub and separate shower

■ The large front Deck can be accessed from the main Living Areas and the Master Bedroom

■ This home is designed with a basement foundation

First floor — 1,212 sq. ft.
Second floor — 620 sq. ft.
Basement — 1,212 sq. ft.

European Flair

No. 98460

This plan features:

Three bedrooms

Two full baths

Large fireplace serving as an attractive focal point for the vaulted Family Room

Decorative column defining the elegant Dining Room

Kitchen including a serving bar for the Family Room and a Breakfast Area

Master Suite topped by a tray ceiling over the Bedroom and a vaulted ceiling over the five-piece Master Bath

Optional Bonus Room for future expansion

This home is designed with a basement and crawlspace foundation options

Main floor — 1,544 sq. ft.
Bonus room — 284 sq. ft.
Garage — 440 sq. ft.
Basement — 1,544

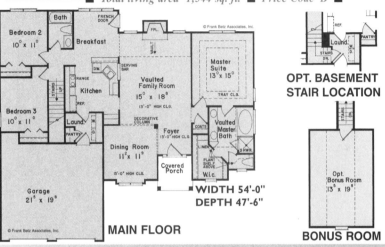

■ *Total living area 1,544 sq. ft.* ■ *Price Code B* ■

OPT. BASEMENT STAIR LOCATION

WIDTH 54'-0"
DEPTH 47'-6"

MAIN FLOOR

BONUS ROOM

Small, But Not Lacking

No. 94116

This plan features:

Three bedrooms

One full and one three-quarter baths

Great Room adjoining the Dining Room for ease in entertaining

Kitchen highlighted by a peninsula counter/snack bar extending work space and offering convenience in serving informal meals or snacks

Split-Bedroom plan allowing for privacy for the Master Bedroom Suite with a private Bath and a walk-in closet

Two additional Bedrooms sharing the full family Bath in the hall

Garage Entry convenient to the Kitchen

This home is designed with a basement foundation

Main floor — 1,546 sq. ft.
Garage — 440 sq. ft.

■ *Total living area 1,546 sq. ft.* ■ *Price Code B* ■

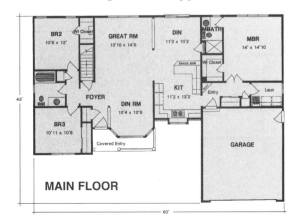

MAIN FLOOR

Informal Country Comfort

■ *Total living area 1,551 sq. ft.* ■ *Price Code B* ■

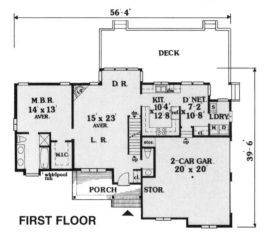

FIRST FLOOR

SECOND FLOOR

No. 99663

■ **This Plan features**

— Three bedrooms

— Two full baths and one half bath

■ Use the large extra Garage Storage Space for your own home shop

■ Relax in the Master Bath's built-in whirlpool tub

■ Right off the Kitchen/Dining Area, the Laundry is right where you need it

■ French doors lead from the Dining Room onto the large rear Deck

■ This home is designed with basement an slab foundation options

First floor — 1,110 sq. ft.
Second floor — 441 sq. ft.
Basement — 1,118 sq. ft.
Garage — 482 sq. ft.

Open Space Living

■ *Total living area 1,551 sq. ft.* ■ *Price Code B* ■

FIRST FLOOR

SECOND FLOOR

No. 90844

■ **This plan features:**

— Three bedrooms

— Two full and one half baths

■ A wraparound Deck providing outdoor Living Space, ideal for a sloping lot

■ Two-and-a-half-story glass wall and two separate doors providing natural light for the Living/Dining Room Area

■ An efficient galley Kitchen with easy acce to the Dining Area

■ A Master Bedroom Suite with a half Bath and ample closet space

■ Another Bedroom on the first floor adjoin full Bath

■ A second floor Bedroom/Studio, with a private Deck, adjacent to a full Bath and a Loft Area

■ This home is designed with a basement foundation

First floor — 1,110 sq. ft.
Second floor — 441 sq. ft.
Basement — 1,118 sq. ft.
Garage — 482 sq. ft.
Porch — 99 sq. ft.

■ *Total living area 1,761 sq. ft.* ■ *Price Code C* ■

No. 93133

This plan features:

Three bedrooms

Two full baths

Open Foyer leads into spacious Living Room highlighted by a wall of windows

Country-size Kitchen with efficient, U-shaped counter, work island, eating Nook with backyard access and nearby Laundry/Garage Entry

French doors open to pampering Master Bedroom with window alcove, walk-in closet and double vanity Bath

Two additional Bedrooms with large closets, share a full Bath

This home is designed with a basement foundation

Main floor — 1,761 sq. ft.
Garage — 658 sq. ft.
Basement — 1,761 sq. ft.

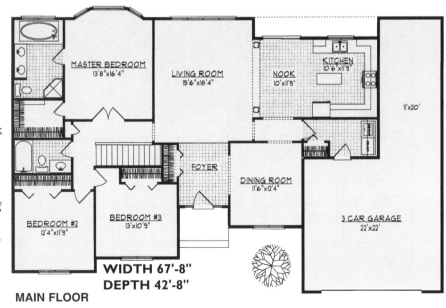

WIDTH 67'-8"
DEPTH 42'-8"

MAIN FLOOR

Ceiling Treatments Add Interest

■ *Total living area 1,553 sq. ft.* ■ *Price Code B* ■

MAIN FLOOR

No. 98412

■ **This plan features:**

— Three bedrooms

— Two full baths

■ A vaulted ceiling over the Family Room and a tray ceiling over the Master Suite

■ Decorative columns accenting the entrance into the Dining Room

■ Great Room with a pass-through from the Kitchen and a fireplace framed by a window to one side and a French door

■ A built-in Pantry and desk adding convenience to the Kitchen

■ This home is designed with basement, slab and crawlspace foundation options

Main floor — 1,553 sq. ft.
Basement — 1,605 sq. ft.
Garage — 434 sq. ft.

Open and Spacious

■ *Total living area 1,553 sq. ft.* ■ *Price Code B* ■

No. 97155

This plan features:

Three bedrooms

Two full and one half baths

The Great Room, the Dining Room and the Kitchen open to each other for a feeling of spaciousness

The Kitchen has an central island work space and is convenient to the Laundry Room

The Master Bedroom has a private Bath and a walk-in closet

The Great Room has a fireplace and direct acccess to the backyard through French doors

This home is designed with a basement foundation

First floor — 846 sq. ft.
Second floor — 707 sq. ft.
Basement — 846 sq. ft.
Garage — 340 sq. ft.

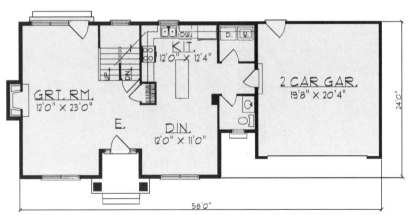

FIRST FLOOR

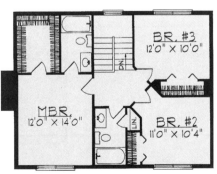

SECOND FLOOR

Rustic Warmth

■ *Total living area 1,764 sq. ft.* ■ *Price Code C* ■

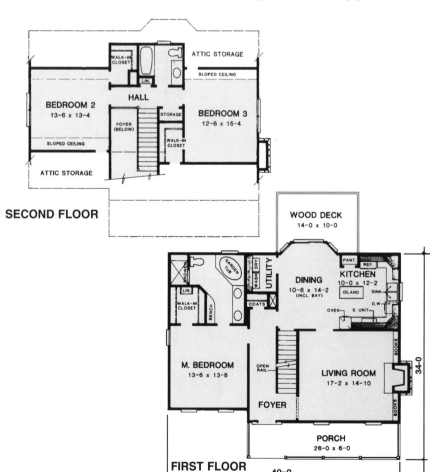

SECOND FLOOR

- BEDROOM 2
  13-6 x 13-4
- HALL
- WALK-IN CLOSET
- LIN.
- ATTIC STORAGE
- SLOPED CEILING
- FOYER (BELOW)
- STORAGE
- BEDROOM 3
  12-8 x 15-4
- SLOPED CEILING
- WALK-IN CLOSET
- ATTIC STORAGE

FIRST FLOOR   40-0

- WOOD DECK
  14-0 x 10-0
- SHOWER
- GARDEN TUB
- LIN.
- WALK-IN CLOSET
- BENCH
- WASH
- DRY
- UTILITY
- COATS
- DINING
  10-6 x 14-2
  (INCL. BAY)
- PANT.
- REF.
- KITCHEN
  10-0 x 12-2
- ISLAND
- SINK
- OVEN
- S. UNIT
- D.W.
- M. BEDROOM
  13-6 x 13-8
- OPEN RAIL
- LIVING ROOM
  17-2 x 14-10
- BOOKS
- FOYER
- BOOKS
- PORCH
  26-0 x 6-0
- 34-0

No. 90440

■ **This plan features:**

— Three bedrooms

— Two full baths

■ A fireplaced Living Room with built-in bookshelves

■ A fully equipped Kitchen with an island

■ A sunny Dining Room with glass sliders to a wood Deck

■ A first floor Master Suite with walk-in closet and lavish Master Bath

■ This home is designed with basement and crawlspace foundation options

First floor — 1,100 sq. ft.
Second floor — 664 sq. ft.
Basement — 1,100 sq. ft.

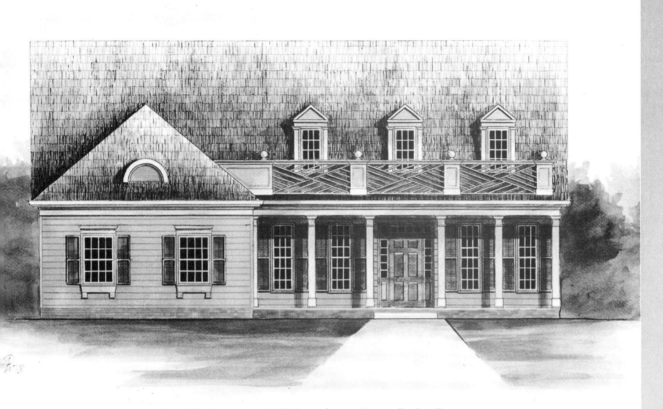

■ *Total living area 1,764 sq. ft.* ■ *Price Code C* ■

No. 98240

This plan features:

Three bedrooms

Two full and one half baths

Interior columns separate the Dining Room and Grand Salon

Featuring a Gazebo-styled Breakfast Room, a Laundry Room and walk-in Pantry, the gourmet Kitchen opens to the vaulted Great Room

The Master Bedroom is privately located on the first floor and has a vaulted ceiling, five-piece Bath and walk-in closet with built-in shelf

This home is designed with a basement and crawlspace foundation options

First floor — 1,296 sq. ft.
Second floor — 468 sq. ft.
Garage — 384 sq. ft.
Porch — 150 sq. ft.

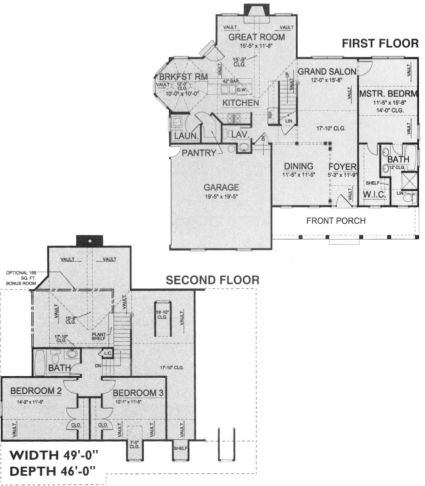

WIDTH 49'-0"
DEPTH 46'-0"

Covered Porches

■ *Total living area 1,554 sq. ft.* ■ *Price Code B* ■

No. 24738

■ This plan features:

— Three bedrooms

— Two full baths

■ There are Covered Porches in both the front and the rear

■ The Bedrooms are located on opposite sides of the home

■ Only columns separate the open floor plan

■ An eating bar expands casual dining options

■ A fireplace warms the home

■ This home is designed with basement and crawlspace foundation options

Main floor — 1,554 sq. ft.
Basement — 1,402 sq. ft.
Garage — 541 sq. ft.
Porch — 219 sq. ft.

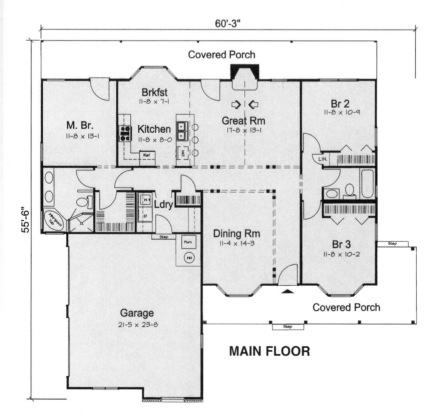

MAIN FLOOR

Convenient Country

■ *Total living area 1,767 sq. ft.* ■ *Price Code C* ■

No. 99045

■ This plan features:

- Three bedrooms

- Two and a half baths

- Expansive Living Room with an inviting fireplace opens to bright Dining Room and Kitchen

- U-shaped Kitchen with peninsula serving counter to Dining Room and nearby Pantry, Laundry and Garage Entry

- Secluded Master Bedroom with two closets and a double vanity Bath

- Two second floor Bedrooms with ample closets and dormer windows share a full Bath

- This home is designed with a basement foundation

First floor — 1,108 sq. ft.
Second floor — 659 sq. ft.
Basement — 875 sq. ft.

SECOND FLOOR

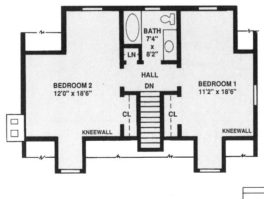

FIRST FLOOR

WIDTH 67'-0"
DEPTH 30'-0"

Cute Starter Home

Total living area 1,557 sq. ft. ■ Price Code B

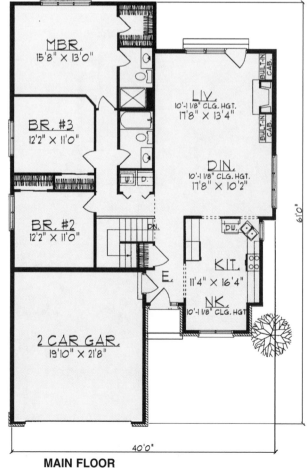

MAIN FLOOR

No. 97152

■ **This plan features:**

– Three bedrooms

– One full and one three-quarter baths

■ Simple design with quality detail provides charm inside and out

■ Spacious Living/Dining Room, with multiple windows and outdoor access, allows comfortable gatherings

■ Open Kitchen/Nook easily accesses Dining Area, Laundry closet and Garage

■ Corner Master Bedroom boasts full view of rear yard, walk-in closet and private Bath

■ Two additional Bedrooms with ample closets share a full Bath

■ This home is designed with a basement foundation

Main floor — 1,557 sq. ft.
Basement — 1,557 sq. ft.
Garage — 400 sq. ft.

■ *Total living area 1,737 sq. ft.* ■ *Price Code B* ■

No. 20100

This plan features:

Three bedrooms

Two full baths

The Foyer opens up into the grand L:iving Room space which features a fireplace and access to a rear Deck through the adjoining Breakfast Room

The Dining Room has an elegant volume ceiling

Quiet corner Master Bedroom features a vaulted ceiling, walk-in closet and plush Bath

Two additional Bedrooms include large closets

This home is designed with basement and crawlspace foundation options

ain floor — 1,737 sq. ft.
asement — 1,727 sq. ft.
arage — 484 sq. ft.

REAR ELEVATION

MAIN FLOOR

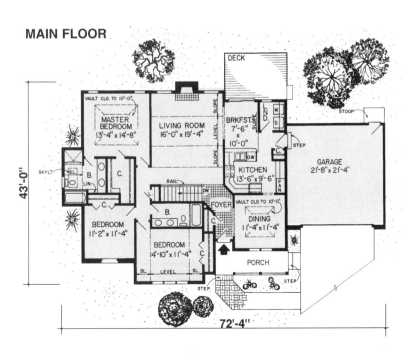

Elegant Charmer

Total living area 1,856 sq. ft. ■ Price Code C

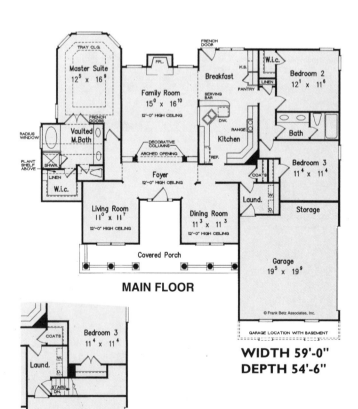

MAIN FLOOR

WIDTH 59'-0"
DEPTH 54'-6"

**OPTIONAL BASEMENT
STAIR LOCATION**

No. 98408

■ **This plan features:**

— Three bedrooms

— Two full baths

■ The foyer with 12-foot ceiling leads past decorative columns in the fireplaced Family Room

■ The Living Room and Dining Room are linked by the Foyer and have windows overlooking the front Porch

■ The Kitchen has a serving bar and is adjacent to the Breakfast Nook which has a French door that opens tot he backyard

■ This home is designed with basement, slab and crawlspace foundation options

Main floor — 1,856 sq. ft.
Garage — 429 sq. ft.

Fireplace Surrounded by Windows

■ *Total living area 1,556 sq. ft.* ■ *Price Code B* ■

No. 99168

This plan features:

- Three bedrooms
- Two full and one half baths
- High ceilings and a fireplace flanked by windows highlight the Living Room
- A five-piece Bath and a large walk-in closet complete the Master Bedroom
- For quick meals, the Kitchen offers a center island eating bar
- A first floor Laundry means fewer trips upstairs
- This home is designed with a basement foundation
- First floor — 1,126 sq. ft.
- Second floor — 430 sq. ft.
- Basement — 1,126 sq. ft.
- Garage — 469 sq. ft.

SECOND FLOOR

FIRST FLOOR

Lavishly Appointed

■ *Total living area 1,845 sq. ft.* ■ *Price Code C* ■

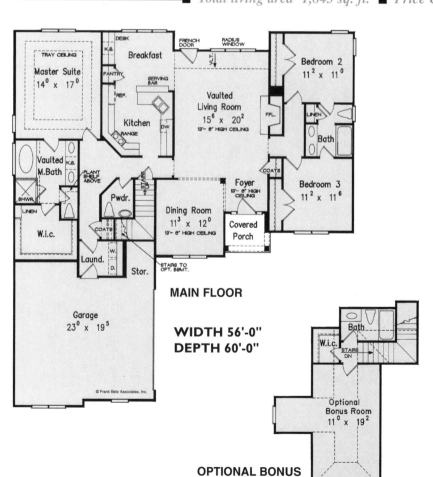

MAIN FLOOR

WIDTH 56'-0"
DEPTH 60'-0"

OPTIONAL BONUS

No. 98425

■ **This plan features:**

— Three bedrooms

— Two full and one half baths

■ The Dining Room, Living Room, Foyer and Master Bath are all crowned by high ceilings

■ The Kitchen, which opens to a sunny Breakfast Area, is enhanced by a serving bar and Pantry

■ The Master Suite is located on opposite side from secondary Bedrooms allowing for privacy

■ The Living Room features a large fireplace and a French door to the rear yard

■ This home is designed with basement and crawlspace foundation options

First floor — 1,845 sq. ft.
Bonus — 409 sq. ft.
Basement — 1,845 sq. ft
Garage — 529 sq. ft

■ *Total living area 1,771 sq. ft.* ■ *Price Code C* ■

No. 24715

This plan features:

Two bedrooms

Two full baths

The Breakfast Bay overlooks the Porch and is open to the Kitchen which includes conveniences such as a built-in desk and a Pantry

Step down into the Great Room, accented by a fireplace with windows on either side

A Screened Porch off the formal Dining Room and an expansive rear Deck expand Living Space to the outdoors

This home is designed with crawlspace, slab and basement/crawlspace combination foundation options

Main floor — 1,771 sq. ft.

Basement — 1,194 sq. ft.

Garage — 517 sq. ft.

CRAWLSPACE/SLAB OPTION

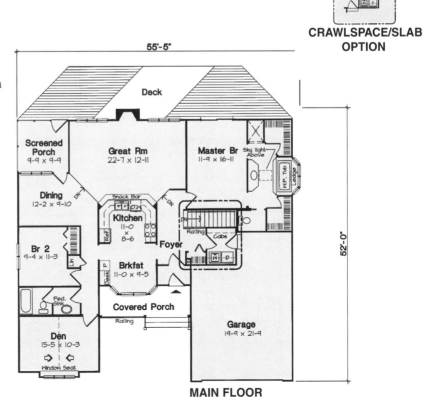

MAIN FLOOR

Family Get-Away

■ *Total living area 1,560 sq. ft.* ■ *Price Code B* ■

No. 34602

■ **This plan features:**

— Three bedrooms

— Two full and one half baths

■ A spacious Great Room with a
two-story ceiling and dormer
window above a massive firepla

■ A combination Dining/Kitchen
with an island work area and
Breakfast Bar opening to a
Great Room and adjacent to the
Laundry/Storage and half Bath

■ A private, two-story Master
Bedroom with a dormer window
walk-in closet, double vanity Ba
and optional Deck with hot tub

■ This home is designed with
basement, slab and crawlspace
foundation options

First floor — 1,061 sq. ft.
Second floor — 499 sq. ft.
Basement — 1,061 sq. ft.

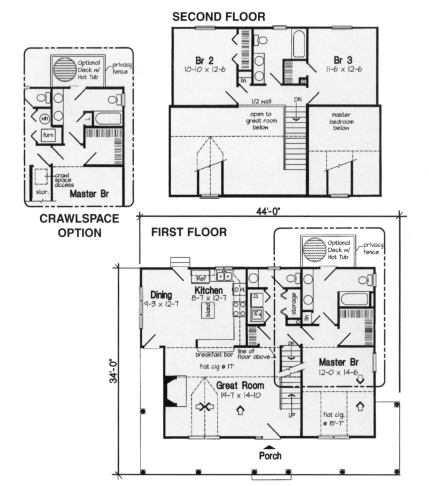

CRAWLSPACE OPTION

SECOND FLOOR

Br 2
10-10 x 12-6

Br 3
11-6 x 12-6

1/2 wall

open to
great room
below

master
bedroom
below

Optional
Deck w/
Hot Tub

privacy
fence

crawl space
access

stor.

Master Br

FIRST FLOOR

44'-0"

34'-0"

Optional
Deck w/
Hot Tub

privacy
fence

Ref

Dining
9-3 x 12-7

Kitchen
8-7 x 12-7
island

storage

breakfast bar
line of
floor above
flat clg @ 17'

Master Br
12-0 x 14-6

Great Room
19-7 x 14-10

UP

DN

flat clg.
@ 15'-7"

Porch

■ *Total living area 1,771 sq. ft.* ■ *Price Code C* ■

No. 24714

Main floor — 1,771 sq. ft.
Basement — 1,194 sq. ft.
Garage — 517 sq. ft.

This plan features:

Two bedrooms

Two full baths

The attractive Covered Porch highlights the curb appeal of this charming home

A cozy window seat and a vaulted ceiling enhance the private Den

The sunken Great Room is accented by a fireplace that is nestled between windows

A Screened Porch, accessed from the Dining Room, extends the Living Space to the outdoors

The Master Bath features a garden tub, separate shower, his and her walk-in closets and a skylight

This home is designed with crawlspace, slab and basement/crawlspace combination foundation options

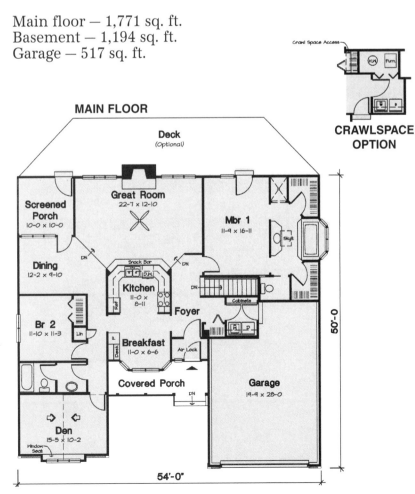

MAIN FLOOR

CRAWLSPACE OPTION

Hillside Haven

■ *Total living area 1,774 sq. ft.* ■ *Price Code C* ■

CRAWLSPACE OPTION

Main floor — 1,774 sq. ft.
Basement — 1,399 sq. ft.
Garage — 551 sq. ft.

No. 20148

■ **This plan features:**

— Three bedrooms

— Two full baths

■ A well-appointed Kitchen that adjoins a cheerful, eight-sided Breakfast Room with access to the wraparound Deck

■ A decorative ceiling in the formal Dining Room which flows into the Living Room

■ A sky-lit Living Room with a built-in wetbar and a fireplace

■ A Master Suite with a decorative ceiling, a window seat, a walk-in closet and a private Master Bath

■ Two additional Bedrooms with ample closet space that share a full Bath

■ This home is designed with basement and crawlspace foundation options

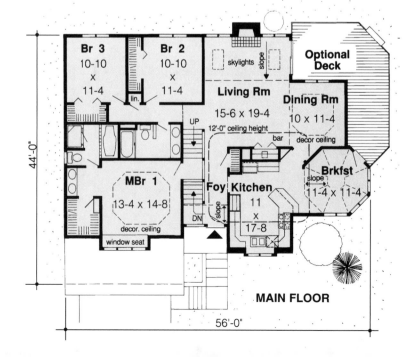

MAIN FLOOR

■ *Total living area 1,561 sq. ft.* ■ *Price Code B* ■

No. 99166

This plan features:

Three bedrooms

One full, one three-quarter and one half baths

The Great Room has a fireplace and triple window

Sliding doors from the Dining Room access the backyard

A Laundry Room and half Bath connect the Garage to the Kitchen

This home is designed with a basement foundation

First floor – 821 sq. ft.
Second floor – 740 sq. ft.
Basement – 821 sq. ft.

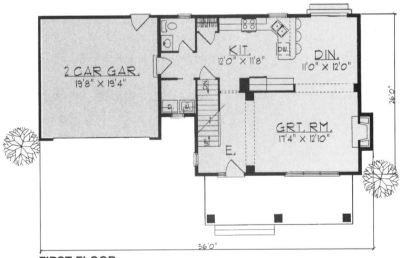

FIRST FLOOR

2 CAR GAR.
19'8" X 19'4"

KIT.
12'0" X 11'8"

DIN.
11'0" X 12'0"

GRT. RM.
17'4" X 12'10"

26'0"

56'0"

SECOND FLOOR

MBR.
13'0" X 13'0"

BR. #2
11'6" X 10'4"

BR. #3
11'6" X 10'4"

Family Friendly

■ *Total living area 1,775 sq. ft.* ■ *Price Code C* ■

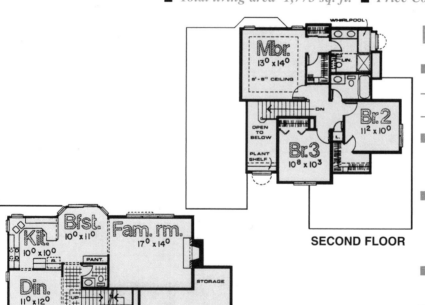

SECOND FLOOR

FIRST FLOOR

No. 97431

■ **This plan features:**

— Three bedrooms

— Two full and one half baths

■ The tiled Entry has convenient access to the Garage, Laundry Room, coat closet and half Bath

■ Luxury in the Master Bedroom defined by the decorative ceiling five-piece whirlpool Bath and two closets

■ The Garage has extra storage space

■ This home is designed with a basement foundation

■ Alternate foundation options available at an additional charge. Please call 1-800-235-5700 for more information.

First floor — 1,032 sq. ft.
Second floor — 743 sq. ft.
Garage — 556 sq. ft.

Traditional Southern Flavor

No. 99641

This plan features:

- Three bedrooms

- Two full baths

- A varied roof line with dormers and a charming colonnaded front Porch sheltering the entrance

- An expansive Living Room enhanced by nine-foot ceilings and a bookcase-flanked fireplace, opening into the Dining Room

- Two mullioned French doors leading from the Dining Room to the rear Terrace

- A Laundry Area serving as a Mudroom between the Garage and Kitchen, also accessed by Terrace

- A Master Suite with a large walk-in closet and compartmented Bath with a separated stall shower, whirlpool tub, double basin vanity and linen closet

- Two additional Bedrooms that share a full Bath

- Bonus Room can be finished into Study or Recreation Room

- This home is designed with basement and slab foundation options

Main floor — 1,567 sq. ft.
Bonus room — 462 sq. ft.
Basement — 1,567 sq. ft.
Garage — 504 sq. ft.

■ Total living area 1,567 sq. ft. ■ Price Code B ■

MAIN FLOOR

BONUS

Foyer Isolates Bedroom Wing

No. 20087

This plan features:

- Three bedrooms

- Two full baths

- A Living Room complete with a window wall flanking a massive fireplace

- A Dining Room with recessed ceilings and a pass-through for convenience

- A Master Suite tucked behind the two-car Garage for maximum noise protection

- A spacious Kitchen with built-ins and access to the two-car Garage

- This home is designed with a basement foundation

Main floor — 1,568 sq. ft.
Basement — 1,568 sq. ft.
Garage — 484 sq. ft.

■ Total living area 1,568 sq. ft. ■ Price Code B ■

MAIN FLOOR

Traditional Ranch

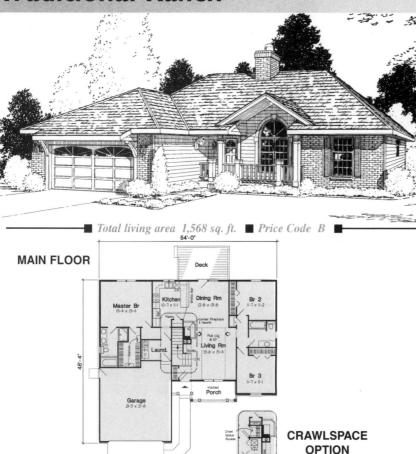

No. 20220

■ **This plan features:**

— Three bedrooms

— Two full baths

■ A large, front Palladian window that give this home great curb appeal, and allows view of the front yard from the Living Room

■ A vaulted ceiling in the Living Room, adding to the architectural interest and t spacious feel of the room

■ Sliding glass doors in the Dining Room t lead to a wood Deck

■ A built-in Pantry, double sink and breakf bar in the efficient Kitchen

■ A Master Suite that includes a walk-in closet and a private Bath with a double vanity

■ Two additional Bedrooms that share a fu Bathroom

■ This home is designed with basement, sl and crawlspace foundation options

Main floor —1,568 sq. ft.
Basement — 1,568 sq. ft.
Garage — 509 sq. ft.

■ Total living area 1,568 sq. ft. ■ Price Code B ■

MAIN FLOOR

CRAWLSPACE OPTION

One-Level with a Twist

No. 20083

■ **This plan features:**

— Three bedrooms

— Two full baths

■ Wide-open living areas that are centrally located

■ A spacious Dining, Living and Kitchen Ar

■ A Master Suite at the rear of the house w a full Bath

■ Two additional Bedrooms that share a fu Bath and a quiet atmosphere that results from an intelligent design

■ This home is designed with basement, sl and crawlspace foundation options

Main floor — 1,575 sq. ft.
Basement — 1,575 sq. ft.
Garage — 475 sq. ft.

■ Total living area 1,575 sq. ft. ■ Price Code B ■

MAIN FLOOR

Terrific Front Porch

■ *Total living area 1,778 sq. ft.* ■ *Price Code C* ■

No. 93261

This plan features:

Three bedrooms

Two full baths

A Country front Porch

An expansive Living Area that includes a fireplace

A Master Suite with a private Master Bath and a walk-in closet, as well as a bay window view of the front yard

An efficient Kitchen that serves the sunny Breakfast Area and the Dining Room with equal ease

A built-in Pantry and a desk add to the conveniences in the Breakfast Area

This home is designed with a basement foundation

Main floor — 1,778 sq. ft.

Basement — 1,008 sq. ft.

Garage — 728 sq. ft.

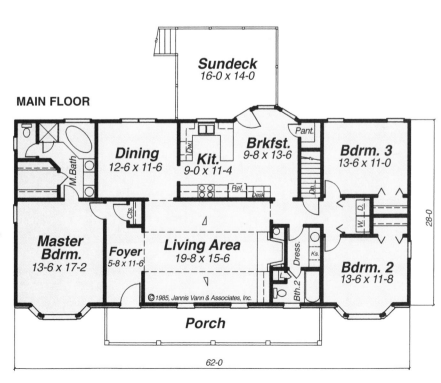

Master Suite Crowns Plan

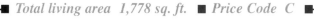

Total living area 1,778 sq. ft. ■ *Price Code C* ■

SECOND FLOOR

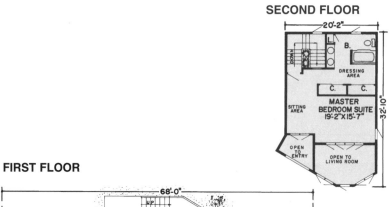

FIRST FLOOR

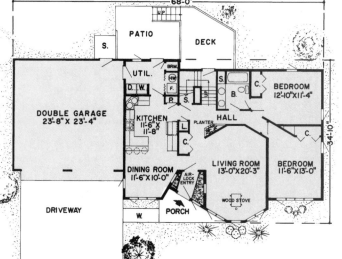

No. 10394

■ This plan features:

— Three bedrooms

— Two full baths

■ A Master Bedroom which occupies the entire second floor

■ A passive solar design

■ A Living Room which rises two stories in the front

■ Skylights in the sloping ceilings the Kitchen and Master Bath

■ This home is designed with basement, slab and crawlspace foundation options

First floor — 1,306 sq. ft.
Second floor — 472 sq. ft.
Garage — 576 sq. ft.

■ *Total living area 1,779 sq. ft.* **■** *Price Code C* **■**

No. 98464

This plan features:

Three bedrooms

Two full baths

A covered Entry reveals a Foyer inside with a 14-foot ceiling

The Family Room has a fireplace, and a French door to the rear yard

The Breakfast Area has a tray ceiling and a bay of windows that overlooks the backyard

The Kitchen has every imaginable convenience, including a walk-in Pantry

The privately located Master Suite has a tray ceiling, a walk-in closet and a private Bath

This home is designed with basement and crawlspace foundation options

Main floor — 1,779 sq. ft.
Basement — 1,818 sq. ft.
Garage — 499 sq. ft.

MAIN FLOOR

OPT. BASEMENT STAIR LOCATION

Charming Brick Ranch

■ *Total living area 1,782 sq. ft.* ■ *Price Code C* ■

No. 92630

■ This plan features:

— Three bedrooms

— Two full baths

■ Sheltered entrance leads into open Foyer and Dining Room defined by columns

■ Vaulted ceiling spans Foyer, Dining Room, and Great Room with corner fireplace and door t rear yard

■ Central Kitchen with separate Laundry and Pantry easily serve Dining Room, Breakfast Area ar Screened Porch

■ Luxurious Master Bedroom offe tray ceiling and French doors to double vanity, walk-in closet an whirlpool tub

■ This home is designed with a basement foundation

Main floor —1,782 sq. ft.
Garage — 407 sq. ft.

MAIN FLOOR

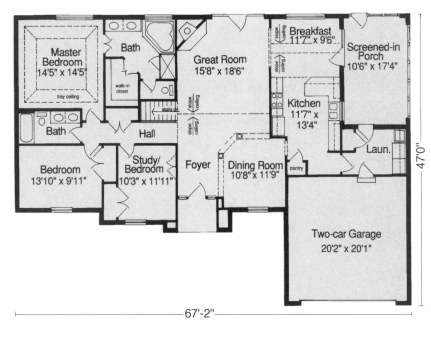

■ *Total living area 1,890 sq. ft.* ■ *Price Code C* ■

No. 93080

This plan features:

Three bedrooms

Two full baths

Tall ceilings and open spaces add to the spaciousness of this elegant home

The formal Dining Room features a 10-foot coffered ceiling

The Kitchen is arranged to maximize available work space and opens into a Breakfast Room

The Living Room includes a fireplace surrounded by built-ins and offers access to a rear Porch

This home is designed with slab and crawlspace foundation options

ain floor — 1,890 sq. ft.
arage — 536 sq. ft.

WIDTH 65'-10"
DEPTH 53'-5"

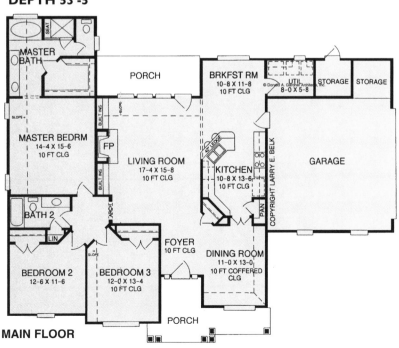

MAIN FLOOR

Breezeway Adds Interest

■ Total living area 1,784 sq. ft. ■ Price Code C ■

No. 90455

■ **This plan features:**

— Three bedrooms

— Two full and one half baths

■ An open-rail staircase, coat close and half Bath highlight the Foye

■ Open to the Dining Room and Breakfast Area, the step-saving Kitchen has direct access to the Laundry Room

■ The Master Bedroom has a five-piece Bath and walk-in closet

■ A balcony overlooking the Foyer connects two additional Bedrooms and a full Bath

■ This home is designed with basement and crawlspace foundation options

First Floor — 1,212 sq. ft.
Second Floor — 572 sq. ft.
Basement — 1,212 sq. ft.
Garage — 484 sq. ft.
Porch — 287 sq. ft.

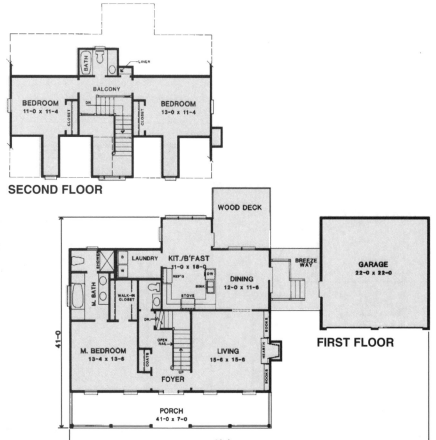

■ *Total living area 1,785 sq. ft.* ■ *Price Code C* ■

No. 24610

This plan features:

Three bedrooms

One full, one three-quarter and one half baths

The Great Room has a focal-point fireplace and a two-story ceiling

The efficient Kitchen has a work island, double sink, a built-in Pantry, and ample storage and counter space

The convenient first floor Laundry Room is near the Kitchen and Garage Entry

The Master Suite has a private Bath and a walk-in closet

This home is designed with basement, slab and crawlspace foundation options

First floor — 891 sq. ft.
Second floor — 894 sq. ft.
Garage — 534 sq. ft.
Basement — 891 sq. ft.

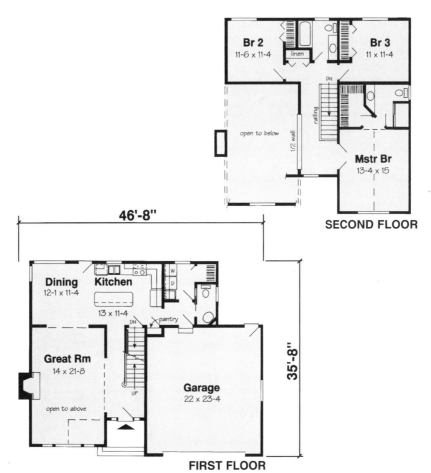

Attention to Details

■ *Total living area 1,575 sq. ft.* ■ *Price Code B* ■

No. 98479

■ **This plan features:**

— Three bedrooms

— Two full baths

■ Breakfast Room and Master Bath have vaulted ceilings

■ Master Suite topped by a tray ceiling

■ Arched openings to the Dining Room from the Family Room and Foyer

■ Master Suite enhanced by a five piece Master Bath and a walk-in closet

■ This home is designed with basement and crawlspace foundation options

Main floor — 1,575 sq. ft
Basement — 1,612 sq. ft.
Garage — 456 sq. ft.

MAIN FLOOR

OPT. BASEMENT STAIR LOCATION

Adapt this Colonial to Your Lifestyle

■ *Total living area 1,587 sq. ft.* ■ *Price Code B* ■

No. 90671

This plan features:

Four bedrooms

Two full baths

A Living Room with a beam ceiling and a fireplace

An eat-in Kitchen efficiently serving the formal Dining Room

A Master Bedroom with his and her closets

Two upstairs Bedrooms sharing a split Bath

This home is designed with a basement foundation

First floor — 1,056 sq. ft.
Second floor — 531 sq. ft.

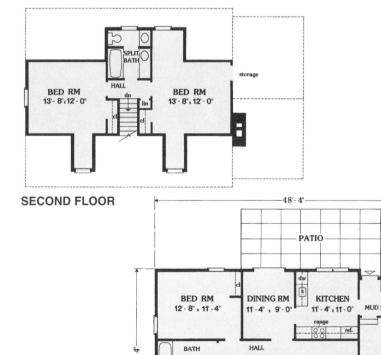

SECOND FLOOR

FIRST FLOOR

Three-Bedroom Ranch

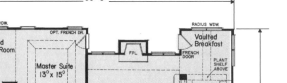

■ *Total living area 1,575 sq. ft.* ■ *Price Code B* ■

MAIN FLOOR

GARAGE LOCATION W/ BASEMENT

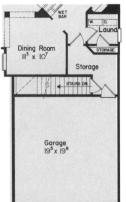

BASEMENT STAIR LOCATION OPTION

No. 98414

■ **This plan features:**

— Three bedrooms

— Two full baths

■ Wetbar located between the Kitchen and the Dining Room

■ Built-in Pantry, a double sink and a snack bar highlight the Kitchen

■ Breakfast Room containing a radius window and a French door to the rear yard

■ Large cozy fireplace framed by windows in the Great Room

■ Master Suite with a vaulted ceiling over the Sitting Area, a Master Bath and a walk-in clos

■ This home is designed with basement and crawlspace foundation options

Main floor — 1,575 sq. ft.
Garage — 459 sq. ft.
Basement — 1,658 sq. ft.

Beautiful Split-Level

■ *Total living area 1,921 sq. ft.* ■ *Price Code C* ■

No. 65157

This plan features:

Three bedrooms

One full and three three-quarter baths

The Living Room and Dining Room share a see-through fireplace

The well-planned Kitchen includes a work space and serving bar that is open to the Dining Room

Three second floor Bedrooms all have ample closet space and private Baths

This home is designed with a basement foundation

Main floor — 1,099 sq. ft.
Lower floor — 822 sq. ft.
Garage — 447 sq. ft.

MAIN FLOOR

WIDTH 60'-0"
DEPTH 41'-0"

LOWER FLOOR

Style and Practicality

■ *Total living area 1,945 sq. ft.* ■ *Price Code C* ■

WIDTH 56'-6"
DEPTH 52'-6"

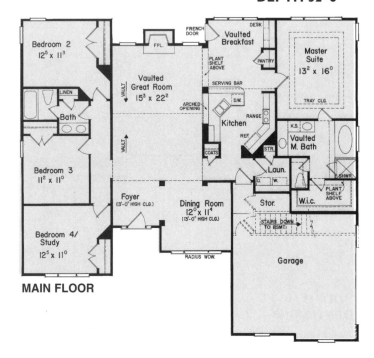

MAIN FLOOR

No. 98435

■ This plan features:

— Four bedrooms

— Two full baths

■ Radius window highlights the exterior and the formal Dining Room

■ Vaulted ceilings enhance the Great Room, which is accented with a fireplace framed by windows

■ Elegant arches separate the Great Room from the efficient Kitchen and sunny Breakfast Room

■ This home is designed with basement and crawlspace foundation options

Main floor — 1,945 sq. ft.

Columned Front Porch Adds Appeal

■ *Total living area 1,594 sq. ft.* ■ *Price Code B* ■

No. 94903

This plan features:

Three bedrooms

Two full and one half baths

Step down from the Entry into the Living Room distinguished by raised-hearth fireplace centered under cathedral ceiling

Open Kitchen and Dinette provide a built-in Pantry, center island/snack bar and a sliding glass door to rear yard

A private Den with French doors strategically located off Dinette

The Master Bedroom offers a decorative ceiling, large walk-in closet and lavish double vanity

This home is designed with a basement foundation

Alternate foundation options available at an additional charge. Please call 1-800-235-5700 for more information.

First floor — 869 sq. ft.
Second floor — 725 sq. ft.
Basement — 869 sq. ft.
Garage — 430 sq. ft.

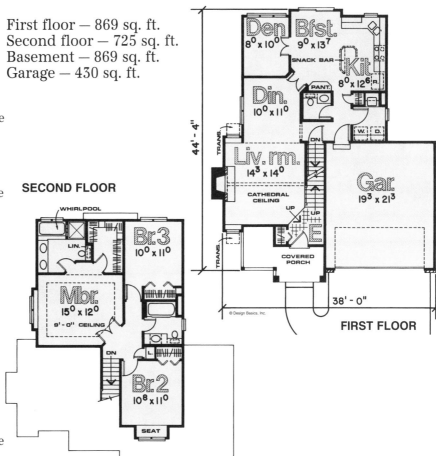

Desirable Split-Bedroom Plan

No. 93419

■ **This plan features:**

— Three bedrooms

— Two full baths

■ A wrapping front Porch has views into the home through windows with transoms

■ The Foyer opens into the large Family Room with an 11-foot ceiling and a fireplace

■ The Kitchen/Dining Room has a center island, a long planning desk and access to the rear Deck

■ The Master Bedroom is set away from the busy areas and features a walk-in closet and a full Bath

■ Two other Bedrooms have bright front windows and ample closet space

■ The two-car Garage has additional Storage Space

■ This home is designed with crawlspace and slab foundation options

Main floor — 1,595 sq. ft.
Garage — 470 sq. ft.

■ *Total living area 1,595 sq. ft.* ■ *Price Code B* ■

MAIN FLOOR

Luxury in One-Story Plan

No. 94827

■ **This plan features:**

_ Three bedrooms

— Two full baths

■ Covered stoop leads into dynamic Activity Room with fireplace, recessed ceiling and adjacent Dining Room and Sun Deck

■ Open Kitchen/Breakfast Room offers loads of counter space and light with nearby Pantry, Laundry and Garage

■ Plush Bedroom Suite shows off a tray ceiling, walk-in closet and garden tub

■ Two additional Bedrooms share a full Bath

■ This home is designed with basement, slab and crawlspace foundation options

Main floor — 1,595 sq. ft.
Basement — 1,595 sq. ft.
Garage — 491 sq. ft.

■ *Total living area 1,595 sq. ft.* ■ *Price Code B* ■

MAIN FLOOR

Compact Design

■ *Total living area 1,811 sq. ft.* ■ *Price Code C* ■

No. 92060

This plan features:

Three bedrooms

One full, one three-quarter and one half baths

A built-in window seat highlights the cozy Living Room

The Family Room, Dining Area and Kitchen flow together effortlessly

For added convenience, the Laundry Room is on the second floor

The Master Bedroom features a cathedral ceiling, huge walk-in closet and three-quarter Bath

Two additional Bedrooms share a full Bath

This home is designed with a basement foundation

First floor — 830 sq. ft.
Second floor — 981 sq. ft.
Basement — 830 sq. ft.

Easy Street

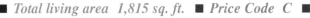

Total living area 1,815 sq. ft. ■ *Price Code C* ■

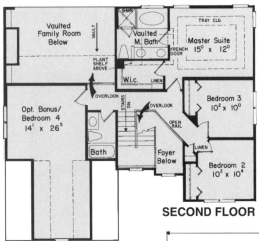

SECOND FLOOR

FIRST FLOOR

No. 97280

■ **This plan features:**

— Three bedrooms

— Two full and one half baths

■ The two-story Foyer is a grand introduction to this home

■ The Living Room and the Dining Room connect through an arched opening

■ The Family Room offers a vaulted ceiling, a fireplace with built-in bookcases and a plant shelf

■ The Master Suite includes a tray ceiling and a French door into the Master Bath

■ This home is designed with basement and crawlspace foundation options

First floor — 1,073 sq. ft.
Second floor — 742 sq. ft.
Bonus — 336 sq. ft.
Basement — 1,073 sq. ft.
Garage — 495 sq. ft.

Corner Sink in the Kitchen

No. 98560

This plan features:

Three bedrooms

Two full and one half baths

The Living Room's cathedral ceiling draws attention to a triple window with transoms

The second floor includes two secondary Bedrooms and a balcony

This home is designed with basement, slab and crawlspace foundation options

First floor – 1,192 sq. ft.

Second floor – 404 sq. ft.

Garage – 410 sq. ft.

Total living area 1,596 sq. ft. ■ *Price Code B*

FIRST FLOOR

SECOND FLOOR

Country Classic

No. 98482

This plan features:

Three bedrooms

Two full and one half baths

The covered Porch adds curb appeal

The vaulted Dining Room is defined by columns and plant shelves

The Kitchen opens to a sunny Breakfast Area and is convenient to the Laundry Room

The Great Room has a vaulted ceiling, a fireplace and access to the backyard through a French door

The Master Suite has a large walk-in closet and pampering Bath

Two additional Bedrooms share a full Bath

This home is designed with basement and crawlspace foundation options

First floor – 1,205 sq. ft.

Second floor – 392 sq. ft.

Bonus – 190 sq. ft.

Basement – 1,137 sq. ft.

Garage – 410 sq. ft.

Total living area 1,597 sq. ft. ■ *Price Code B*

FIRST FLOOR

SECOND FLOOR

195

Country Living

■ *Total living area 1,815 sq. ft.* ■ *Price Code C* ■

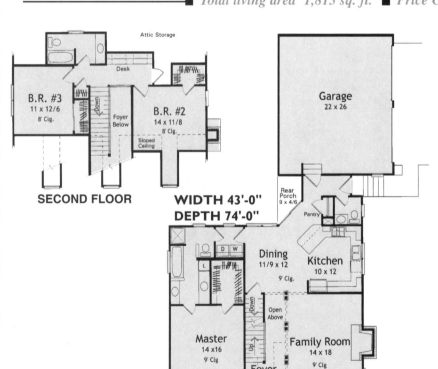

SECOND FLOOR

WIDTH 43'-0"
DEPTH 74'-0"

FIRST FLOOR

No. 93452

■ **This plan features:**

— Three bedrooms

— Two full and one half baths

■ The full-width Porch, dormers and cupola highlight Country charm

■ The Foyer opens to the Master Bedroom, a colonnaded Family Room with fireplace and a Dining Area

■ The Kitchen features an angled serving peninsula, Pantry, half Bath, Laundry Room, Dining Area and sliding doors to the rear Porch

■ Two additional Bedrooms share full Bath, built-in desk and extra storage in the Attic

First floor — 1,256 sq. ft.
Second floor — 559 sq. ft.
Basement — 1,256 sq. ft.
Garage — 569 sq. ft.
Porch — 296 sq. ft.

Sunny Character

■ *Total living area 1,819 sq. ft.* ■ *Price Code C* ■

No. 20158

This plan features:

Three bedrooms

Two and one half baths

A Kitchen with easy access to Screened Porch

A Master Suite including walk-in closet and luxury Bath

A second floor balcony linking two Bedrooms

This home is designed with a basement foundation

First floor — 1,293 sq. ft
Second floor — 526 sq. ft.
Basement — 1,286 sq. ft.
Garage — 484 sq. ft.

SECOND FLOOR

Br 3
10-8 x 12

Balcony DN

Br 2
12 x 13-4

open to below

plant shelf

FIRST FLOOR

MBr 1
14-8 x 13-4

decor. ceiling

Deck

skylight

Living Rm
20 x 13-4

slope

Ldry

Balcony above DN

Kitchen
15-6 x 13-4

decor. ceiling

Garage
21-4 x 21-4

Screened Porch

Foyer UP

Dining Rm
11 x 12

44'-0"

68'-0"

Vacation In Style

■ *Total living area 1,600 sq. ft.* ■ *Price Code B* ■

No. 92803

■ **This plan features:**

— Four bedrooms

— Two full baths

■ A long wooden Deck and a Screened Porc providing outdoor Living Space

■ An expansive Great Room/Dining Area with a fireplace and glass on three sides

■ An efficient Kitchen with ample Storage Space and an open counter separating it from the Dining Area

■ A Master Bedroom with windows on two sides and a walk-in closet adjacent to a fu Bathroom

■ Three additional Bedrooms, with windo on two sides, sharing two full Baths

■ This home is designed with crawlspace, slab and pier/post combination foundati options

Main floor — 1,600 sq. ft.

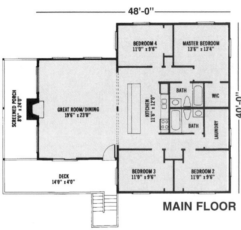

MAIN FLOOR

Easy Living Plan

■ *Total living area 1,600 sq. ft.* ■ *Price Code B* ■

No. 98406

■ **This plan features:**

— Three bedrooms

— Two full and one half baths

■ Kitchen, Breakfast Bay and Family Room blend into a spacious open Living Area

■ Convenient Laundry Center is tucked int the rear of the Kitchen

■ Luxurious Master Suite is topped by a tra ceiling while a vaulted ceiling is in the B

■ Two roomy secondary Bedrooms share th full Bath in the hall

■ This home is designed with basement, sl and crawlspace foundation options

First floor — 828 sq. ft.
Second floor — 772 sq. ft.
Basement — 828 sq. ft.
Garage — 473 sq. ft.

FIRST FLOOR

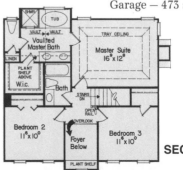

SECOND FLOOR

Total living area 1,949 sq. ft. ■ *Price Code C* ■

No. 64006

This plan features:

- Three bedrooms

- Two full baths

- The formal Living and Dining Rooms are separated by a Foyer which opens into the large Den, featuring a fireplace, box-beam ceiling and access to a rear Porch

- The well-planned Kitchen opens to a bay-windowed Eating Area

- A Mudroom entrance off the Garage provides a handy spot for raincoats and kicking off muddy boots

- The Master Bedroom includes a walk-in closet and Dressing Area

- This home is designed with slab and crawlspace foundation options

- Main floor — 1,949 sq. ft.
- Garage — 465 sq. ft.
- Porch — 512 sq. ft.

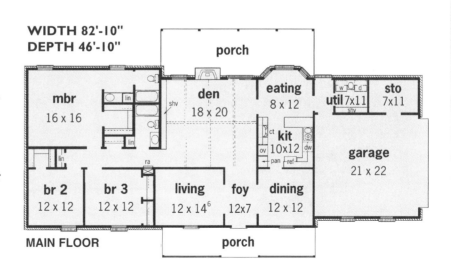

WIDTH 82'-10"
DEPTH 46'-10"

porch

mbr 16 x 16

den 18 x 20

eating 8 x 12

util 7x11

sto 7x11

kit 10x12

garage 21 x 22

br 2 12 x 12

br 3 12 x 12

living 12 x 14⁶

foy 12x7

dining 12 x 12

MAIN FLOOR

porch

Quaint Side Entrance

■ *Total living area 1,829 sq. ft.* ■ *Price Code C* ■

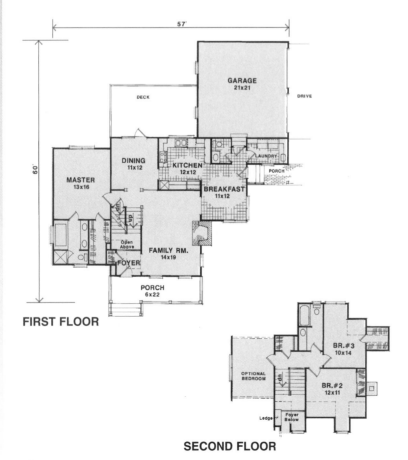

FIRST FLOOR

SECOND FLOOR

No. 93423

■ **This plan features:**

— Three bedrooms

— Two full and one half baths

■ The tiled Kitchen, Breakfast Area and Laundry Room can handle the muddy shoes and paws of an active family

■ An optional Bedroom adds extra space to the Living Area of this home

■ This home is designed with a basement foundation

First floor — 1,339 sq. ft.
Second floor — 490 sq. ft.
Garage — 491 sq. ft.
Porch — 173 sq. ft.
Bonus — 145 sq. ft.

■ *Total living area 1,830 sq. ft.* ■ *Price Code C* ■

No. 90457

This plan features:

Three bedrooms

Two full and one half baths

The drive-under Garage is ideal for a sloping lot

Efficient and inviting, the Kitchen has a Pantry and Dining Area with front door access to the rear Deck

The Bonus Room and Attic provides ample Storage Space

A bay window, luxurious Bath with Spa tub, double vanity and two spacious closets highlight the Master Bedroom

This home is designed with basement and crawlspace foundation options

First floor — 1,224 sq. ft.
Second floor — 606 sq. ft.
Basement — 1,204 sq. ft.
Porch — 130 sq. ft.
Bonus — 306 sq. ft.

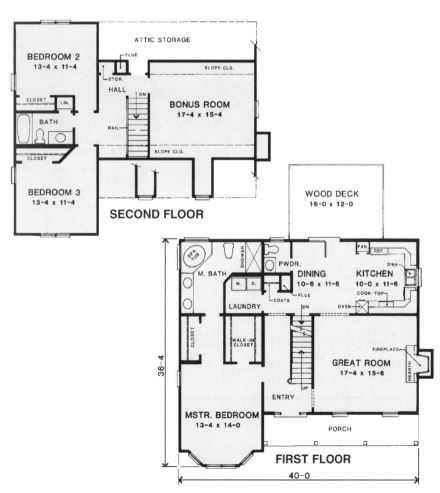

Brick Beauty

■ *Total living area 1,994 sq. ft.* ■ *Price Code C* ■

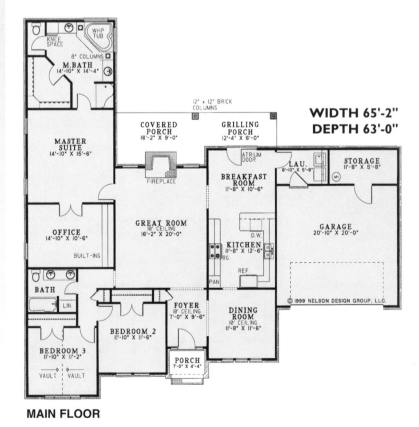

MAIN FLOOR

No. 82080

■ **This plan features:**

— Three bedrooms

— Two full baths

■ High-ceilinged Foyer opens to a large fireplaced Great Room with access to a Covered Porch

■ Formal Dining Room flows into efficiently designed Kitchen, which in turn flows into a lovely Breakfast Room offering access to a Grilling Porch

■ Master Bedroom Suite includes an Office with built-ins that could also be used as a private Sitting Room

■ This home is designed with basement, slab and crawlspace foundation options

Main floor — 1,994 sq. ft.
Garage — 417 sq. ft.

Carefree Convenience

No. 10674

This plan features:

Three bedrooms

Two full baths

A galley Kitchen, centrally located between the Dining, Breakfast and Living Room Areas

A huge Family Room which exits onto the Patio

A Master Suite with double closets and vanities; two additional Bedrooms share a full Bath

This home is designed with a slab foundation

Main floor — 1,600 sq. ft.

Garage — 465 sq. ft.

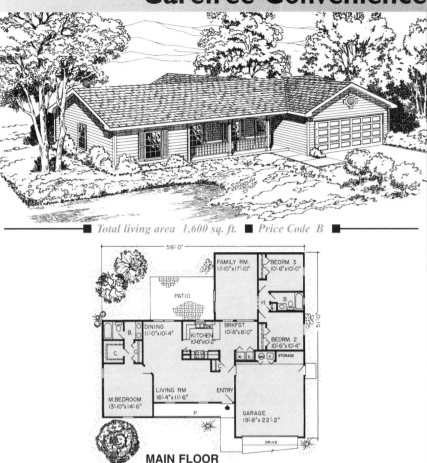

■ *Total living area 1,600 sq. ft.* ■ *Price Code B* ■

MAIN FLOOR

Exciting Ceilings

No. 20191

This plan features:

Three bedrooms

Two full baths

A brick hearth fireplace in the Living Room

An efficient Kitchen, with an island and double sinks, flows into the Dining Room, which features a decorative ceiling

A private Master Suite with a decorative ceiling and a Master Bath

Two additional Bedrooms that share a full Bathroom

This home is designed with a basement foundation

Main floor — 1,606 sq. ft.

Basement — 1,575 sq. ft.

Garage — 545 sq. ft.

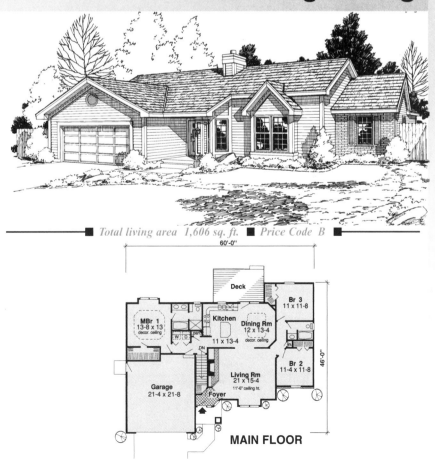

■ *Total living area 1,606 sq. ft.* ■ *Price Code B* ■

MAIN FLOOR

Country-Style Home

■ *Total living area 1,833 sq. ft.* ■ *Price Code C* ■

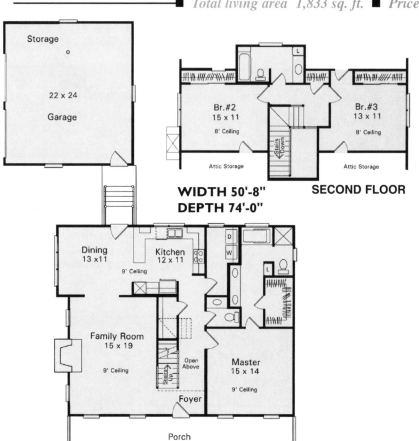

Storage

22 x 24

Garage

Br.#2
15 x 11
8' Ceiling

Br.#3
13 x 11
8' Ceiling

Attic Storage

Attic Storage

WIDTH 50'-8"
DEPTH 74'-0"

SECOND FLOOR

Dining
13 x 11
9' Ceiling

Kitchen
12 x 11

D
W
L

Family Room
15 x 19
9' Ceiling

Open
Above

Master
15 x 14
9' Ceiling

Stairs
Up

Foyer

Porch
39/6 x 8

FIRST FLOOR

No. 93432

■ **This plan features:**

— Three bedrooms

— Two full and one half baths

■ A Country-style front Porch provides a warm welcome

■ The Family Room is highlighted by a fireplace and front windows

■ The Dining Room is separated from the U-shaped Kitchen by an extended counter

■ The first floor Master Suite pampers the owners with a walk-in closet and a five-piece Bath

■ There are two additional Bedrooms with a convenient Bath in the hall

■ This home is designed with crawlspace and slab foundation options

First floor — 1,288 sq. ft.
Second floor — 545 sq. ft.
Garage — 540 sq. ft.

■ *Total living area 1,834 sq. ft.* ■ *Price Code C* ■

No. 98564

This plan features:

Three bedrooms

Two full baths

Privacy is key in the Master Bedroom, which boasts a decorative tray ceiling and a bay Sitting Area overlooking the rear yard

The upstairs Game Room is ideal for setting up computer games and spacious enough for a pool table

The Kitchen with ample counter space opens to the Breakfast Nook, where a tile floor makes upkeep easy

This home is designed with crawlspace and slab foundation options

Lower floor — 1,552 sq. ft.

Upper floor — 282 sq. ft.

Garage — 422 sq. ft.

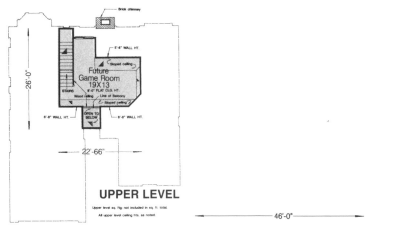

UPPER LEVEL

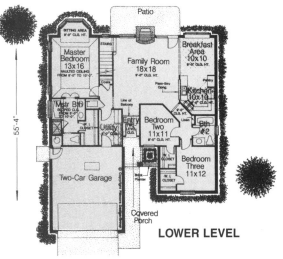

LOWER LEVEL

Unfinished Lower Level

■ Total living area 1,609 sq. ft. ■ Price Code B ■

No. 97235

■ **This plan features:**

— Three bedrooms

— Two full baths

■ A wide staircase leads to the Great Room, which has views into the Kitchen and Breakfast Area

■ The Master Suite, with French doors and covered Porch, occupies one side of the home

■ This home is designed with a basement foundation

Upper floor — 1,509 sq. ft.
Lower floor — 100 sq. ft.

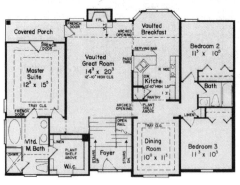

UPPER FLOOR

LOWER FLOOR

WIDTH 49'-0"
DEPTH 34'-4"

Interesting Roof Height Lines

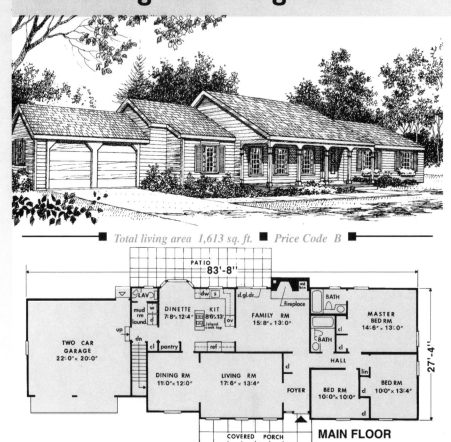

■ Total living area 1,613 sq. ft. ■ Price Code B ■

MAIN FLOOR

No. 90601

■ **This plan features:**

— Three bedrooms

— Two full and one half baths

■ A spacious Family Room with a heat-circulating fireplace, which is visible from the Foyer

■ A large Kitchen with a cooktop island, opening into the Dinette Bay

■ A Master Suite with his and her closets and a private Master Bath

■ Two additional Bedrooms which share a full Bath in the hall

■ Formal Dining and Living Rooms, flowing into each other for easy entertaining

■ This home is designed with basement and slab foundation options

Main floor — 1,613 sq. ft.
Basement — 1,060 sq. ft.
Garage — 461 sq. ft.

■ *Total living area 1,835 sq. ft.* ■ *Price Code C* ■

No. 91517

This plan features:

Three bedrooms

Two full and one half baths

Two-story Living Room with corner fireplace opens to Dining Area and Kitchen for ease in entertaining

Comfortable Family Room with French doors to raised Deck and easy access to Laundry and half Bath

Secluded Master Suite with arched window below vaulted ceiling, plus a walk-in closet and double vanity Bath

This home is designed with a basement foundation

First floor — 1,022 sq. ft.
Second floor — 813 sq. ft.
Garage — 1,077 sq. ft.

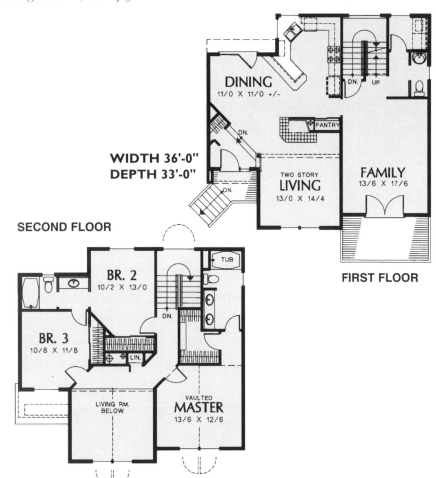

WIDTH 36'-0"
DEPTH 33'-0"

SECOND FLOOR

FIRST FLOOR

Secluded Vacation Retreat

■ *Total living area 1,837 sq. ft.* ■ *Price Code C* ■

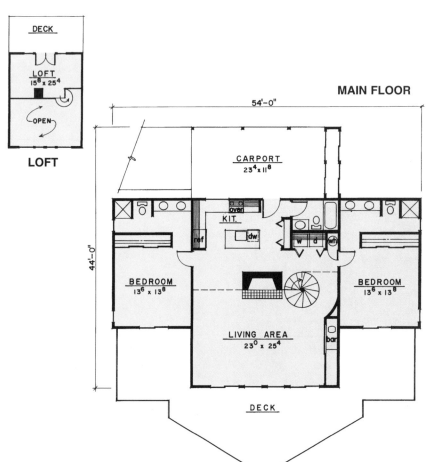

MAIN FLOOR

LOFT

No. 91704

■ This plan features:

— Two bedrooms

— One full and two three-quarter baths

■ A vaulted ceiling in the Living Area with a large masonry fireplace and circular stairway

■ A wall of windows along the full cathedral height of the Living Area

■ A Kitchen with ample storage and counter space including a sink and a chopping-block island

■ Private full Baths for each of the Bedrooms with 10-foot closets

■ A Loft with windowed doors opening to a Deck

■ This home is designed with a crawlspace foundation

Main floor — 1,448 sq. ft.
Loft — 389 sq. ft.
Carport — 312 sq. ft.

Bathed in Natural Light

No. 98416

This plan features:

Three bedrooms

Two full and one half baths

A high, arched window illuminates the Foyer and adds style to the exterior of the home

Vaulted ceilings in the formal Dining Room, Breakfast Room and Great Room create volume

The Master Suite is crowned with a decorative tray ceiling

The Master Bath has a double vanity, oval tub, separate shower and a walk-in closet

The Loft, with the option of becoming a fourth Bedroom, highlights the second floor

This home is designed with basement and crawlspace foundation options

First floor — 1,133 sq. ft.

Second floor — 486 sq. ft.

Basement — 1,133 sq. ft.

Bonus — 134 sq. ft.

Garage — 406 sq. ft.

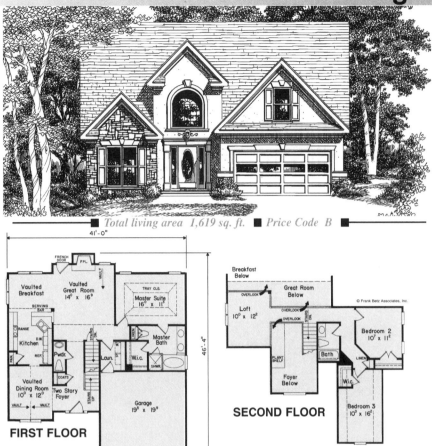

■ *Total living area 1,619 sq. ft.* ■ *Price Code B* ■

A Traditional Ranch

No. 99174

This plan features:

Three bedrooms

Two full and one half baths

Spacious covered Porches on the front and the rear of the home

The two-car Garage offers the option of a third bay or extra Storage Space

Columns and a lowered soffit define the separation of Kitchen from Living Room

The Master Bedroom features a private Bath with separate shower and large walk-in closet

This home is designed with a basement foundation

Main floor — 1,859 sq. ft.

Garage — 750 sq. ft.

■ *Total living area 1,859 sq. ft.* ■ *Price Code C* ■

REAR ELEVATION

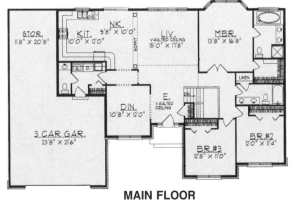

WIDTH 69'-8"
DEPTH 43'-0"

MAIN FLOOR

Convenient Floor Plan

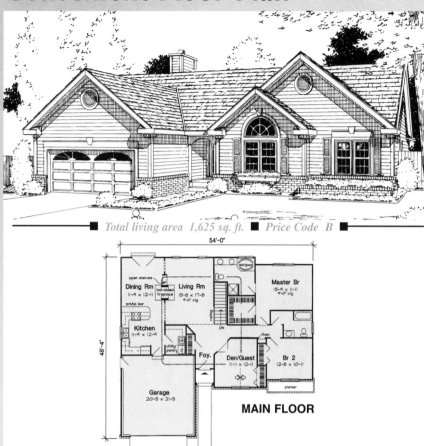

Total living area 1,625 sq. ft. ■ Price Code B ■

MAIN FLOOR

No. 24701

■ **This plan features:**

— Three bedrooms

— Two full baths

■ Central Foyer leads to Den/Guest Room with arched window below vaulted ceilin and Living Room accented by two-sided fireplace

■ Efficient, U-shaped Kitchen with peninsu counter/Breakfast Bar serving Dining Room and adjacent to Utility/Pantry

■ Master Suite features large walk-in closet and private Bath with double vanity and whirlpool tub

■ Two additional Bedrooms with ample closet space share full Bath

■ This home is designed with basement, sla and crawlspace foundation options

Main floor — 1,625 sq. ft.
Basement — 1,625 sq. ft.
Garage — 455 sq. ft.

Designed for Efficiency

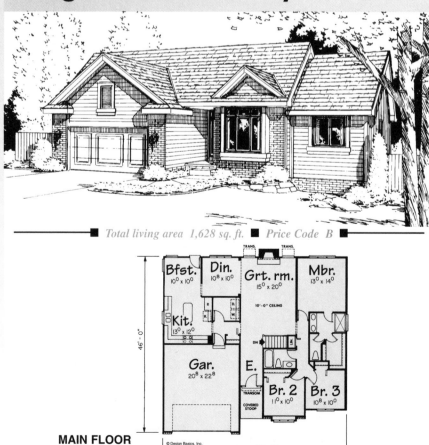

Total living area 1,628 sq. ft. ■ Price Code B ■

MAIN FLOOR

No. 97445

■ **This plan features:**

— Three bedrooms

— Two full baths

■ The covered stoop shelters the front Entrance to the home

■ Windows with transoms above flank the cozy fireplace in the Great Room

■ A box window highlights one of the secondary Bedrooms

■ The Master Bedroom has a private Bath

■ The Kitchen has a center work island and bright Breakfast Area

■ The Dining Room opens to the Great Roo

■ This home is designed with a basement foundation

■ Alternate foundation options available at additional charge. Please call 1-800-235-57 for more information.

Main floor — 1,628 sq. ft.
Garage — 487 sq. ft.

■ *Total living area 1,840 sq. ft.* ■ *Price Code C* ■

No. 96819

This plan features:

Three bedrooms

Two full and one half baths

This traditionally styled home offers a versatile floor plan adaptable to any lifestyle

To the left of the Foyer is a room that can be used as a Study, Office or even a Guest Room

Just beyond the Foyer, the large Great Room opens up to include a fireplace surrounded by built-ins and a bay-windowed Nook

A deep wraparound Porch offers opportunity to expand the home's living spaces to the out-of-doors

This home is designed with basement, slab and crawlspace foundation options

First floor — 1,014 sq. ft.
Second floor — 826 sq. ft.
Garage — 690 sq. ft.

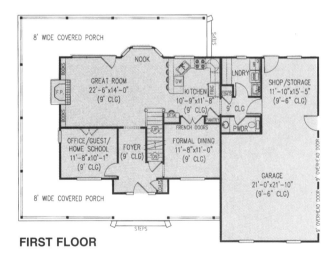

FIRST FLOOR

WIDTH 62'-7"
DEPTH 45'-0"

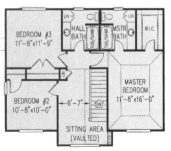

SECOND FLOOR

Wraparound Porch Adds Style

■ Total living area 1,846 sq. ft. ■ Price Code C ■

SECOND FLOOR

FIRST FLOOR

No. 99491

■ **This plan features**

— Four bedrooms

— Two full and one half baths

■ The two-story Entry of this home includes a large coat closet and a plant shelf

■ The volume ceiling and arched window in the front Bedroom add a touch of elegance

■ Master Suite has his and her walk-in closets, corner windows and a private Bath area with a double vanity and whirlpool tub

■ This home is designed with basement and slab foundation options

■ Alternate foundation options available at an additional charge. Please call 1-800-235-5700 for more information.

First floor — 919 sq. ft.
Second floor — 927 sq. ft.
Garage — 414 sq. ft.

© Design Basics, Inc.

Relaxed Style

■ *Total living area 1,868 sq. ft.* ■ *Price Code C* ■

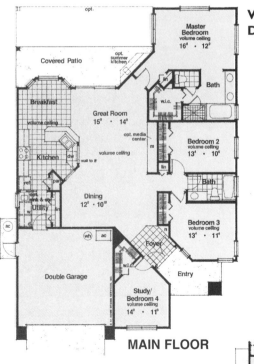

WIDTH 45'-0"
DEPTH 66'-0"

MAIN FLOOR

OPTIONAL GARAGE

No. 63114

■ **This plan features:**

— Three or four bedrooms

— Two full baths

■ Volume ceilings throughout this open floor plan add to the feeling of spaciousness

■ The angled Kitchen ends in a bay-windowed Breakfast Room

■ The Study could be used as a fourth Bedroom

■ The large Master Bedroom has windows on three sides

■ This home is designed with a slab foundation

Main floor — 1,868 sq. ft.
Garage — 400 sq. ft.

Delightful Home

■ *Total living area 1,853 sq. ft.* ■ *Price Code D* ■

SECOND FLOOR

observation deck

master
13'-0" x 14'-0"
vault. clg.

am kitchen

open to grand room below

down

© The Sater Group, Inc.

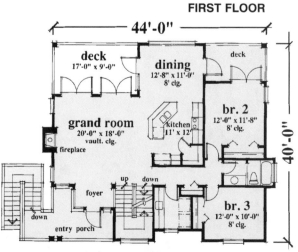

FIRST FLOOR

44'-0"

40'-0"

deck
17'-0" x 9'-0"

dining
12'-8" x 11'-0"
8' clg.

deck

grand room
20'-0" x 18'-0"
vault. clg.

fireplace

kitchen
11' x 12'

br. 2
12'-0" x 11'-8"
8' clg.

up   down

foyer

down

entry porch

br. 3
12'-0" x 10'-0"
8' clg.

No. 94248

■ **This plan features:**

— Three bedrooms

— Two full baths

■ Grand Room with a fireplace, vaulted ceiling and double French doors to the rear Deck

■ Kitchen and Dining Room open continue the overall feel of spaciousness

■ Kitchen has a large walk-in Pantry, island with a sink and dishwasher, creating a perfect triangular work space

■ This home is designed with a pier/post foundation

■ Alternate foundation options available at an additional charge Please call 1-800-235-5700 for more information.

First floor — 1,342 sq. ft.
Second floor — 511 sq. ft.

No. 97435

This plan features:

- Three bedrooms
- Two full and one half baths
- The Entry opens to a private Den
- The Kitchen, Breakfast Area and Family Room open to each other
- The Family Room has nine-foot ceilings and a fireplace
- The Master Bedroom has a walk-in closet and a whirlpool Bath
- Two additional Bedrooms share a full Bath
- This home is designed with a basement foundation
- Alternate foundation options available at an additional charge. Please call 1-800-235-5700 for more information.

First floor — 874 sq. ft.
Second floor — 754 sq. ft.
Garage — 512 sq. ft.

■ Total living area 1,628 sq. ft. ■ Price Code B ■

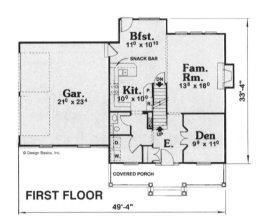

FIRST FLOOR

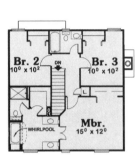

SECOND FLOOR

Distinguished Plan

No. 90398

This plan features:

- Two bedrooms, optional den/third bedroom
- Two full baths
- A vaulted ceiling Living Room with cozy fireplace
- Columns dividing the Living and Dining Rooms, and half-walls separating the Kitchen and Breakfast Room
- A luxurious Master Suite with a private sky-lit Bath, double vanities and a generous walk-in closet
- This home is designed with a basement foundation

Main floor — 1,630 sq. ft.

■ Total living area 1,630 sq. ft. ■ Price Code B ■

MAIN FLOOR

Demonstrative Detail

■ *Total living area 1,854 sq. ft.* ■ *Price Code C* ■

SECOND FLOOR

BR.#3
11x12

BR.#2
11x13

OPTIONAL BONUS
12x23

FIRST FLOOR

PORCH
5 x 16

BREAKFAST
11x12

KITCHEN
10x11

FAMILY ROOM
18x15

MASTER
13x15

DINING
10x12

FOYER

GARAGE
20x23

Drive

Workbench

No. 93410

■ **This plan features:**

— Three bedrooms

— Two full and one half baths

■ Keystone arched windows, stone and stucco combine with shutter and a flower box to create an eye catching elevation

■ The Foyer accesses the Dining Room, Family Room or the Master Suite

■ The Family Room has a sloped ceiling and is accented by a fireplace with windows to either side

■ This home is designed with a basement foundation

First floor — 1,317 sq. ft.
Second floor — 537 sq. ft.
Bonus — 312 sq. ft.
Basement — 1,317 sq. ft.
Garage — 504 sq. ft.

■ *Total living area 1,855 sq. ft.* ■ *Price Code C* ■

No. 93458

This plan features:

Three bedrooms

Two full and one half baths

The angled staircase with built-in niche creates a stunning Foyer

Large closets in the Foyer and Garage entry add to the comfort of this home

A peninsula counter opens the Kitchen to the sunny Breakfast Area

The Master Bedroom features a five-piece Bath, walk-in closet and access to Attic Storage

This home is designed with a basement foundation

First floor — 990 sq. ft.

Second floor — 865 sq. ft.

Basement — 990 sq. ft.

Garage — 498 sq. ft.

Porch — 106 sq. ft.

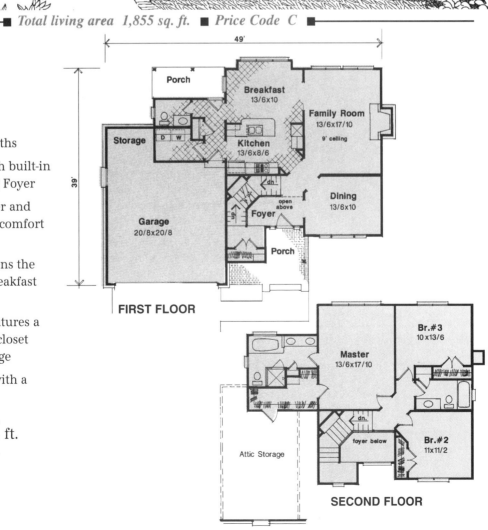

Cozy Corners and Open Spaces

■ *Total living area 1,631 sq. ft.* ■ *Price Code B* ■

MAIN FLOOR

No. 93418

■ **This plan features:**

— Three bedrooms

— Two full baths

■ A covered front Porch is supported by columns

■ Inside, the Foyer has a nine-foot ceiling

■ The entrance to the Family Room is accented by columns, while a fireplace li beyond them

■ The Kitchen is separated from the Dining Room by an angled counter

■ A Porch and Deck in the rear are accessed by a door in the Dining Room

■ The Master Bedroom has a decorative, te foot ceiling, a walk-in closet and a private Bath in the hallway

■ Two additional Bedrooms are brightened by front-wall windows and share a full B

■ A two-car, drive-under Garage completes this plan

■ This home is designed with a basement foundation

Main floor — 1,631 sq. ft.
Basement — 1,015 sq. ft.
Garage — 616 sq. ft.

Beautiful From Front to Back

■ *Total living area 1,519 sq. ft.* ■ *Price Code B* ■

FIRST FLOOR

SECOND FLOOR

No. 65198

■ **This plan features:**

— Three bedrooms

— One full and one three-quarter baths

■ The Dining Room is open to the exception galley Kitchen which offers additional seating at a curved breakfast bar

■ An angled second floor balcony overlooks the slope-ceiling Living Room

■ Three second floor Bedrooms share a generously proportioned Bath, which includes a separate shower

■ Convenient coat closets are at every entrance to this home

■ A large Laundry Room tucked behind the Kitchen

■ This home is designed with a basement foundation

First floor — 788 sq. ft.
Second floor — 731 sq. ft.
Garage — 266 sq. ft.

Brick Beauty

■ *Total living area 1,856 sq. ft.* ■ *Price Code C* ■

No. 97707

This plan features:

Three bedrooms

Two full and one half baths

The stylish Foyer is complemented by a well-positioned turned staircase

The full-sized Great Room is enhanced by a large fireplace and oversized windows

The Laundry Room is conveniently located just steps from the Kitchen and Garage

The formal Dining Room has a stepped ceiling

This home is designed with a slab foundation

First floor — 980 sq. ft.
Second floor — 876 sq. ft.
Bonus — 325 sq. ft.
Basement — 980 sq. ft.
Garage — 577 sq. ft.

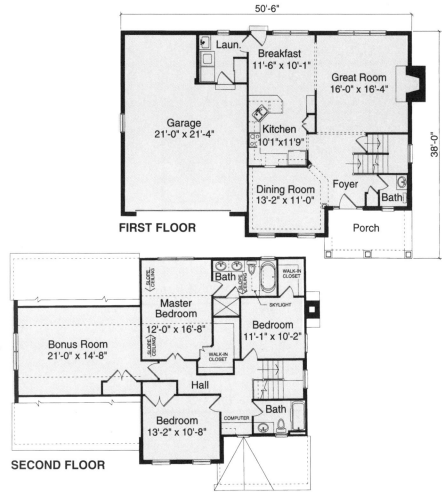

Classic Cottage

■ *Total living area 1,594 sq. ft.* ■ *Price Code B* ■

No. 97762

■ **This plan features:**

— Three bedrooms

— Two full baths

■ The Breakfast Area features a lovely and efficient built-in bench under a bay window

■ Double doors open to the Library which features built-ins on two walls — or this versatile room could be finished as a Bedroom

■ Dramatic Great Room features slope ceiling and fireplace

■ This home is designed with a basement foundation

Main floor — 1,594 sq. ft.
Basement — 1,594 sq. ft.
Garage — 512 sq. ft.
Porch — 125 sq. ft.

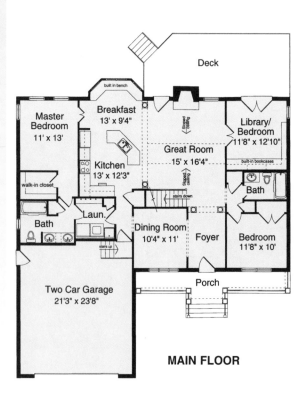

MAIN FLOOR

OPTIONAL THIRD BEDROOM

WIDTH 52'-8"
DEPTH 55'-5"

Exciting Ceilings Add Appeal

■ *Total living area 1,475 sq. ft.* ■ *Price Code B* ■

No. 93455

This plan features:

Three bedrooms

Two full baths

The wrap-around Porch says "welcome" to your friends and neighbors

The Great Room is truly great with a high ceiling and fireplace

Center island in Kitchen provides extra work space and open to the Dining Room, which offers access to a rear Porch

The Master Bedroom includes a walk-in closet and compartmentalized Bath

This home is designed with a slab and crawlspace foundation

Main floor — 1,475 sq. ft.

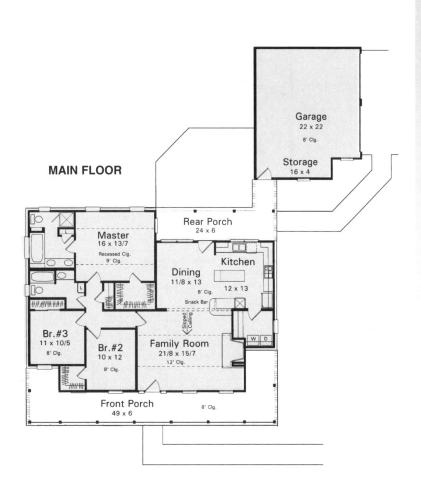

MAIN FLOOR

For the Growing Family

■ *Total living area 1,862 sq. ft.* ■ *Price Code C* ■

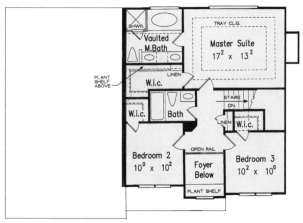

SECOND FLOOR

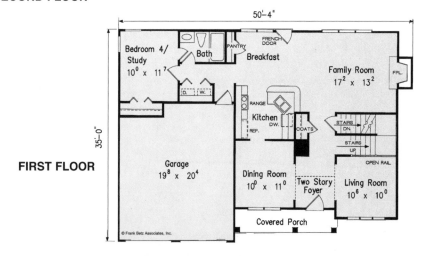

FIRST FLOOR

No. 98473

■ This plan features:

— Three or four bedrooms

— Three full baths

■ Formal areas are located to either side of the two-story Foyer

■ An open-rail staircase adorns the Living Room while the Dining Room features access to Kitchen

■ Kitchen equipped with a corner double sink and a wraparound snack bar is open to the Family Room and Breakfast Area

■ Secondary Bedroom or Study privately located in the left rear corner of the home with direct access to a full Bath

■ This home is designed with basement and crawlspace foundation options

First floor — 1,103 sq. ft.
Second floor — 759 sq. ft.
Basement — 1,103 sq. ft.
Garage — 420 sq. ft.

o. 97933

his plan features:

hree bedrooms

wo full baths

his charming home with classic exterior
etails offers lovely, open public spaces

he Family Room features a fireplace and
pens to a rear covered Porch

he Morning Lounge, which offers convenient
ccess to that same rear Porch, is open to the
ell-planned, center-island Kithcen

he secluded Master Bedroom features a tray
eiling and truly ample closet space

wo secondary Bedrooms at the front of the
ome include generous closet space

his home is designed with a basement
oundation

lternate foundation options available at an
dditional charge. Please call 1-800-235-5700
or additional information.

in floor — 1,724 sq. ft.
rage — 460 sq. ft.

■ *Total living area 1,724 sq. ft.* ■ *Price Code B* ■

WIDTH 50'-0"
DEPTH 50'-0"

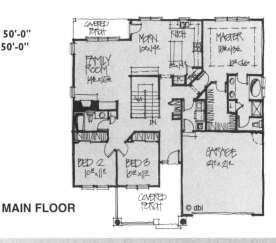

MAIN FLOOR

o. 98337

his plan features:

hree bedrooms

wo full baths

he two-story Foyer opens to the Living Room

he angled Kitchen opens to the Dining Area
nd a sunny Breakfast Area

he Living Room has a vaulted ceiling, and a
replace, and opens to the Dining Area

he Master Suite has a Sitting Area, walk-in
loset and spacious Bath

wo additional Bedrooms share a full Bath

his home is designed with a basement
oundation

in floor — 1,633 sq. ft.
sement — 1,633 sq. ft.
rage — 450 sq. ft.

■ *Total living area 1,633 sq. ft.* ■ *Price Code B* ■

MAIN FLOOR

Classic Exterior/Modern Interior

■ Total living area 1,876 sq. ft. ■ Price Code C ■

Bedroom
10'5" x 12'

Foyer Below

Bedroom
11'6" x 11'5"

Hall

Bath

Bonus Bedroom
10' x 18'2"

SECOND FLOOR

WIDTH 56'-2"
DEPTH 48'-0"

Screened-in Porch

Master Bedroom
14'1" x 15'1"

Great Room
16'8" x 15'4"

Dining Area
10'1" x 14'1"

Bath

Laun.

Dressing

Foyer

Kitchen
13'2" x 11'8"

pantry

Porch

Two-car Garage
20' x 27'5"

FIRST FLOOR

No. 92674

■ This plan features:

— Three or four bedrooms

— Two full and one half baths

■ Front Porch leads into an open Foyer and Great Room beyond, accented by a sloped ceiling, corner fireplace and multiple windows

■ An efficient Kitchen with a cooktop island, walk-in Pantry, a bright Dining Area and nearby Screened Porch, Laundry and Garage entry

■ Deluxe Master Bedroom wing with a decorative ceiling, large walk-in closet and plush Bath

■ This home is designed with a basement foundation

First floor — 1,348 sq. ft.
Second floor — 528 sq. ft.
Basement — 1,300 sq. ft.
Bonus — 195 sq. ft.

Brilliance in Brick and Fieldstone

■ *Total living area 1,640 sq. ft.* ■ *Price Code B* ■

o. 98580

his plan features:

hree bedrooms

wo full baths

tately appearance of the
ntrance and arched windows
ives style to modest plan

lub of home is the Great Room,
pening to Study/Formal Dining
rea, covered Patio and
ining/Kitchen

n efficient Kitchen features a
antry, serving ledge and bright
ining Area

laster Bedroom wing offers
ccess to covered Patio, a huge
valk-in closet and a whirlpool
ath

his home is designed with a slab
oundation

in floor — 1,640 sq. ft.

rage — 408 sq. ft.

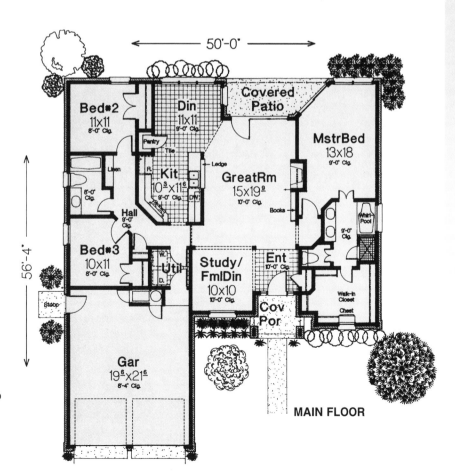

MAIN FLOOR

New England Cottage

Photography supplied by The Meredith Corp.

■ *Total living area 1,881 sq. ft.* ■ *Price Code C* ■

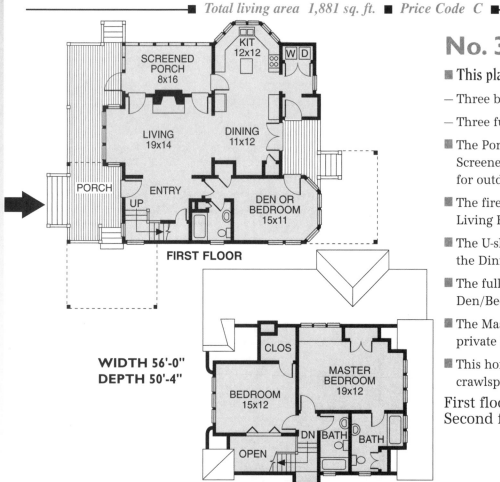

FIRST FLOOR

WIDTH 56'-0"
DEPTH 50'-4"

SECOND FLOOR

No. 32032

■ **This plan features:**

— Three bedrooms

— Three full baths

■ The Porch and the Screened Porch add options for outdoor entertaining

■ The fireplace warms the Living Room

■ The U-shaped Kitchen is open to the Dining Room

■ The full Bath is located next to Den/Bedroom

■ The Master Bedroom has a private Bath

■ This home is designed with a crawlspace foundation

First floor — 1,109 sq. ft.
Second floor — 772 sq. ft.

Split-Bedroom Design

■ *Total living area 1,646 sq. ft.* ■ *Price Code B* ■

No. 98920

This plan features:

- Three bedrooms
- Two full baths
- A bay window extends the Dining Room
- This plan features a well-planned Kitchen
- The Master Bedroom has a tray ceiling
- The secondary Bedrooms have walk-in closets
- This home is designed with crawlspace and slab foundation options
- Main floor — 1,646 sq. ft.

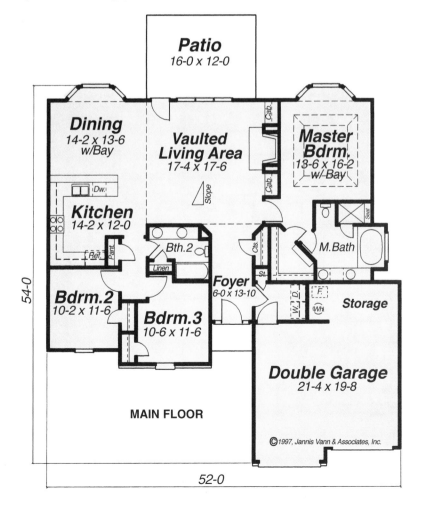

Patio
16-0 x 12-0

Dining
14-2 x 13-6
w/Bay

Vaulted
Living Area
17-4 x 17-6

Master
Bdrm.
13-6 x 16-2
w/ Bay

Kitchen
14-2 x 12-0

Bth.2

M.Bath

Bdrm.2
10-2 x 11-6

Bdrm.3
10-6 x 11-6

Foyer
6-0 x 13-10

Storage

Double Garage
21-4 x 19-8

54-0

52-0

MAIN FLOOR

©1997, Jannis Vann & Associates, Inc.

Keystones, Arches and Gables

■ *Total living area 1,642 sq. ft.* ■ *Price Code B* ■

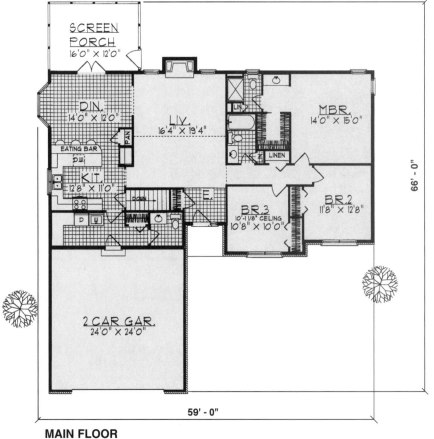

SCREEN PORCH 16'0" X 12'0"

DIN. 14'0" X 12'0"

LIV. 16'4" X 19'4"

MBR. 14'0" X 15'0"

EATING BAR

KIT. 12'8" X 11'0"

BR.3 10'8" ceiling 10'8" X 10'0"

BR.2 11'8" X 12'8"

2 CAR GAR. 24'0" X 24'0"

59' - 0"

66' - 0"

MAIN FLOOR

No. 93171

■ **This plan features:**

— Three bedrooms

— One full, one three-quarter and one half baths

■ Tiled Entry opens to Living Roo with focal-point fireplace

■ U-shaped Kitchen with a built-i Pantry, eating bar and nearby Laundry/Garage Entry

■ Comfortable Dining Room with bay window and French doors Screened Porch, expanding Livi Area outdoors

■ Corner Master Bedroom offers great walk-in closet and private Bathroom

■ Two additional Bedrooms with ample closets and double windows share a full Bath

■ This home is designed with a basement foundation

Main floor — 1,642 sq. ft.

■ *Total living area 1,883 sq. ft.* ■ *Price Code C* ■

o. 97121

his plan features:

hree bedrooms

wo full and one half baths

he Entry opens into the Great
Room and Dining Room

A step-saving Kitchen features an
ating bar, Pantry and Nook with
rench door access to the
ackyard

Convenient to the Garage and
Master Bedroom, the Laundry
Room has an easy-maintenance
loor and separate closet

he Master Bedroom includes a
rivate Bath with garden tub and
arge walk-in closet

his home is designed with a
asement foundation

st floor — 1,365 sq. ft.
cond floor — 518 sq. ft.

SECOND FLOOR

FIRST FLOOR

Spacious Country Charm

■ *Total living area 1,887 sq. ft.* ■ *Price Code C* ■

SECOND FLOOR

WIDTH 52'-8"
DEPTH 40'-0"

FIRST FLOOR

No. 94107

■ **This plan features:**

— Three bedrooms

— Two full and one half baths

■ Comfortable front Porch leads into bright two-story Foyer

■ Pillars frame entrance to forma Dining Room highlighted by ba window

■ Expansive Great Room accente by hearth fireplace and triple window opens to Kitchen/Dini Area

■ Efficient Kitchen with loads of counter and Storage Space, and Dining Area with window acce to rear yard

■ Corner Master Bedroom offers triple window

■ This home is designed with a basement foundation

First floor — 961 sq. ft.
Second floor — 926 sq. ft.
Garage — 548 sq. ft.

Friendly Facade

■ *Total living area 1,892 sq. ft.* ■ *Price Code C* ■

No. 90850

This plan features:

Three bedrooms

Two full and one half baths

A covered Country Porch that welcomes guests and family

A spacious Living Room with a stone fireplace and an elegant bay window

A formal Dining Room that views the front Porch

An efficient Kitchen situated conveniently between the Dining Room and the Family Area

A first floor Master Suite

This home is designed with a basement foundation

First floor — 1,190 sq. ft.
Second floor — 702 sq. ft.
Basement — 1,178 sq. ft.

WIDTH 37'-0"
DEPTH 29'-0"

FIRST FLOOR

FAMILY 10-0×20-0
KITCHEN
DINING 10-0×10-0
FOYER
Porch
up
railing
dn
Hall
lin.
Ens.
Bath
MBR 11-0×13-0
LIVINGROOM 18-0×17-0

SECOND FLOOR

attic
attic
Bath
BR 2 14-0×13-0
dn
BR 3 11-0×13-0
linen
storage
attic

Column Accents

■ *Total living area 1,894 sq. ft.* ■ *Price Code C* ■

SECOND FLOOR

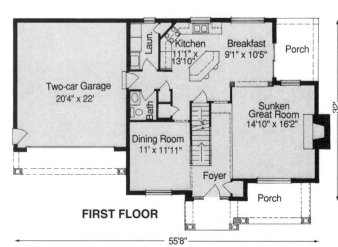

FIRST FLOOR

No. 92659

■ **This plan features:**

— Three bedrooms

— Two full and one half baths

■ The Foyer opens to the Dining Room and sunken Great Room with fireplace

■ An angled counter with eating bar, Pantry and Breakfast Area with sliding-door access to the Porch highlight the Kitchen

■ Bedrooms radiate off a center h that features a built-in Comput Center

■ This home is designed with a basement foundation

First floor — 922 sq. ft.
Second floor — 972 sq. ft.
Bonus — 267 sq. ft.
Basement — 882 sq. ft.
Garage — 447 sq. ft.

Modern Slant on a Country Theme

■ *Total living area 1,648 sq. ft.* ■ *Price Code B* ■

No. 96513

This plan features:

Three bedrooms

Two full and one half baths

Country-style front Porch highlighting exterior which is enhanced by dormer windows

Great Room accented by a quaint, corner fireplace and a ceiling fan

Dining Room flowing from the Great Room for easy entertaining

Kitchen graced by natural light from attractive bay window and featuring a convenient snack bar for quick meals

This home is designed with crawlspace and slab foundation options

Main floor — 1,648 sq. ft.
Garage — 479 sq. ft.

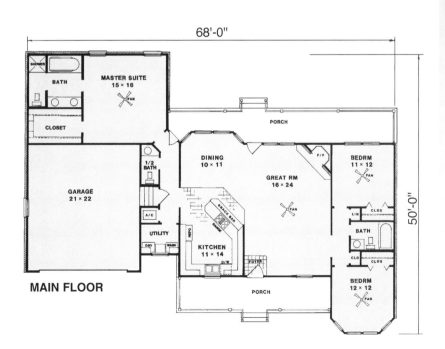

MAIN FLOOR

Office with Private Entrance

■ Total living area 1,564 sq. ft. ■ Price Code B ■

FIRST FLOOR

4,60 X 6,50
15'-4" X 21'-8"

3,90 X 2,70
13'-0" X 9'-0"

3,90 X 3,00
13'-0" X 10'-0"

3,90 X 3,60
13'-0" X 12'-0"

3,60 X 4,50
12'-0" X 15'-0"

11,7 m
39'-0"

15,0 m
50'-0"

No. 65372

■ **This plan features:**

— Two bedrooms

— One full and one three-quarter baths

■ The Living and Dining Areas are open to the well-planned Kitchen in this flowing plan

■ The center-island Kitchen features an Eating Nook

■ An Office or Study at the front of this home offers plenty of natural light and a separate entrance from the front Porch

■ Two second floor Bedrooms share a three-quarter Bath

■ This home is designed with a basement foundation

First floor — 983 sq. ft.
Second floor — 581 sq. ft.
Garage — 336 sq. ft.
Basement — 983 sq. ft.

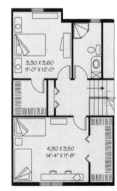

3,30 X 3,60
11'-0" X 12'-0"

4,30 X 3,50
14'-4" X 11'-8"

SECOND FLOOR

Total living area 1,650 sq. ft. ■ *Price Code B* ■

o. 97442

his plan features:

hree bedrooms

wo full baths

. desk in the Kitchen allows
arents to supervise homework

. bay window extends the
Breakfast Nook

he plan features an open-rail
taircase to the Basement

. whirlpool tub is located in the
Master Bath

Double windows are found in
oth of the secondary Bedrooms

his home is designed with a
asement foundation

lternate foundation options
vailable at an additional charge.
lease call 1-800-235-5700 for more
nformation.

in floor — 1,650 sq. ft.
rage — 529 sq. ft.

MAIN FLOOR

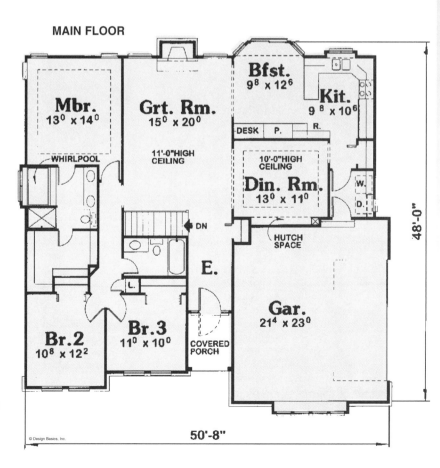

Impressive Brick and Wood Facade

■ Total living area 1,651 sq. ft. ■ Price Code B ■

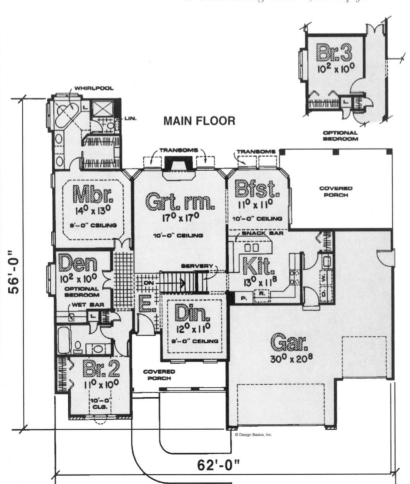

WHIRLPOOL

MAIN FLOOR

Br. 3
10² x 10⁰

OPTIONAL
BEDROOM

LIN.

TRANSOMS   TRANSOMS

Mbr.
14⁰ x 13⁰
9'-0" CEILING

Grt. rm.
17⁰ x 17⁰
10'-0" CEILING

Bfst.
11⁰ x 11⁰
10'-0" CEILING

COVERED
PORCH

SNACK BAR

Den
10² x 10⁰
OPTIONAL
BEDROOM

SERVERY

Kit.
13⁰ x 11⁸

WET BAR

DN

Din.
12⁰ x 11⁰
9'-0" CEILING

P.

Gar.
30⁰ x 20⁸

Br. 2
11⁰ x 10⁰
10'-0" CLG.

COVERED
PORCH

56'-0"

62'-0"

© Design Basics, Inc.

No. 94921

■ This plan features:

— Two or three bedrooms

— Two full baths

■ Covered front and rear Porches
   expand Living Space outside

■ Handy serving area located
   between formal Dining Room
   expansive Great Room

■ French doors lead into Den wit
   wetbar

■ Den can easily convert to third
   Bedroom

■ This home is designed with a
   basement foundation

■ Alternate foundation options
   available at an additional char
   Please call 1-800-235-5700 for
   information.

Main floor — 1,651 sq. ft.
Basement — 1,651 sq. ft.
Garage — 480 sq. ft.

Filled With Light

■ *Total living area 1,650 sq. ft.* ■ *Price Code B* ■

No. 94938

This plan features:

Three bedrooms

Two full and one half baths

Inviting covered Porch leads into large Foyer with coat closet and views of fireplaced Great Room

The second floor Master Bedroom offers serenity, a whirlpool tub and plenty of closet space

This home is designed with a basement foundation

Alternate foundation options available at an additional charge. Please call 1-800-235-5700 for additional information.

First floor — 891 sq. ft.
Second floor — 759 sq. ft.
Basement — 891 sq. ft.
Garage — 484 sq. ft.

WIDTH 44'-0"
DEPTH 40'-0"

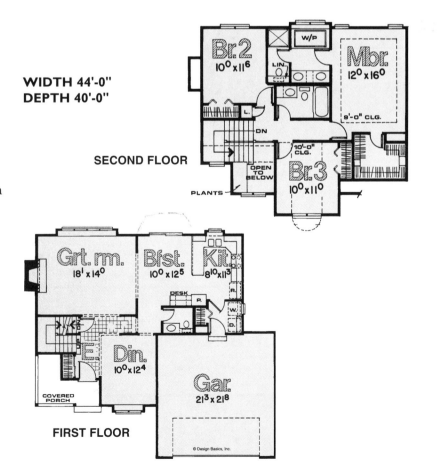

Charm and Efficiency

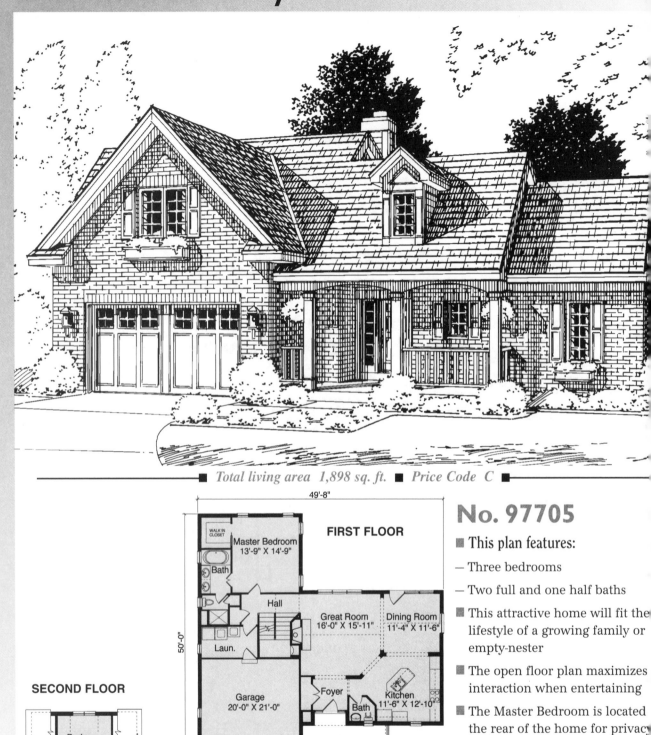

■ *Total living area 1,898 sq. ft.* ■ *Price Code C* ■

FIRST FLOOR

WALK IN CLOSET

Master Bedroom
13'-9" X 14'-9"

Bath

Hall

Great Room
16'-0" X 15'-11"

Dining Room
11'-4" X 11'-6"

Laun.

Foyer

Kitchen
11'-6" X 12'-10"

Garage
20'-0" X 21'-0"

Bath

Porch

49'-8"

50'-0"

SECOND FLOOR

Bedroom
11'-0"X12'-4"

Bath

Computer Loft

WALK IN CLOSET

Bedroom
11'-0"X13'-10"

No. 97705

■ **This plan features:**

— Three bedrooms

— Two full and one half baths

■ This attractive home will fit the lifestyle of a growing family or empty-nester

■ The open floor plan maximizes interaction when entertaining

■ The Master Bedroom is located the rear of the home for privacy

■ Upstairs are the secondary Bedrooms, a Bath and a Loft

■ A two-car Garage accesses the Laundry Room

■ This home is designed with a basement foundation

First floor —1,283 sq. ft.
Second floor — 615 sq. ft.
Basement — 1,283 sq. ft.
Garage — 420 sq. ft.

Cozy Front and Back Porches

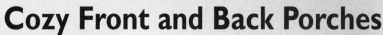

No. 96523

This plan features:

- Three bedrooms
- Two full baths
- A spacious Great Room is highlighted by a corner fireplace and access to the rear Porch
- The Dining Area, with views of the front yard, is separated from the Kitchen by an eating bar
- The private Master Suite is tucked into the rear left corner of the home
- A tray ceiling, a whirlpool tub and a walk-in closet highlight the Master Suite
- Two additional Bedrooms are located on the opposite side of the home, a full Bath is between the Bedrooms
- This home is designed with crawlspace and slab foundation options

Main floor — 1,652 sq. ft.
Garage — 497 sq. ft.

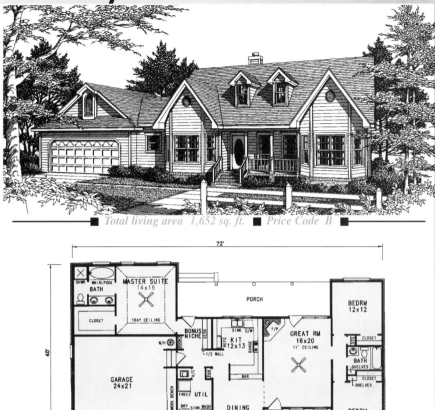

Total living area 1,652 sq. ft. ■ *Price Code B*

MAIN FLOOR

Attractive Ceiling Treatments

No. 96506

This plan features:

- Three bedrooms
- Two full and one half baths
- Great Room and Master Suite with step-up ceiling treatments
- A cozy fireplace providing warm focal point in the Great Room
- Open layout between Kitchen, Dining and Great Room lending a more spacious feeling
- Pampering Master Suite features five-piece, private Bath and walk-in closet
- Two additional Bedrooms located at opposite end of home from the Master Suite sharing the full Bath in the hall
- This home is designed with crawlspace and slab foundation options

Main floor — 1,654 sq. ft.
Garage — 480 sq. ft.
Porch — 401 sq. ft.

Total living area 1,654 sq. ft. ■ *Price Code B* ■

MAIN FLOOR

WIDTH 68'-0"
DEPTH 46'-0"

Perfect Porches

■ *Total living area 1,899 sq. ft.* ■ *Price Code C* ■

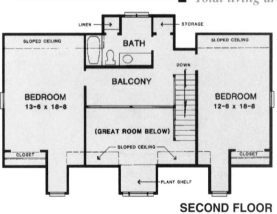

SECOND FLOOR

FIRST FLOOR

No. 90477

■ This plan features:

— Three bedrooms

— Two full baths

■ Full-width front and rear Porch add plenty of outdoor living spaces

■ The Country Kitchen features a center island, Laundry closet and Pantry

■ A focal-point fireplace and door the rear Porch creates a warm and inviting Great Room

■ The Master Bedroom has a full walk-in closet and Bath with two vanities

■ This home is designed with a crawlspace foundation

First floor — 1,012 sq. ft.
Second floor — 887 sq. ft.
Porch — 562 sq. ft.

No. 97615

This plan features:

- Three bedrooms

- Two full baths

- An arched opening with decorative columns accents the Dining Room

- Ample cabinet and counter space, a built-in pantry and serving bar add to the appealing kitchen

- French doors to the outdoors or an optional bay window will personalize your sunny Breakfast Room

- A vaulted ceiling crowns the Great Room which also features a fireplace

- Lavish Master Suite is topped by a tray ceiling

- This home is designed with a basement foundation

- Main floor — 1,571 sq. ft.
- Bonus — 334 sq. ft.
- Basement — 1,642 sq. ft.
- Garage — 483 sq. ft.

■ *Total living area 1,571 sq. ft.* ■ *Price Code B* ■

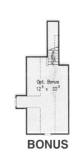

WIDTH 64'-0"
DEPTH 52'-0"

MAIN FLOOR

BONUS

No. 97760

This plan features:

- Three bedrooms

- Two full baths

- A 10-foot ceiling tops the Foyer

- Columns accent the Great Room and a fireplace adds a focal point to the room

- The Dining Area has a sunny bay window and accesses the Screened Porch through sliders

- The Kitchen includes a peninsula counter that can serve as a snack bar for after-school snacks or meals on the go

- The Master Suite has a 10-foot ceiling and a plush Bath

- This home is designed with a basement foundation

- Main floor — 1,611 sq. ft.
- Garage — 430 sq. ft.
- Porch — 163 sq. ft.

■ *Total living area 1,611 sq. ft.* ■ *Price Code B* ■

WIDTH 66'-4"
DEPTH 43'-10"

MAIN FLOOR

241

Designed For Busy Lifestyle

■ *Total living area 1,663 sq. ft.* ■ *Price Code B* ■

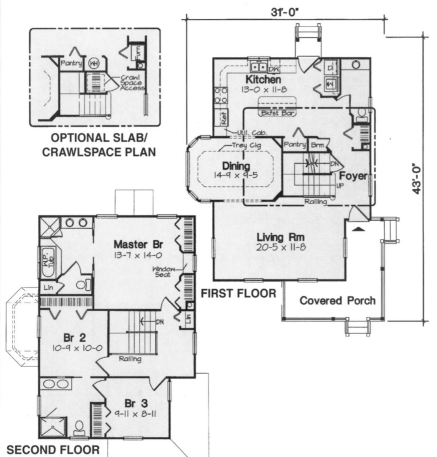

**OPTIONAL SLAB/
CRAWLSPACE PLAN**

FIRST FLOOR

SECOND FLOOR

No. 24729

■ **This plan features:**

— Three bedrooms

— One full, one three-quarter and one half baths

■ This home has been designed f today's family with their busy lifestyle in mind

■ The Living Room is large and adjoins with the Dining Room ease when entertaining

■ A tray ceiling tops the Dining Room adding elegance and sty to the room

■ The Master Suite includes a Sp tub, a separate shower and a compartmentalized toilet

■ This home is designed with basement, slab and crawlspace foundation options

First floor — 850 sq. ft.
Second floor — 813 sq. ft.
Porch — 150 sq. ft.

■ *Total living area 1,666 sq. ft.* ■ *Price Code B* ■

No. 94923

This plan features:

Three bedrooms

Two full baths

Brick and stucco enhance the dramatic front elevation and volume entrance

Inviting Entry leads into expansive Great Room with hearth fireplace framed by transom windows

Bay window Dining Room topped by decorative ceiling is convenient to the Great Room and the Kitchen/Breakfast Area

This home is designed with a basement foundation

Alternate foundation options available at an additional charge. Please call 1-800-235-5700 for more information.

Main floor — 1,666 sq. ft.

Basement — 1,666 sq. ft.

Garage — 496 sq. ft.

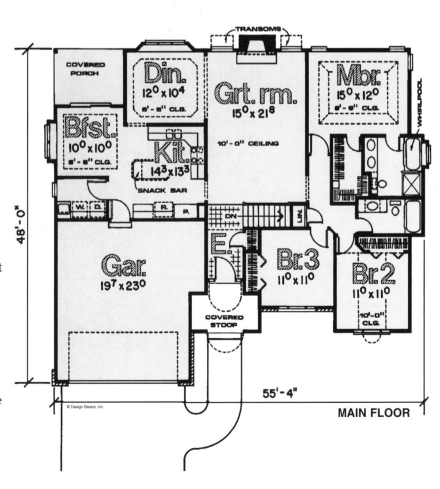

Beautiful Stucco & Stone

Total living area 1,913 sq. ft. ■ **Price Code C** ■

For the Farm

FIRST FLOOR

48'-0"

SEAT
SH·WR
Vaulted M.Bath
PLANT SHELF ABOVE
W.l.c.
LINEN
FRENCH DOOR
Master Suite
12⁴ x 16⁰
TRAY CEILING
STAIRS DN
STAIRS UP
Two Story Foyer
Sitting Room
9⁴ x 10⁰
FPL
FRENCH DOOR
Vaulted Family Room
14⁶ x 22⁵
Dining Room
11⁹ x 11⁰
Covered Porch
FRENCH DOOR
RANGE
DW.
Kitchen
Breakfast
REF. DESK
KB.
PANTRY
W. T.B.
Pwdr.
COATS
Laund.
Garage
20⁰ x 20³
50'-10"

© Frank Betz Associates, Inc.

SECOND FLOOR

Convert attic to a bedroom

VAULT
Bedroom 2
11⁷ x 11⁰
W.l.c.
Family Room Below
Attic
OPEN RAIL
OVERLOOK
Bath
Bedroom 3
11⁰ x 10⁶
STAIRS DN
OPEN RAIL
Foyer Below
LINEN
Opt. Bonus Room
12⁰ x 23⁷

No. 98445

■ **This plan features:**

— Three bedrooms

— Two full and one half baths

■ This home is accented by keystone arches and a turret-sty roof

■ The two-story Foyer includes a half Bath

■ The vaulted Family Room is highlighted by a fireplace and a French door to the rear yard

■ This home is designed with basement and crawlspace foundation options

First floor — 1,398 sq. ft.
Second floor — 515 sq. ft.
Bonus — 282 sq. ft.
Basement — 1,398 sq. ft.
Garage — 421 sq. ft.

Impressive Curb Appeal

© Frank Betz Associates, Inc.

■ *Total living area 1,917 sq. ft.* ■ *Price Code C* ■

No. 97605

This plan features:

Four bedrooms

Two full and one half baths

An entrance hall off the two-story Foyer has a Laundry Room with sink, Powder Room and access to the Garage

The efficient Kitchen has a Pantry, serving bar and pass-through to the vaulted Great Room with fireplace

Natural light floods the vaulted Breakfast Area with French door access to the backyard

This home is designed with basement and crawlspace foundation options

First floor — 1,305 sq. ft.
Second floor — 612 sq. ft.
Basement — 1,305 sq. ft.
Garage — 468 sq. ft.

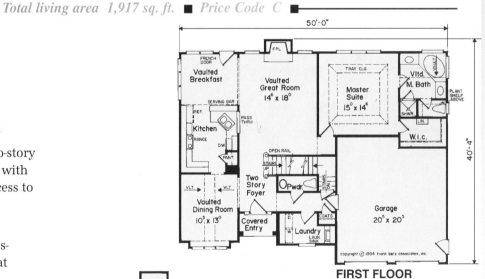

For the Farm.

FIRST FLOOR

SECOND FLOOR

Look of Yesteryear

■ *Total living area 1,926 sq. ft.* ■ *Price Code C* ■

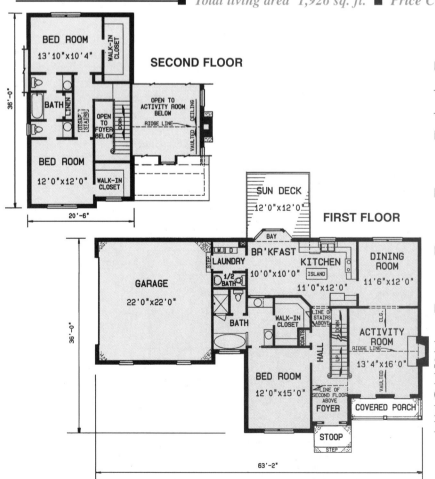

SECOND FLOOR

BED ROOM
13'10"x10'4"

WALK-IN CLOSET

BATH

LINEN

OPEN TO FOYER BELOW

OPEN TO ACTIVITY ROOM BELOW

RIDGE LINE

VAULTED CEILING

BED ROOM
12'0"x12'0"

WALK-IN CLOSET

36'-0"

20'-6"

FIRST FLOOR

SUN DECK
12'0"x12'0"

BAY

GARAGE
22'0"x22'0"

LAUNDRY

1/2 BATH

BR'KFAST
10'0"x10'0"

KITCHEN
ISLAND
11'0"x12'0"

DINING ROOM
11'6"x12'0"

BATH

WALK-IN CLOSET

COATS

LINE OF STAIRS ABOVE

DOWN

UP

CLG.

ACTIVITY ROOM
RIDGE LINE
13'4"x16'0"

VAULTED

HALL

BED ROOM
12'0"x15'0"

LINE OF SECOND FLOOR ABOVE

FOYER

COVERED PORCH

STOOP

STEP

36'-0"

63'-2"

No. 94813

■ This plan features:

— Three bedrooms

— Two full and two half baths

■ Keystone windows and brick siding create plenty of curb appeal

■ The Activity Room has a vaulted ceiling, fireplace and private covered Porch

■ Conveniently located between the Kitchen and Garage is the Laundry Area and half Bath

■ This home is designed with a basement foundation

First floor — 1,235 sq. ft.
Second floor — 691 sq. ft.
Basement — 1264 sq. ft.
Garage — 507 sq. ft.
Deck — 144 sq. ft.
Porch — 55 sq. ft.

Terrific Starter Home

o. 97149

his plan features:

hree bedrooms

wo full and one half baths

he Foyer opens to the luxurious
iving Room with a cozy fireplace
rrounded by built-in cabinets

he Kitchen, open to the Dining Area,
fers a unique use of space with the
ppliances around the perimeter

he first floor Master Bedroom is
eal for a getaway

wo additional Bedrooms share a
ll Bath and have ample closet space

his home is designed with a basement
undation

st floor – 1,168 sq. ft.
ond floor – 498 sq. ft.

■ Total living area 1,666 sq. ft. ■ Price Code B ■

FIRST FLOOR

SECOND FLOOR

Old-Fashioned Country Porch

o. 93219

his plan features:

hree bedrooms

wo full and one half baths

traditional front Porch, with matching
rmers above and a Garage hidden below,
ading into an open, contemporary layout

Living Area with a cozy fireplace visible
om the Dining Room for warm entertaining

U-shaped, efficient Kitchen featuring a
rner double sink and pass-through to the
ining Room

convenient half Bath with a Laundry center
the first floor

spacious, first floor Master Suite with a
vish Bath that includes a double vanity,
alk-in closet and an oval corner window tub

n the second floor, two large Bedrooms with
rmer windows share a full Bath

his home is designed with a basement
undation

st floor – 1,057 sq. ft.
ond floor – 611 sq. ft.
ement – 511 sq. ft.
age – 546 sq. ft.

■ Total living area 1,668 sq. ft. ■ Price Code B ■

FIRST FLOOR

SECOND FLOOR

247

Central Kitchen

■ *Total living area 1,928 sq. ft.* ■ *Price Code C* ■

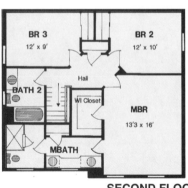

SECOND FLOOR

- BR 3 — 12' x 9'
- BR 2 — 12' x 10'
- Hall
- BATH 2
- W Closet
- MBR — 13'3 x 16'
- MBATH

No. 94144

■ **This plan features:**

— Three bedrooms

— One full, one three-quarter and one half baths

■ The Foyer opens to the Living Room and central Kitchen

■ An informal Entry features two closets, Laundry Room and half Bath, and connects the Garage and Kitchen

■ Family activities are easily accommodated in the expansiv Family Room and Dining Area

■ The Kitchen opens to the Dinir Area and has views of the fireplace in the Family Room

■ This home is designed with a basement foundation

First floor — 1,132 sq. ft.
Second floor — 796 sq. ft.
Basement — 1,132 sq. ft.
Garage — 529 sq. ft.

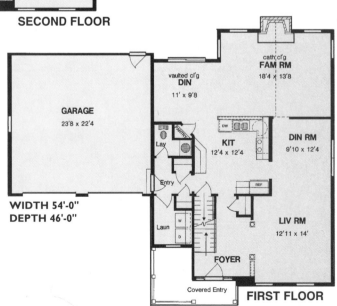

FIRST FLOOR

- GARAGE — 23'8 x 22'4
- WIDTH 54'-0"
- DEPTH 46'-0"
- FAM RM — 18'4 x 13'8 — cath'l cl'g
- DIN — 11' x 9'8 — vaulted cl'g
- DIN RM — 9'10 x 12'4
- KIT — 12'4 x 12'4
- Lay
- Entry
- REF
- DW
- PANTRY
- LIV RM — 12'11 x 14'
- Laun — W D
- FOYER
- Covered Entry

■ *Total living area 1,929 sq. ft.* ■ *Price Code C* ■

No. 96901

■ **This plan features:**

- Three bedrooms

- Two full and one half baths

■ The Great Room features a fireplace, an open-rail staircase with balcony and a plant ledge over the opening into the Dining Room

■ Well-equipped and efficient, the Kitchen has an angled sink and walk-in Pantry

■ Double doors lead to the Master Suite with five-piece Bath and walk-in closet

■ This home is designed with a slab foundation

First floor — 1,383 sq. ft.
Second floor — 546 sq. ft.
Bonus — 320 sq. ft.
Garage — 475 sq. ft.
Deck — 120 sq. ft
Porch — 68 sq. ft.

WIDTH 50'-6"
DEPTH 42'-10"

Keystones and Arched Windows

Total living area 1,670 sq. ft. ■ *Price Code B*

MAIN FLOOR

No. 98432

■ **This plan features:**

— Three bedrooms

— Two full baths

■ A large, arched window in the Dining Room offers eye-catching appeal

■ A decorative column helps to define the Dining Room from the Great Room

■ A fireplace and French door to the rear yard can be found in the Great Room

■ An efficient Kitchen includes a serving bar, Pantry and pass-through to the Great Room

■ A vaulted ceiling over the Breakfast Room

■ Two additional Bedrooms share a full Bathroom

■ This home is designed with basement, slab and crawlspace foundation options

Main floor — 1,670 sq. ft.

Country-Style Ranch

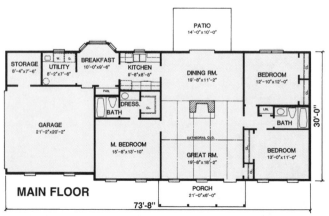

Total living area 1,670 sq. ft. ■ *Price Code B*

No. 90409

■ **This plan features:**

— Three bedrooms

— Two full baths

■ A massive fireplace separating Living and Dining Rooms

■ A Master Suite with a walk-in closet and compartmentalized Bath

■ A galley Kitchen between the Breakfast Room and Dining Room

■ This home is designed with basement, slab and crawlspace foundation options

Main floor — 1,670 sq. ft.
Basement — 1,670 sq. ft.
Garage — 427 sq. ft.

MAIN FLOOR

Front Porch of Yesteryear

■ *Total living area 1,930 sq. ft.* ■ *Price Code C* ■

No. 93290

This plan features:

- Three bedrooms
- Two full and one half baths
- The open Foyer is flanked by the formal Living and Dining Rooms
- The Breakfast Nook has a bay window overlooking the rear yard and spacious Deck
- The luxurious Master Bedroom has a decorative tray ceiling, an oversized walk-in closet and a plush Bath
- The secondary Bedrooms include generous closet space and share a full Bath
- This home is designed with a basement foundation

First floor — 981 sq. ft.
Second floor — 899 sq. ft.
Lower floor — 50 sq. ft.
Basement — 425 sq. ft.
Garage — 558 sq. ft.

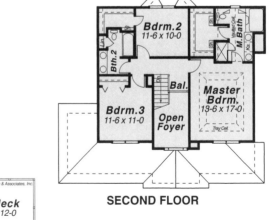

SECOND FLOOR

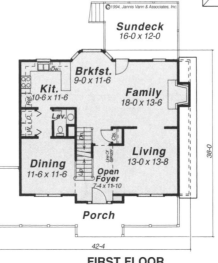

FIRST FLOOR

Windows for Natural Lighting

■ *Total living area 1,931 sq. ft.* ■ *Price Code C* ■

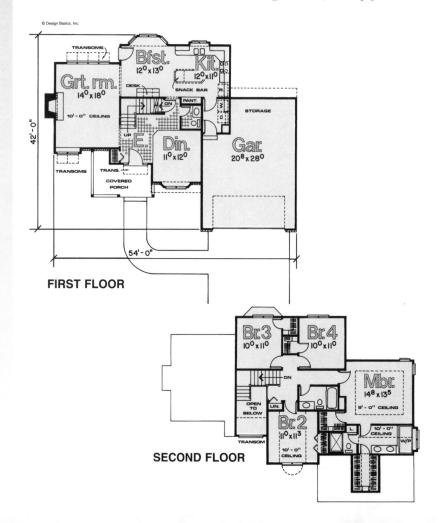

FIRST FLOOR

SECOND FLOOR

No. 94902

■ **This plan features:**

— Four bedrooms

— Two full and one half baths

■ A covered front Porch, sidelights and a transom window highlight the Entry to this home

■ The Great Room features a hearth fireplace, transom windows and a 10-foot ceiling

■ The Kitchen has a convenient center island and is open to the Breakfast Room

■ This home is designed with a basement foundation

■ Alternate foundation options available at an additional charge. Please call 1-800-235-5700 for more information.

First floor — 944 sq. ft.
Second floor — 987 sq. ft.
Basement — 944 sq. ft.
Garage — 557 sq. ft.

Spectacular Sophistication

■ *Total living area 1,933 sq. ft.* ■ *Price Code C* ■

No. 94944

This plan features:

Four bedrooms

Two full and one half baths

The tiled Foyer has a coat closet and leads to the formal Dining Room and Great Room

An inviting fireplace and windows on two walls highlight the Great Room

The Kitchen has a work island and is open to the Breakfast Area

This home is designed with basement and slab foundation options

Alternate foundation options available at an additional charge. Please call 1-800-235-5700 for more information.

First floor — 941 sq. ft.
Second floor — 992 sq. ft.
Basement — 941 sq. ft.
Garage — 480 sq. ft.

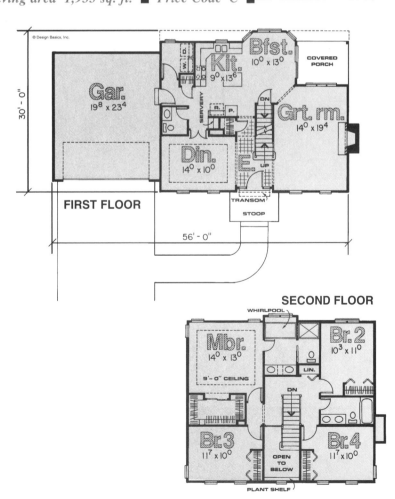

Covered Porch Gazebo

Total living area 1,938 sq. ft. ■ *Price Code C* ■

No. 97430

■ This plan features:

— Three bedrooms

— Two full and one half baths

■ Enjoy summer dining on the covered Porch Gazebo

■ The Kitchen features a snack bar, Breakfast Area and view of the fireplace in the Family Room

■ A whirlpool Bath, huge walk-in closet and Bonus space create a wonderful Master Suite

■ Two additional Bedrooms share a full Bath

■ This home is designed with a basement foundation

■ Alternate foundation options available at an additional charge. Please call 1-800-235-5700 for more information.

First floor — 1,091 sq. ft.
Second floor — 847 sq. ft.
Garage — 482 sq. ft.

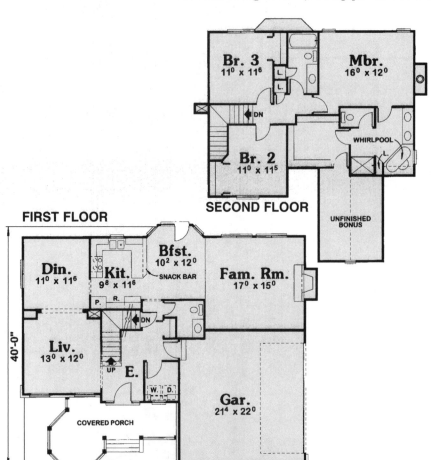

Towering Windows

No. 91071

This plan features:

Three bedrooms

Two full baths

A wraparound Deck above a three-car Garage with plenty of work/Storage Space

Both the Dining and Living Areas have vaulted ceilings above French doors to the Deck

An octagon-shaped Kitchen with a view, a cooktop peninsula and an open counter to the Dining Area

A Master Bedroom on the upper floor, with an over-sized closet, a private Bath and an optional Loft

Two additional Bedrooms sharing a full Bathroom

This home is designed with crawlspace and slab foundation options

Main floor — 1,329 sq. ft.

Upper floor — 342 sq. ft.

Garage — 885 sq. ft.

Deck — 461 sq. ft.

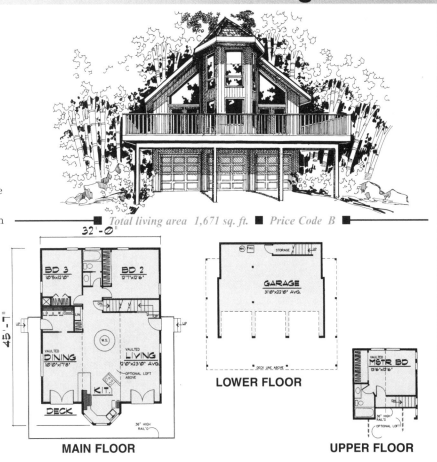

■ *Total living area 1,671 sq. ft.* ■ *Price Code B* ■

MAIN FLOOR

LOWER FLOOR

UPPER FLOOR

Easy One-Floor Living

No. 98423

This plan features:

Three bedrooms

Two full baths

A spacious Family Room topped by a vaulted ceiling and highlighted by a large fireplace and a French door to the rear yard

A serving bar open to the Family Room and the Dining Room, a Pantry and a peninsula counter adding more efficiency to the Kitchen

A tray ceiling over the Master Bedroom and a vaulted ceiling over the Master Bath

A vaulted ceiling over the Sitting Room in the Master Suite

Two additional roomy Bedrooms share a full Bath

This home is designed with basement, slab and crawlspace foundation options

Main floor — 1,671 sq. ft.

Basement — 1,685 sq. ft.

Garage — 400 sq. ft.

■ *Total living area 1,671 sq. ft.* ■ *Price Code B* ■

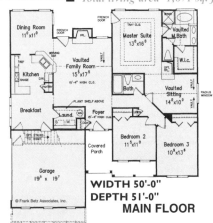

WIDTH 50'-0"
DEPTH 51'-0"
MAIN FLOOR

Room to Expand

■ Total living area 1,675 sq. ft. ■ Price Code B ■

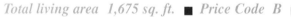

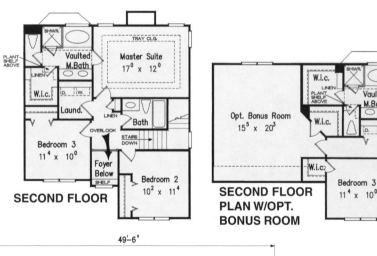

SECOND FLOOR

Master Suite 17⁰ x 12⁰
Vaulted M.Bath
PLANT SHELF ABOVE
LINEN
W.i.c.
Laund.
Bedroom 3 11⁴ x 10⁰
LINEN
Bath
OVERLOOK
STAIRS DOWN
Foyer Below
SHELF
Bedroom 2 10² x 11⁴

SECOND FLOOR PLAN W/OPT. BONUS ROOM

Opt. Bonus Room 15⁵ x 20³
W.i.c.
LINEN
PLANT SHELF ABOVE
Vaulted M.Bath
W.i.c.
W.i.c.
Bedroom 3 11⁴ x 10⁰

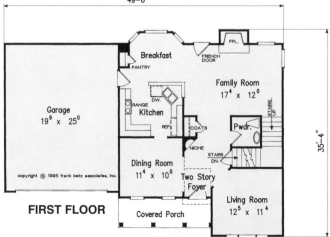

FIRST FLOOR

49'-6"
Garage 19⁹ x 25⁰
Breakfast
PANTRY
FPL.
FRENCH DOOR
Family Room 17⁴ x 12⁰
RANGE
DW.
Kitchen
REF.
COATS
Pwr.
STAIRS UP
NICHE
Dining Room 11⁴ x 10⁰
STAIRS DN.
Two Story Foyer
Covered Porch
Living Room 12⁵ x 11⁴
35'-4"
copyright © 1995 frank betz associates, inc.

No. 98431

■ **This plan features:**

— Three bedrooms

— Two full and one half baths

■ An impressive two-story Foyer

■ The Kitchen is equipped with ample cabinet and counter space

■ Spacious Family Room flows from the Breakfast Bay and is highlighted by a fireplace and a French door to the rear yard

■ The Master Suite is topped by a tray ceiling and is enhanced by a vaulted, five-piece Master Bath

■ This home is designed with basement, slab and crawlspace foundation options

First floor — 882 sq. ft.
Second floor — 793 sq. ft.
Bonus room — 416 sq. ft.
Basement — 882 sq. ft.
Garage — 510 sq. ft.

■ *Total living area 1,672 sq. ft.* ■ *Price Code B* ■

No. 34011

This plan features:

Three bedrooms

Two full baths

A Master Suite with huge his and her walk-in closets and private Bath

A second and third Bedroom with ample closet space

A Kitchen equipped with an island counter and flowing easily into the Dining and Family Rooms

A Laundry Room conveniently located near all three Bedrooms

This home is designed with basement, slab and crawlspace foundation options

Main floor— 1,672 sq. ft.
Garage — 566 sq. ft.

Fit for a Family

■ *Total living area 1,948 sq. ft.* ■ *Price Code C* ■

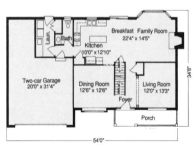

FIRST FLOOR

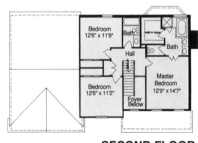

SECOND FLOOR

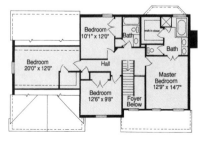

ALTERNATE SECOND FLOOR

No. 92636

■ **This plan features:**

— Three bedrooms

— Two full and one half baths

■ Inviting Porch leads into central Foyer and banister staircase

■ Formal Living and Dining Room enhanced by decorative window

■ Expansive Family Room with coz fireplace and bright bay window

■ L-shaped Kitchen with work island and Breakfast Area with sliding glass door to rear yard

■ Handy half Bath, Laundry and Garage entry off Kitchen

■ This home is designed with a basement foundation

First floor — 1,113 sq. ft.
Second floor — 835 sq. ft.
Alternate Second — 245 sq. ft.
Basement — 927 sq. ft.
Garage — 400 sq. ft.

■ *Total living area 1,956 sq. ft.* ■ *Price Code C* ■

No. 9964

This plan features:

Four bedrooms

Two full baths

A wood-burning fireplace warming the Living and Dining Rooms, which provide access to the large wooden Sun Deck

Two first floor Bedrooms with access to a full Bath

Two ample-sized second floor Bedrooms

A Recreation Room with a cozy fireplace and convenient Bath

This home is designed with a basement foundation

first floor — 896 sq. ft.

second floor — 456 sq. ft.

basement — 864 sq. ft.

Maximum Use of Minimum Space

■ *Total living area 1,676 sq. ft.* ■ *Price Code B* ■

No. 96537

■ **This plan features:**

— Four bedrooms

— Two full baths

■ There is a workbench and Storage Space i the Garage

■ The huge Great Room has a corner fireplace

■ The galley Kitchen opens into the Dining Room

■ The Master Suite has a ceiling fan

■ One of the secondary Bedrooms can be used as a Study

■ This home is designed with crawlspace ar slab foundation options

Main floor — 1,676 sq. ft.
Garage — 420 sq. ft.
Porch — 225 sq. ft.

MAIN FLOOR

WIDTH 65'-0"
DEPTH 41'-0"

Rustic Styling

■ *Total living area 1,677 sq. ft.* ■ *Price Code B* ■

No. 99914

■ **This plan features:**

— Two bedrooms

— Two full baths

■ A large Sun Deck wraps around this rustic home

■ The Living Room and Dining Room are combined

■ The Living Room has a gas fireplace and sliders to the Deck

■ The large Kitchen features an angled counter

■ There is a Bedroom, Bath and an ample Utility Room on the first floor

■ Upstairs, the Master Bedroom has two closets and a private Deck

■ Relax in the whirlpool tub in the Master Bath

■ This home is designed with basement and crawlspace foundation options

First floor — 1,064 sq. ft.
Second floor — 613 sq. ft.

WIDTH 28'-0"
DEPTH 40'-0"

FIRST FLOOR

SECOND FLOOR

Enticing Two-Story Traditional

■ *Total living area 1,960 sq. ft.* ■ *Price Code C* ■

No. 34027

This plan features:

Four bedrooms

Two and one half baths

A Porch serving as a wonderful, relaxing area to enjoy the outdoors

A Dining Room with a decorative ceiling and easy access to the Kitchen

A Kitchen/Utility Area with access to the Garage

A Living Room with double doors into the Family Room which features a fireplace and access to the Patio

This home is designed with basement and crawlspace foundation options

First floor — 955 sq. ft.

Second floor — 1,005 sq. ft.

Garage — 484 sq. ft.

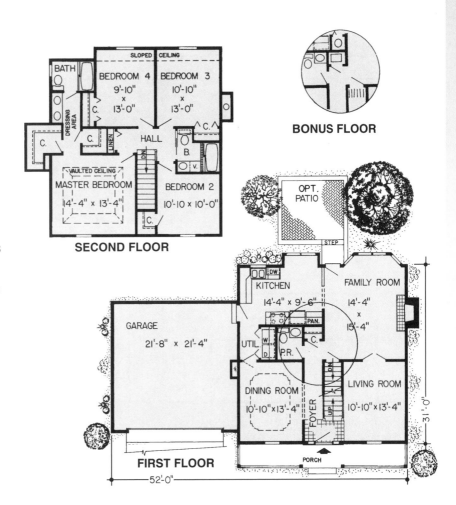

Great Lines and Ample Storage

No. 97153

■ **This plan features:**

— Three bedrooms

— Two full and one half baths

■ Behind the two-car Garage is 160 sq. ft. of Storage or Shop Space

■ Enjoy family dining in the Dining Area's bright bay window

■ Plenty of natural light floods the interior, thanks to large windows

■ For the comfort of your guests, a half Bath is just inside the Entry

■ This home is designed with a basement foundation

First floor — 881 sq. ft.
Second floor — 798 sq. ft.
Basement — 881 sq. ft.
Garage — 553 sq. ft.

Total living area 1,679 sq. ft. ■ *Price Code B*

Secluded Master Suite

No. 92527

■ **This plan features:**

— Three bedrooms

— Two full baths

■ A convenient one-level design with an open floor plan between the Kitchen, Breakfast Area and Great Room

■ A vaulted ceiling and a cozy fireplace in the spacious Great Room

■ A well-equipped Kitchen using a peninsula counter as an eating bar

■ A Master Suite with a luxurious Master Bath

■ Two additional Bedrooms having use of a full Bath

■ This home is designed with crawlspace and slab foundation options

Main floor — 1,680 sq. ft.
Garage — 538 sq. ft.

Total living area 1,680 sq. ft. ■ *Price Code B*

Double Gables

■ *Total living area 1,966 sq. ft.* ■ *Price Code C* ■

No. 97154

This plan features:

Three bedrooms

Two full and one half baths

There are practically no interior walls separating rooms on the first floor

The full-width Great Room has a focal-point fireplace

Access to the backyard is through sliding doors in the Nook

An eating counter, built-in Pantry and convenient Laundry Room creates an efficient Kitchen

This home is designed with a basement foundation

First floor — 1,136 sq. ft.
Second floor — 830 sq. ft.
Basement — 1,136 sq. ft.
Garage — 400 sq. ft.

SECOND FLOOR

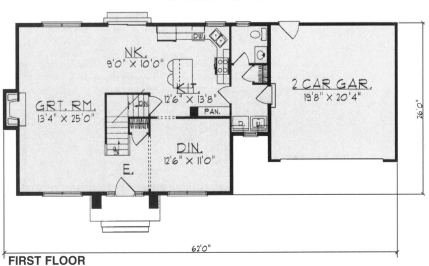

FIRST FLOOR

Quaint Curb Appeal

■ *Total living area 1,966 sq. ft.* ■ *Price Code C* ■

SECOND FLOOR

Attic Storage

Bedroom #3
14 x 12
8' Clg.

Bedroom #2
13/9 x 11/5
8' Clg.
Sloped Clg.

Stairs Down

Linen

FIRST FLOOR

Garage & Storage
22 x 25/10

WIDTH 48'-2"
DEPTH 67'-5"

Rear Porch
18 x 7/10

Kitchen
11/10 x 10/5

Breakfast
14/3 x 10/5
9' Clg.

Stairs Up

Pantry

W
D

Stairs Down

Desk

Family Room
14 x 18/8
9' Clg.

Dining
11 x 11/5
9' Clg.

Master Bedroom
13/9 x 16/8
9' Clg.

Foyer
8/9 x 5/10

Front Porch
40 x 7/10

No. 93451

■ **This plan features:**

— Three bedrooms

— Two full and one half baths

■ Opening from the Foyer is a central Dining Room and Family Room with fireplace

■ The U-shaped Kitchen has a cent[ral] island, Breakfast Area with Frenc[h] door leading to the rear Porch, and built-in desk and Pantry

■ Two additional Bedrooms share [a] full Bath and access to extra storage in the Attic

■ Privately located, the Master Bedroom has two walk-in closets and spacious Bath

■ This home is designed with a basement foundation

First floor — 1,409 sq. ft.
Second floor — 557 sq. ft.
Garage — 548 sq. ft.
Porch — 316 sq. ft.

Compact and Appealing

No. 20075

This plan features:

Three bedrooms

Two full baths

A fireplaced Living Room and formal Dining Room with extra-wide doorways

A centrally located Kitchen for maximum convenience

A Master Bedroom with a vaulted ceiling, a private Master Bath and walk-in closet

This home is designed with a basement foundation

Main floor — 1,682 sq. ft.

Basement — 1,682 sq. ft.

Garage — 484 sq. ft

■ *Total living area 1,682 sq. ft.* ■ *Price Code B* ■

MAIN FLOOR

Inviting Front Porch

No. 93298

This plan features:

Three bedrooms

Two full and one half baths

Detailed gables and inviting front Porch create a warm welcoming facade

Open Foyer features an angled staircase, a half Bath and a coat closet

The expansive informal Living Area at the rear of the home features a fireplace and opens onto the Sun Deck

The efficient Kitchen has easy access to both the formal and informal Dining Areas

Master Bedroom includes a walk-in closet and compartmented private Bath

Two secondary Bedrooms share a Bath with a double vanity

This home is designed with basement, slab and crawlspace foundation options

Main floor — 797 sq. ft.

Second floor — 886 sq. ft.

Basement — 797 sq. ft.

Garage — 414 sq. ft.

■ *Total living area 1,683 sq. ft.* ■ *Price Code B* ■

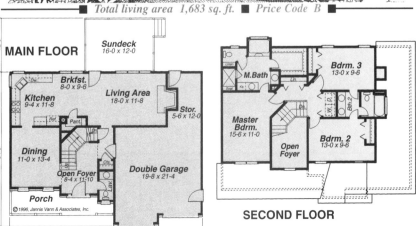

Elegantly Styled

Total living area 1,969 sq. ft. ■ *Price Code C*

SECOND FLOOR

FIRST FLOOR

No. 92696

■ **This plan features:**

— Three bedrooms

— Two full and one half baths

■ An angled staircase and balcony with built-in computer desk highlight the two-story Foyer

■ The Great Room features a fireplace and opens to the Breakfast Bay and gourmet Kitchen

■ A Bonus Room with built-in window seat could be an additional Bedroom or Game Room

■ This home is designed with a basement foundation

First floor — 1,420 sq. ft.
Second floor — 549 sq. ft.
Bonus — 268 sq. ft.
Basement — 1,420 sq. ft.
Garage — 532 sq. ft.
Porch — 57 sq. ft.

■ *Total living area 1,970 sq. ft.* ■ *Price Code C* ■

No. 92668

This plan features:

- Three bedrooms

- Two full and one half baths

- A Bonus Loft and Room over the Garage can become one or two additional rooms

- A rear staircase accesses the second floor

- The first floor Great Room has a two-story, sloped ceiling

- This home is designed with a basement foundation

First floor — 1,497 sq. ft.
Second floor — 473 sq. ft.
Garage — 468 sq. ft.
Basement — 1,420 sq. ft.
Bonus — 401 sq.ft.

FIRST FLOOR

SECOND FLOOR

For the Farm.

Cozy and Comfortable

■ Total living area 1,683 sq. ft. ■ Price Code B ■

FIRST FLOOR

SECOND FLOOR

No. 94117

■ **This plan features:**

— Three bedrooms

— One full, one three-quarter and one half baths

■ A welcoming Covered Entry with sidelight door leads into the Foyer

■ Combination Dining and Living Room ad a spacious feel

■ Views from the Kitchen and Dining Area the fireplace in the Family Room

■ This home is designed with a basement foundation

First floor — 999 sq. ft.
Second floor — 684 sq. ft.
Basement — 975 sq. ft.
Garage — 480 sq. ft.

Dramatic Staircase

■ Total living area 1,684 sq. ft. ■ Price Code B ■

WIDTH 40'-0"
DEPTH 44'-0"

FIRST FLOOR

SECOND FLOOR

No. 93905

■ **This plan features:**

— Three bedrooms

— One full, one three-quarter and one half baths

■ A box window in the Living Room looks o to the Porch

■ Instant appeal in the dramatic Entry, highlighted by the open-rail staircase

■ The built-in desk and serving bar create a efficient Kitchen

■ Optional Bonus Room offers room for expansion

■ This home is designed with a basement foundation

First floor — 913 sq. ft.
Second floor — 771 sq. ft.
Garage — 483 sq. ft.

National Treasure

■ *Total living area 1,978 sq. ft.* **■** *Price Code C* **■**

No. 24400

This plan features:

Three bedrooms

Two full and one half baths

A wraparound covered Porch

Decorative ceilings in the fireplaced Living Room

A large Kitchen with central island/Breakfast Bar

This home is designed with basement, slab and crawlspace foundation options

First floor — 1,034 sq. ft.
Second floor — 944 sq. ft.
Basement — 98°4 sq. ft.
Garage & Storage — 675 sq. ft.

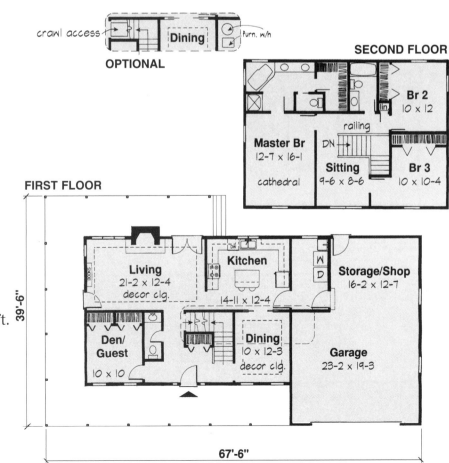

Arched Windows

■ *Total living area 1,986 sq. ft.* ■ *Price Code C* ■

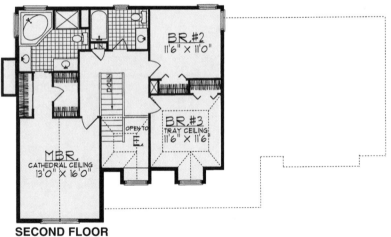

SECOND FLOOR

- BR.#2
  11'6" X 11'0"
- BR.#3
  TRAY CEILING
  11'6" X 11'6"
- M.B.R.
  CATHEDRAL CEILING
  13'0" X 16'0"

No. 99164

■ **This plan features:**

— Three bedrooms

— Two full and one half baths

■ Tile flooring provides easy
  maintenance in the Entry,
  Kitchen, Laundry Room and half
  Bath

■ The Family Room has a fireplace
  and is open to the Kitchen and
  Nook

■ Double doors connect the Living
  Room and Family Room

■ Tray ceilings crown the two-story
  Entry and a Bedroom

■ This home is designed with a
  basement foundation

First floor — 1,065 sq. ft.
Second floor — 921 sq. ft.
Basement — 1,065 sq. ft.

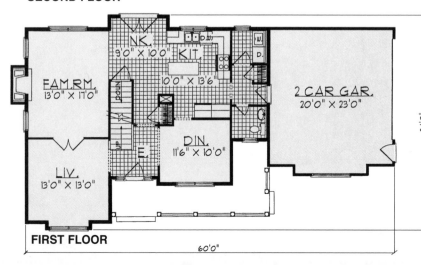

FIRST FLOOR

- NK.
  9'0" X 10'0"
- KIT.
  10'0" X 13'6"
- FAM.RM.
  13'0" X 17'0"
- 2 CAR GAR.
  20'0" X 23'0"
- DIN.
  11'6" X 10'0"
- LIV.
  13'0" X 13'0"

60'0"

34'0"

Elegant Styling

■ *Total living area 1,690 sq. ft.* ■ *Price Code B* ■

No. 97207

This plan features:

Three bedrooms

Two full and one half baths

The Great Room has a vaulted ceiling and a fireplace

The Kitchen has an angled counter and is open to the Dining Room and the Breakfast Area

The Master Suite has a tray ceiling, a walk-in closet and a private Bath

The two-story Foyer has a balcony overlooking the Great Room

This home is designed with basement, slab and crawlspace foundation options

First floor – 1,236 sq.ft.
Second floor – 454 sq. ft.
Basement – 1,236 sq. ft.
Garage – 462 sq. ft.

Elegant Ceiling Treatments

■ *Total living area 1,692 sq. ft.* ■ *Price Code B* ■

MAIN FLOOR

BONUS

No. 97254

■ **This plan features:**

— Three bedrooms

— Two full baths

■ A cozy wrapping front Porch sheltering entrance

■ Dining Room defined by columns at the entrances

■ Kitchen highlighted by a peninsula counter/serving bar

■ Breakfast Room flowing from the Kitchen

■ Vaulted ceiling highlighting the Great Room which also includes a fireplace

■ Master Suite crowned in a tray ceiling over the Bedroom, plus a Sitting Room and plush Master Bath

■ This home is designed with basement and crawlspace foundation options

Main floor — 1,692 sq. ft.
Bonus — 358 sq. ft.
Basement — 1,705 sq. ft.
Garage — 472 sq. ft.

WIDTH 54'-0"
DEPTH 56'-6"

Peaks and Arches Add Interest

■ *Total living area 1,659 sq. ft.* ■ *Price Code B* ■

SECOND FLOOR

WIDTH 38'-0"
DEPTH 36'-0"

SECOND FLOOR

No. 65251

■ **This plan features:**

— Three bedrooms

— One full and one half baths

■ As you step into this home, you know you're in for a special treat as you view the stairway ahead or the sunken Living Room

■ The Living Room offers plenty of options for entertaining, thanks to its circular design, two-story height and angled fireplace shared by the Dining Room

■ The Kitchen is conveniently located with easy access to the Dining Room and the Living Room

■ Off the main Living Spaces, a half Bath, a second coat closet and a large Mudroom complete the first floor

■ On the second floor, three Bedrooms share a full Bath that has twin vanities, and a separate shower and tub

■ This home is designed with a basement foundation

First floor — 917 sq. ft.
Second floor — 742 sq. ft.
Garage — 300 sq. ft.

■ *Total living area 1,297 sq. ft.* ■ *Price Code A* ■

No. 67020

This plan features:

Three bedrooms

Two full baths

Foyer opens into fireplaced Great Room

The efficiently planned Kitchen includes a Dining Area

The Master Suite at the rear of the home includes a double vanity Bath with separate shower

The Garage includes a Storage Room

Bonus Room could be used as a Fourth Bedroom or as a Family Room

This home is designed with a slab foundation

Main floor — 1,297 sq. ft.
Bonus — 299 sq. ft.
Garage — 448 sq. ft.

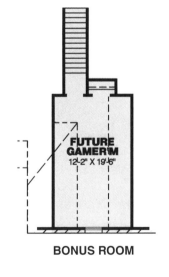

BONUS ROOM

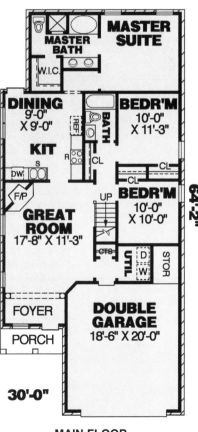

MAIN FLOOR

Inviting Welcome

■ *Total living area 1,997 sq. ft.* ■ *Price Code C* ■

WIDTH 64'-0"
DEPTH 57'-0"

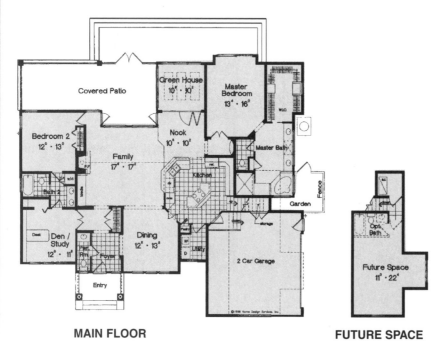

MAIN FLOOR

FUTURE SPACE

No. 63049

■ **This plan features:**

— Three bedrooms

— Two full and one half baths

■ The Family Room and Dining Nook flow together, with both rooms providing access to the covered Patio

■ The tiled Kitchen features a Pantry, plenty of work space , and access to the Utility Room and Garage

■ The Master Bedroom is tucked into the right rear corner of the home for privacy

■ The Den/Study is located off the main hall from the Foyer with a half Bath close by

■ This home is designed with a basement foundation

Main floor — 1,997 sq. ft.
Garage — 502 sq. ft.
Bonus — 310 sq. ft.

Master Retreat Crowns Home

■ *Total living area 1,695 sq. ft.* ■ *Price Code B* ■

No. 19422

This plan features:

Two bedrooms

Two full baths

A unique four-sided fireplace separates the Living Room, Dining Area and Kitchen

A well-equipped Kitchen featuring a cook island, a walk-in Pantry and easy access to Dining Area and Laundry Room

A three-season Screened Porch and Deck beyond adjoining Dining Room, Living Room, and second Bedroom

This home is designed with basement and crawlspace foundation options

First floor — 1,290 sq. ft.
Second floor — 405 sq. ft.
Porch — 152 sq. ft.
Garage — 513 sq. ft.

SECOND FLOOR

FIRST FLOOR

WIDTH 50'-8"
DEPTH 61'-8"

Four Bedroom Family Favorite

■ *Total living area 1,705 sq. ft.* ■ *Price Code B* ■

WIDTH 45'-0"
DEPTH 45'-0"

SECOND FLOOR

FIRST FLOOR

No. 96524

■ This plan features:

— Four bedrooms

— Two full and one half baths

■ The large fireplaced Great Room opens to the Dining Room, which offers access to a rear Porch through a lovely set of French doors

■ The secluded Master Bedroom Suite includes a large walk-in closet and a private Bath with separate shower

■ Three additional Bedrooms and full Bath comprise the second floor of this family-ready home

■ This home is designed with slab and crawlspace foundation options

First floor — 1,056 sq. ft.
Second floor — 649 sq. ft.
Garage — 562 sq. ft.

Enchanting Entry

■ *Total living area 1,994 sq. ft.* ■ *Price Code C* ■

No. 34679

This plan features:

Three bedrooms

Two full and one half baths

Split Entry leads down to Family Room, Utility Room, Den, half Bath and two-car Garage

Up a half-flight of stairs leads to the large Living Room highlighted by a double window

Dining Room convenient to Living Room and Kitchen

Efficient Kitchen with rear yard access and room for eating

Corner Master Bedroom offers an over-sized closet and private Bath

This home is designed with a basement foundation

Upper floor — 1,331 sq. ft.
Lower floor — 663 sq. ft.
Garage — 584 sq. ft.

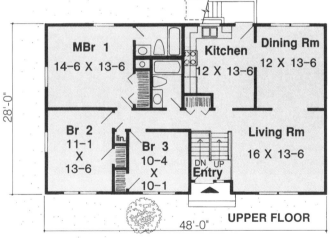

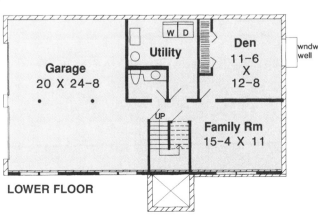

Gables and Arches

■ Total living area 1,845 sq. ft. ■ Price Code C ■

WIDTH 57'-2"
DEPTH 54'-10"

MAIN FLOOR

No. 90466

■ **This plan features:**

— Three bedrooms

— Two full and one half baths

■ Elegant columns define the spaces between the Dining Room and the large, fireplaced Great Room, which features built-ins and access to a rear Deck

■ The galley-style Kitchen opens to a bright Breakfast Area

■ The Garage includes extra space for storage and opens to the house through a convenient Mudroom/Laundry Room

■ The secluded Master Bedroom includes his and her walk-in closets and a compartmentalized Bath

■ Two secondary Bedrooms each have their own water closet and share a bath tub

■ This home is designed with slab and crawlspace foundation options

Main floor — 1,845 sq. ft.
Garage — 512 sq. ft.

Plenty of Living Space

■ Total living area 1,700 sq. ft. ■ Price Code B ■

MAIN FLOOR

No. 24250

■ **This plan features:**

— Three bedrooms

— Two full baths

■ A sunken Living Room that includes a vaulted ceiling and a fireplace with oversized windows framing it

■ A center island and an eating Nook in the Kitchen that has more than ample counter space

■ A formal Dining Room that adjoins the Kitchen, allowing for easy entertaining

■ A spacious Master Suite including a vaulted ceiling and lavish Bath

■ Secondary Bedrooms with custom ceiling treatments and use of full Bath

■ This home is designed with basement and crawlspace foundation options

Main floor — 1,700 sq. ft.
Garage — 462 sq. ft.

■ *Total living area 1,995 sq. ft.* ■ *Price Code C* ■

No. 98484

This plan features:

- Three bedrooms
- Two full and one half baths
- The impressive two-story Foyer greets guests
- The formal areas, the Living Room and the Dining Room, are located at the front of the home
- The Master Suite includes a tray ceiling, a French door, and a vaulted ceiling in the Master Bath and walk-in closet
- This home is designed with basement and crawlspace foundation options

First floor — 1,071 sq. ft.
Second floor — 924 sq. ft.
Bonus — 280 sq. ft.
Basement — 1,071 sq. ft.
Garage — 480 sq. ft.

FIRST FLOOR

SECOND FLOOR

Stupendous Design

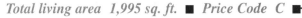
Total living area 1,995 sq. ft. ■ Price Code C

Bedroom #2
10-11 x 13-0

(Open to
Below)

Bedroom #4
10-5 x 11-4

Bedroom #3
11-0 x 10-8

SECOND FLOOR

**SLAB/CRAWLSPACE
OPTION**

44'-0"

Nook
10-11 x 10-0

Great Room
18-6 x 15-6

Master Bedroom
13-5 x 13-0

(Open to
Above)

Kitchen
10-11 x
15-11

M. Bath

54'-0"

Dining Room
10-11 x 12-0

Covered
Porch

Garage
19-5 x 21-11

FIRST FLOOR

No. 20230

■ **This plan features:**

— Four bedrooms

— Two full and one half baths

■ A Covered Porch entry opens to
the formal Dining Room and
Great Room beyond

■ A bright Kitchen with loads of
counter space easily serves the
eating Nook, Great Room and
Dining Room

■ The Master Bedroom Suite
privately pampers its owners wit
two walk-in closets and a plush
Bath

■ This home is designed with
basement, slab and crawlspace
foundation options

First floor — 1,365 sq. ft.
Second floor — 630 sq. ft.
Basement — 1,419 sq. ft.
Garage — 426 sq. ft.

Neighborhood Favorite

No. 97923

This plan features:

Three bedrooms

Two full baths

The Entry opens to the large, fireplaced Great Room to the left and through French doors to the Kitchen and Breakfast Room to the rear

The Kitchen offers ample counter space and a serving bar open to the bright Breakfast Room

The Master Suite commands the entire front of the second floor with its spacious Bedroom, compartmentalized Bath and large walk-in closet

This home is designed with a basement foundation

Alternate foundation options available at an additional charge. Please call 1-800-235-5700 for additional information.

First floor — 1,099 sq. ft.

Second floor — 601 sq. ft.

Garage — 347 sq. ft.

■ *Total living area 1,700 sq. ft.* ■ *Price Code B* ■

WIDTH 46'-0"
DEPTH 41'-4"

REAR ELEVATION

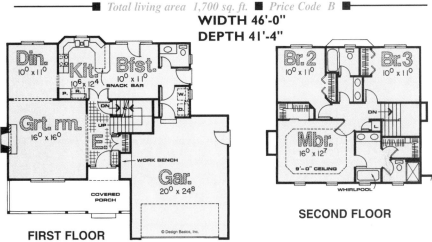

FIRST FLOOR

SECOND FLOOR

Elegantly Styled

No. 98449

This plan features:

Three bedrooms

Two full and one half baths

Architectural details create eye-catching appeal to this home's facade

The two-story Foyer is flanked by the formal Living and Dining Rooms

A convenient Kitchen with angled snack bar has easy access to the Dining Room, Breakfast Area, backyard and the Laundry/Garage

Open and comfortable, the Family Room is highlighted by a fireplace and windows

The Master Suite is enhanced by a tray ceiling and a plush Bath with a vaulted ceiling

The second floor offers an optional Bonus Room for future expansion

This home is designed with basement and crawlspace foundation options

First floor — 922 sq. ft.

Second floor — 778 sq. ft.

Bonus room — 369 sq. ft.

Garage & Storage — 530 sq. ft.

■ *Total living area 1,700 sq. ft.* ■ *Price Code B* ■

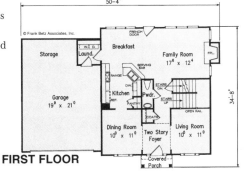

FIRST FLOOR

SECOND FLOOR

Tradition with Flair

Total living area 1,996 sq. ft. ■ Price Code C ■

WIDTH 62'-0"
DEPTH 38'-0"

FIRST FLOOR

SECOND FLOOR

No. 94143

■ **This plan features:**

— Three bedrooms

— Two full baths and one half bath

■ A large Master Suite boasts a big walk-in closet and fully appointed Bath

■ Guests walk past the covered Entry and into the impressive two-story Foyer

■ The two-story Family Room will make the fireplace that much cozier

■ This home is designed with a basement foundation

First floor — 1,132 sq. ft.
Second floor — 864 sq. ft.
Basement — 1,116 sq. ft.
Garage — 462 sq. ft.

Distinctive Design

Total living area 1,998 sq. ft. ■ Price Code C ■

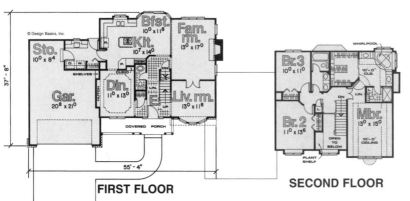

FIRST FLOOR

SECOND FLOOR

No. 94904

■ **This plan features:**

— Three bedrooms

— Two full and one half baths

■ Living Room is distinguished by warmth o bayed window and French doors leading t Family Room

■ Built-in curio cabinet adds interest to form Dining Room

■ Well-appointed Kitchen with island cook-to and Breakfast Area designed to save you steps adjoined Laundry and Garage entry

■ Family Room with focal-point fireplace for informal gatherings

■ Secondary Bedrooms share a double vanit Bath

■ This home is designed with a basement foundation

■ Alternate foundation options available at a additional charge. Please call 1-800-235-570 for more information.

First floor — 1,093 sq. ft.
Second floor — 905 sq. ft.
Basement — 1,093 sq. ft.
Garage — 527 sq. ft.

Perfect for a Growing Family

■ *Total living area 2,133 sq. ft.* ■ *Price Code D* ■

No. 99124

This plan features:

- Four bedrooms
- Two full and one half baths
- Sliding doors in the Breakfast Area offer great views onto the back garden
- A conveniently located Kitchen serves all rooms well
- The roomy Master Suite includes a large closet and a Spa tub
- This home is designed with a basement foundation

First floor — 1,099 sq. ft.
Second floor — 1,034 sq. ft.
Basement — 1,099 sq. ft.

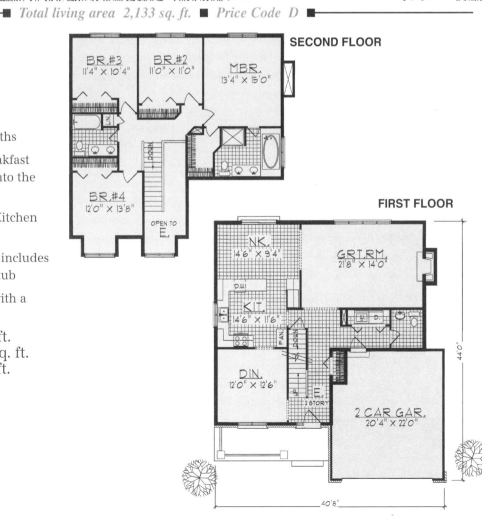

Columned Porch

■ *Total living area 2,136 sq. ft.* ■ *Price Code D* ■

WIDTH 56'-0"
DEPTH 42'-0"

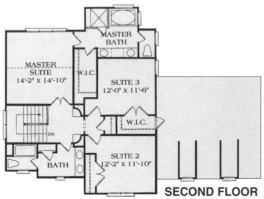

No. 96904

■ **This plan features:**

— Three bedrooms

— Two full and one half baths

■ The Foyer leads into the formal Dining Room that is topped by a decorative ceiling

■ The Gathering Room has a fireplace and opens to the Deck through a French door

■ Conveniently located, the Laundr Room connects the Kitchen and the Garage

■ This home is designed with a crawlspace foundation

First floor — 1,066 sq. ft.
Second floor — 1,070 sq. ft.
Garage — 466 sq. ft.

Porch Adorns Elegant Bay

No. 20093

This plan features:

- Three bedrooms
- Two and one half baths
- A Master Suite with a romantic bay window and full Bath
- Bedrooms with huge closets and use of the full hall Bath
- A roomy island Kitchen with a modern, efficient layout
- A formal Dining Room with a recessed decorative ceiling
- Sloping skylit ceilings illuminating the fireplaced Living Room
- A rear Deck accessible from both the Kitchen and the Living Room
- This home is designed with a basement foundation

First floor — 1,027 sq. ft.
Second floor — 974 sq. ft.
Basement — 978 sq. ft.
Garage — 476 sq. ft.

■ *Total living area 2,001 sq. ft.* ■ *Price Code D* ■

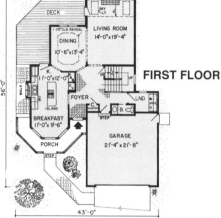

FIRST FLOOR

SECOND FLOOR

Two-Story Foyer

No. 94142

This plan features:

- Three bedrooms
- Two full and one half baths
- The two-story Foyer open to a private Study
- The Great Room has a volume ceiling and corner windows
- The Kitchen has a center-island workspace and is open to the Dining Area
- The Master Suite has a walk-in closet and a plush, five-piece Bath
- Two additional Bedrooms share a full Bath
- This home is designed with a basement foundation

First floor — 1,182 sq. ft.
Second floor — 821 sq. ft.
Basement — 1,182 sq. ft.
Garage — 426 sq. ft.
Porch — 57 sq. ft.

■ *Total living area 2,003 sq. ft.* ■ *Price Code D* ■

FIRST FLOOR

WIDTH 57'-4"
DEPTH 37'-8"

SECOND FLOOR

285

Elegant Entertaining

No. 93434

This plan features:

— Four bedrooms

— Two full and one half baths

■ A switch-back, open-rail staircase overlooking the two-story Foyer

■ Vaulted ceilings and a fireplace flanked b quarter-round transom windows in the Family Room

■ Privacy in the Master Bedroom with its own Porch and Bath

■ Three additional Bedrooms sharing a full Bath with twin vanities

■ This home is designed with a basement foundation

First floor — 1,318 sq. ft.
Second floor — 690 sq. ft.
Basement — 1,318 sq. ft.
Garage — 446 sq. ft.

Total living area 2,008 sq. ft. ■ *Price Code D*

FIRST FLOOR

SECOND FLOOR

Craftsman Cottage

No. 93450

This plan features:

— Three bedrooms

— Two full and one half baths

■ The Foyer opens from the covered Porch the Family Room with fireplace

■ A center island with serving bar and amp cabinet space highlights the L-shaped Kitchen

■ Dual closets and a luxurious, five-piece B create a comfortable Master Bedroom

■ The Kid's Living Area is a private place fo homework or relaxing

■ Extra living space is available in the optional Bonus Room

■ This home is designed with a basement foundation

First floor — 1,269 sq. ft.
Second floor — 741 sq. ft.
Bonus — 313 sq. ft.
Basement — 1,269 sq. ft.
Garage — 514 sq. ft.

Total living area 2,010 sq. ft. ■ *Price Code D*

WIDTH 43'-0"
DEPTH 69'-4"

FIRST FLOOR

SECOND FLOOR

Master Suite with Private Sun Deck

■ *Total living area 2,139 sq. ft.* ■ *Price Code D* ■

No. 91411

This plan features:

Four bedrooms

Two full and one half baths

A sunken Living Room, formal Dining Room and island Kitchen enjoying an expansive view of the Patio and backyard

A fireplaced Living Room keeping the house toasty after the sun goes down

Skylights brightening the balcony and Master Bath

This home is designed with basement, slab and crawlspace foundation options

Main floor — 1,249 sq. ft.
Upper floor — 890 sq. ft.
Garage — 462 sq. ft.

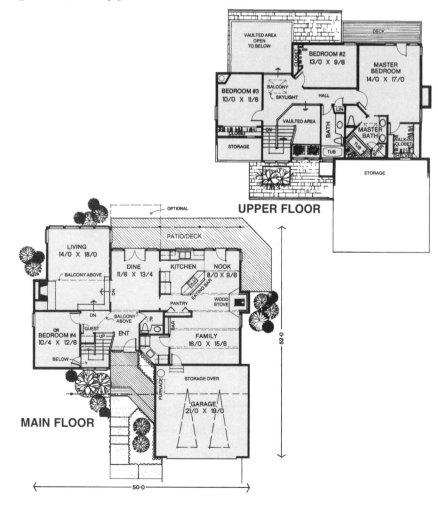

UPPER FLOOR

MAIN FLOOR

Perfect for the Growing Family

© Donald A. Gardner Architects, Inc.

■ *Total living area 2,148 sq. ft.* ■ *Price Code D* ■

No. 61096

■ This plan features:

— Four bedrooms

— Two full baths

■ Terrific family Ranch offers convenient one-floor living

■ The Great Room features a decorative ceiling, a fireplace, an French doors

■ The well-planned Kitchen opens up to a sunny Breakfast Room

■ Secluded Master Suite includes generous walk-in closet, double vanity and separate shower

■ Three additional Bedrooms on th opposite side of the home make this plan family-perfect

■ This home is designed with slab and crawlspace foundation options

Main floor — 2,148 sq. ft.
Garage — 477 sq. ft.

MAIN FLOOR

WIDTH 63'-0"
DEPTH 52'-8"

■ *Total living area 2,148 sq. ft.* ■ *Price Code D* ■

No. 93442

This plan features:

Three bedrooms

Two full and one half bath

Dining Room with direct access to the Kitchen, yet can be made private by the pocket door

Kitchen made efficient by a cooktop island, an abundance of counter space and a built-in Pantry

Sun Room adjoining Kitchen and the Family Room

Fireplace and a fourteen-foot ceiling highlighting the Family Room

This home is designed with crawlspace and slab foundation options

Main floor — 1,626 sq. ft.
Second floor — 522 sq. ft.
Basement — 1,626 sq. ft.
Garage — 522 sq. ft.
Bonus — 1,626 sq. ft.

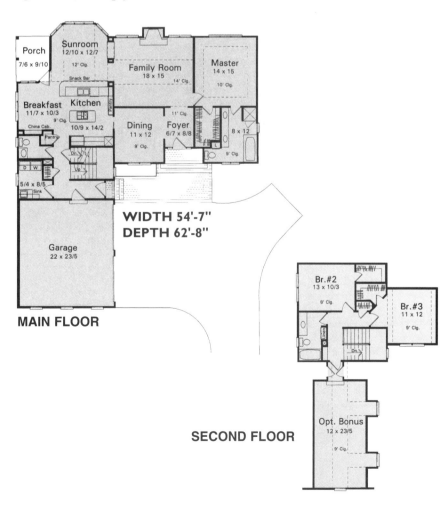

WIDTH 54'-7"
DEPTH 62'-8"

MAIN FLOOR

SECOND FLOOR

A Traditional Approach

■ *Total living area 2,013 sq. ft.* ■ *Price Code D* ■

No. 94109

■ **This plan features:**

– Four bedrooms

– Two full and one half baths

■ A covered Entry leading to a two-story Foyer

■ A well-appointed Kitchen with direct acce to the Garage

■ A bright and sunny Dinette for informal eating

■ An expansive Family Room highlighted b a large fireplace

■ A roomy Master Suite including a private Bath and a walk-in closet

■ This home is designed with a basement foundation

First floor — 1,025 sq. ft.
Second floor — 988 sq. ft.

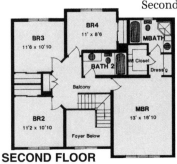

Computer Balcony

■ *Total living area 2,017 sq. ft.* ■ *Price Code D* ■

No. 92697

■ **This plan features:**

– Three bedrooms

– Two full and one half baths

■ The Kitchen in this design is positioned between the eating areas for convenience

■ A U-shape staircase leads to an second floc balcony that makes a perfect spot for the family computer

■ This home is designed with a basement foundation

First floor — 1,432 sq. ft.
Second floor — 585 sq. ft.
Basement — 1,432 sq. ft.

Luxurious Master Bedroom

■ *Total living area 2,151 sq. ft.* ■ *Price Code D* ■

No. 97613

This plan features:

Three bedrooms

Two full and one half baths

The Foyer has a two-story ceiling, half Bath, Laundry Room and coat closet

The two-story Family Room has a fireplace flanked by windows and opens to the Kitchen and Breakfast Area

A Sitting Room, tray ceiling, vaulted Bath and huge, walk-in closet highlight the Master Bedroom

This home is designed with basement and crawlspace foundation options

First floor — 1,092 sq. ft.
Second floor — 1,059 sq.ft.
Basement — 1,081 sq. ft.
Garage — 445 sq.ft.

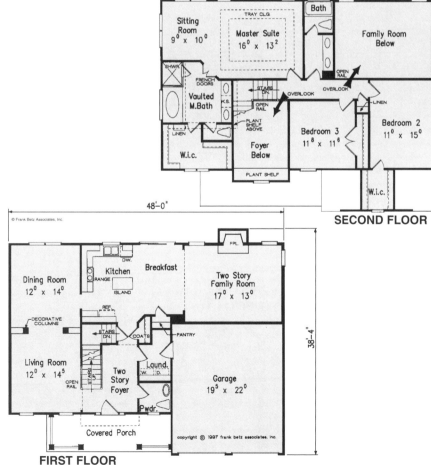

Customized for Sloping View Site

■ *Total living area 2,162 sq. ft.* ■ *Price Code D* ■

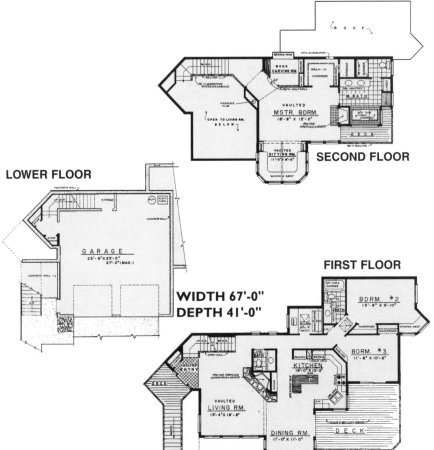

SECOND FLOOR

LOWER FLOOR

GARAGE
25'-6" X 23'-0"
27'-0" (MAX.)

WIDTH 67'-0"
DEPTH 41'-0"

FIRST FLOOR

No. 91343

■ **This plan features:**

— Three bedrooms

— Two full and one half baths

■ A stone-faced fireplace and vaulted ceiling in the Living Roo

■ An island food preparation cent with a sink and a breakfast bar i the Kitchen

■ Sliding glass doors leading from the Dining Room to the adjacen Deck

■ This home is designed with basement/crawlspace combination foundation option

First floor — 1,338 sq. ft.
Second floor — 763 sq. ft.
Lower floor — 61 sq. ft.
Garage — 779 sq. ft.

■ *Total living area 2,162 sq. ft.* ■ *Price Code D* ■

No. 97608

This plan features:

Three bedrooms

Two full and one half baths

The Kitchen and Family Room share a wetbar making entertaining easy in this open home

The Kitchen has a Breakfast Area, center island, Pantry and views of the Family Room fireplace

A stunning and vaulted Bath highlights the spacious Master Bedroom with Sitting Area

This home is designed with basement and crawlspace foundation options

First floor — 1,169 sq. ft.
Second floor — 993 sq. ft.
Bonus — 309 sq. ft.
Basement — 1,169 Sq. ft.
Garage — 523 sq. ft.

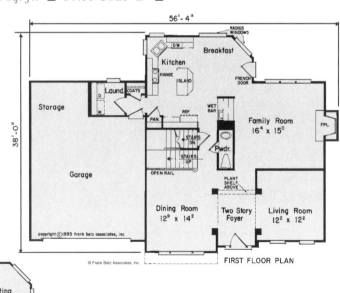

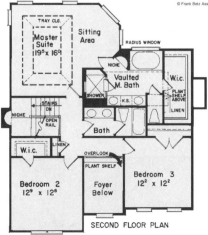

Four Bedroom Country Classic

Photography supplied by the Meredith Corporation

Photography supplied by The Meredith Corp.

■ *Total living area 2,175 sq. ft.* ■ *Price Code D* ■

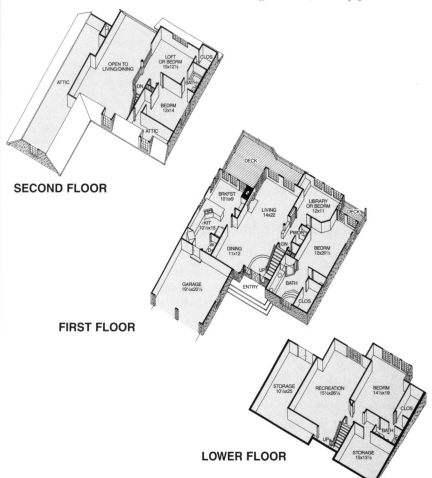

SECOND FLOOR

FIRST FLOOR

LOWER FLOOR

No. 19410

■ **This plan features:**

— Four or Five bedrooms

— Three full and one half baths

■ Enter into the combination Livi
and Dining Area of this versatile
home and view the great outdoo
through tall windows

■ A Library can be used as a fifth
Bedroom

■ The first floor Master Bedroom
includes a private Deck

■ This spacious home offers volun
ceilings and plenty of storage

■ This home is designed with a
basement foundation

First floor — 1,600 sq. ft.
Second floor — 576 sq. ft.
Lower floor — 1,509 sq. ft.
Garage — 413 sq. ft.

Comfortable Vacation Living

No. 98714

This plan features:

- Three bedrooms

- One full, two three-quarter and one half baths

- A wraparound Deck offering views and access into the Living Room

- A sunken Living Room with a vaulted ceiling, and a raised-hearth fireplace adjoining the Dining Area

- An open Kitchen with a corner sink and windows, an eating bar and a walk-in Storage/Pantry

- Two private Bedroom Suites with sliding glass doors leading to a Deck, walk-in closets and plush Baths

- Loft Area with a walk-in closet, attic access, and a private Bath and a Deck

- This home is designed with a crawlspace foundation

First floor — 1,704 sq ft

Second floor — 313 sq. ft.

■ *Total living area 2,017 sq. ft.* ■ *Price Code D* ■

FIRST FLOOR

WIDTH 58'-0"
DEPTH 48'-0"

SECOND FLOOR

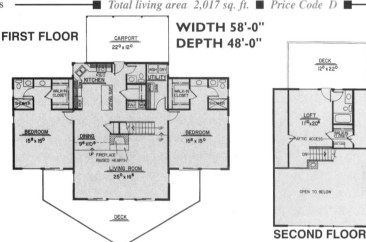

Family Faire

No. 97100

This plan features:

- Four bedrooms

- One full, one half and one three-quarter baths

- The two-story Entry, with large coat closet, opens to the Study at the front of the house and the large, fireplaced Great Room at the rear of the house

- The Eat-in-Kitchen features a sunny bump-out, efficient L-shaped counter configuration and center-island work area

- The second-floor Master Bedroom has a cathedral ceiling, large walk-in closet and three-quarter Bath

- Three additional second floor Bedrooms have ample closet space and share a full Bath

- This home is designed with a basement foundation

First floor — 995 sq. ft.

Second floor — 1,125 sq. ft.

Garage — 995 sq. ft.

■ *Total living area 2,120 sq. ft.* ■ *Price Code D* ■

FIRST FLOOR

WIDTH 56'-4"
DEPTH 35'-8"

SECOND FLOOR

Private Master Suite Patio

■ *Total living area 2,175 sq. ft.* ■ *Price Code D* ■

FIRST FLOOR

No. 98517

■ **This plan features:**

— Four bedrooms

— Two full and one half baths

■ The Breakfast Nook and Great Room access the partially Covered Patio

■ The Master Bedroom ceiling stretches 11-feet-high

■ This home is designed with a sla foundation

First floor — 1,472 sq. ft.
Second floor — 703 sq. ft.
Garage — 540 sq. ft.

SECOND FLOOR

■ *Total living area 2,135 sq. ft.* ■ *Price Code D* ■

No. 65137

This plan features:

Four bedrooms

Two full and one half baths

Pocket doors in the Solarium and an airlock Entry are energy savings features of this home

Built-in cabinets offers ample storage in the Laundry Room and Kitchen

This home is designed with a basement foundation.

First floor — 1,085 sq. ft.
Second floor — 1,050 sq. ft.
Basement — 1,050 sq. ft.
Garage — 440 sq. ft.

SECOND FLOOR

For the Farm

FIRST FLOOR

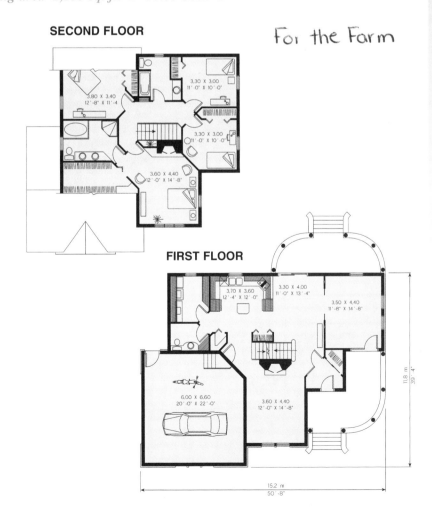

A Modern Twist

■ Total living area 2,024 sq. ft. ■ Price Code D ■

FIRST FLOOR

SECOND FLOOR

No. 93287

■ **This plan features:**

— Three bedrooms

— Two full and one half baths

■ Brick detailing and keystones highlight the elevation

■ Two-story Foyer opens to formal Living Dining Rooms

■ Expansive Family Room with a hearth fireplace between built-in shelves and D access

■ U-shaped Kitchen with serving counter, Breakfast Alcove and nearby Garage Ent

■ Elegant Master Bedroom with a decorati ceiling, large walk-in closet and a double vanity Bath

■ Two additional Bedrooms share a full B Laundry and Bonus Area

■ This home is designed with a basement foundation

First floor — 987 sq. ft.
Second floor — 965 sq. ft.
Basement — 899 sq. ft.

Friendly Colonial

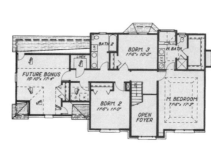

■ Total living area 2,031 sq. ft. ■ Price Code D ■

No. 90606

■ **This plan features:**

— Four bedrooms

— Two and one half baths

■ A beautiful, circular stair ascending fro the central Foyer and flanked by the for Living Room and Dining Room

■ Exposed beams, wood paneling and a br fireplace wall in the Family Room

■ A separate Dinette opening to an efficien Kitchen

■ This home is designed with a basement foundation

First floor — 1,099 sq. ft.
Second floor — 932 sq. ft.
Garage — 476 sq. ft.

FIRST FLOOR

SECOND FLOOR

■ *Total living area 2,178 sq. ft.* ■ *Price Code D* ■

No. 92569

This plan features:

Four bedrooms

Two full and one half baths

Formal areas are located in traditional location, to the front of the home and flanking the Foyer

The expansive Den is enhanced by a fireplace and built-in cabinets and shelves

The island Kitchen features a built-in desk, Pantry and extensive counter and Storage Space

Informal meals can be easily served in the adjoining room to the Kitchen

This home is designed with crawlspace and slab foundation options

First floor — 1,170 sq. ft.
Second floor — 1,008 sq. ft.
Garage — 484 sq. ft.

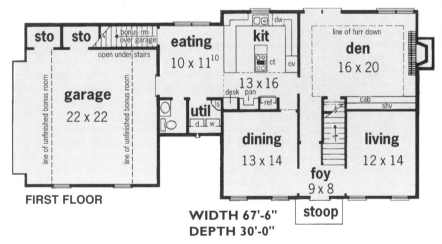

FIRST FLOOR

WIDTH 67'-6"
DEPTH 30'-0"

SECOND FLOOR

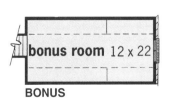

BONUS

Appealing Farmhouse

■ *Total living area 2,089 sq. ft.* ■ *Price Code D* ■

FIRST FLOOR

WIDTH 56'-0"
DEPTH 38'-0"

SECOND FLOOR

No. 65135

■ This plan features:

— Three bedrooms

— Two full and one half baths

■ Interior doors provide privacy options in the Study and Living Rooms

■ Luxurious amenities in the Master Suite include a fireplace, large walk-in closet and Bath with separate tub and shower

■ This home is designed with a basement foundation

First floor — 1,146 sq. ft.
Second floor — 943 sq. ft.
Bonus — 313 sq. ft.
Basement — 483 sq. ft.

Prairie-Style Retreat

No. 32109

■ *Total living area 2,038 sq. ft.* ■ *Price Code D* ■

This plan features:

Three bedrooms

Two full and one half baths

Shingle siding, tall expanses of glass and wrapping Decks accent the exterior

The octagonal shaped Living Room has a two-story ceiling and French doors

The Kitchen is enhanced by a cooktop island

The first floor Master Suite offers a private Bath

Two additional, second floor Bedrooms share the full Bath in the hall

This home is designed with a basement foundation

First floor — 1,213 sq. ft.

Second floor — 825 sq. ft.

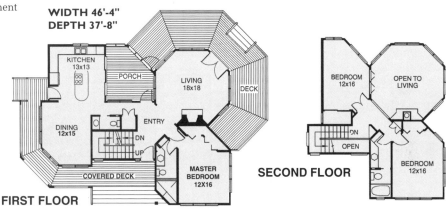

WIDTH 46'-4"
DEPTH 37'-8"

FIRST FLOOR

SECOND FLOOR

Attractive Covered Entry

No. 24736

■ *Total living area 2,044 sq. ft.* ■ *Price Code D* ■

This plan features:

Three bedrooms

Two full and one half baths

The angled, covered Porch welcomes everyone to this home

The Great Room is accented by a vaulted ceiling and a fireplace

The spacious Kitchen offers a Pantry and a Breakfast Bay

The Master Bedroom wing has a bay window, a decorative ceiling, two walk-in closets and a plush Bath

On the second floor, two additional Bedrooms share a full Bath, a Loft and a Computer Center

This home is designed with basement, slab and crawlspace foundation options

First floor — 1,403 sq. ft.

Second floor — 641 sq. ft.

Basement — 1,394 sq. ft.

Garage — 680 sq. ft.

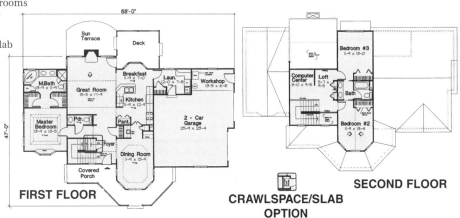

FIRST FLOOR

CRAWLSPACE/SLAB OPTION

SECOND FLOOR

Ready for the Future

■ *Total living area 2,119 sq. ft.* ■ *Price Code D* ■

FIRST FLOOR

SECOND FLOOR

No. 65378

■This plan features:

— Three bedrooms

— Two full and one half baths

■ A wrap-around Porch provides ample space for outdoor entertaining

■ French doors off the Foyer provide privacy in the Computer Room

■ The Media Room includes the warmth of a fireplace while viewing the large-screen television

■ Pampering amenities in the Master Suite include a corner fireplace and a luxurious Bath with an angled tub

■ The home is designed with a basement foundation

First floor — 1,132 sq. ft.
Second floor — 987 sq. ft.
Basement — 1,132 sq. ft.
Garage — 556 sq. ft.

Old-Fashioned Yet Contemporary

■ *Total living area 2,052 sq. ft.* ■ *Price Code D* ■

FIRST FLOOR

SECOND FLOOR

© Frank Betz Associates, Inc.

No. 98407

■This plan features:

— Four bedrooms

— Three full baths

■ A two-story Foyer is flanked by the Living Room and the Dining Room

■ The Family Room features a fireplace and French door

■ The bayed Breakfast Nook and Pantry are adjacent to the Kitchen

■ The Master Suite with a trayed ceiling has an attached Bath with a vaulted ceiling and radius window

■ Upstairs are two additional Bedrooms, a full Bath, a Laundry closet and a Bonus Room

■ This home is designed with basement, slab and crawlspace foundation options

First floor — 1,135 sq. ft.
Second floor — 917 sq. ft.
Bonus — 216 sq. ft.
Basement — 1,135 sq. ft.
Garage — 452 sq. ft.

Polished & Poised

■ *Total living area 2,101 sq. ft.* ■ *Price Code D* ■

No. 92610

This plan features:

Three bedrooms

Two full and one half baths

Lovely Foyer with striking staircase opens to sunken Great Room, which features a fireplace and access to a rear Deck

The Dining Room features a large bay window

The well-planned Kitchen is open to a bright Breakfast Room, which in turn, is open to the Great Room

The private Master Bedroom is enhanced by a spectacular ceiling, walk-in closet and a deluxe Bath

This home is designed with a basement foundation

First floor – 1,626 sq. ft.
Second floor – 475 sq. ft.
Basement – 1,512 sq. ft.
Garage – 438 sq. ft.

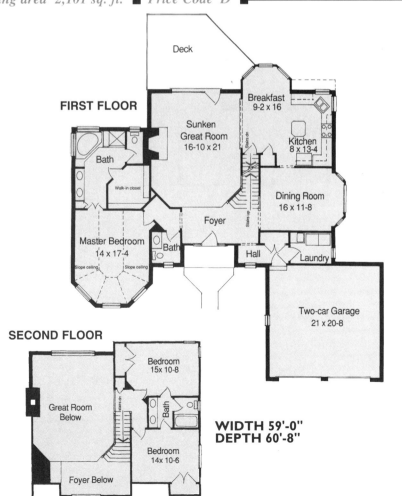

FIRST FLOOR

Deck

Breakfast 9-2 x 16

Sunken Great Room 16-10 x 21

Kitchen 8 x 13-4

Bath

Walk-in closet

Dining Room 16 x 11-8

Foyer

Master Bedroom 14 x 17-4

Bath

Slope ceiling   Slope ceiling

Hall

Laundry

Two-car Garage 21 x 20-8

SECOND FLOOR

Bedroom 15x 10-8

Great Room Below

Bath

Bedroom 14 x 10-6

Foyer Below

WIDTH 59'-0"
DEPTH 60'-8"

Porch Adds Charm

■ *Total living area 2,193 sq. ft.* ■ *Price Code D* ■

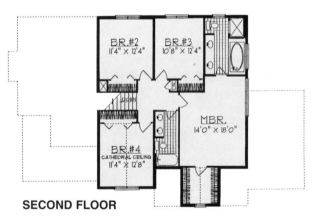

SECOND FLOOR

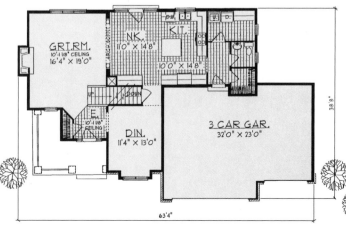

FIRST FLOOR

No. 97120

■ **This plan features:**

— Four bedrooms

— Two full and one half baths

■ An arched soffit divides the Great Room and the Kitchen/Breakfast Nook

■ A walk-in closet near the three-car Garage is handy for storage

■ This home is designed with a basement foundation

First floor — 1,113 sq. ft.
Second floor — 1,080 sq. ft.
Basement — 1,113 sq. ft.

Impeccable Style

■ *Total living area 2,198 sq. ft.* ■ *Price Code D* ■

No. 97710

This plan features:

Three bedrooms

Two full and one half baths

Brick, stone and interesting rooflines showcase the impeccable style of this home

Inside, a deluxe staircase highlights the Foyer

The Dining Room has a bay window at one end and columns at the other

The U-shaped Kitchen has an island in its center

The two-story Great Room has a warm fireplace

This home is designed with a basement foundation

First floor — 1,706 sq. ft.
Second floor — 492 sq. ft.
Basement — 1,706 sq. ft.

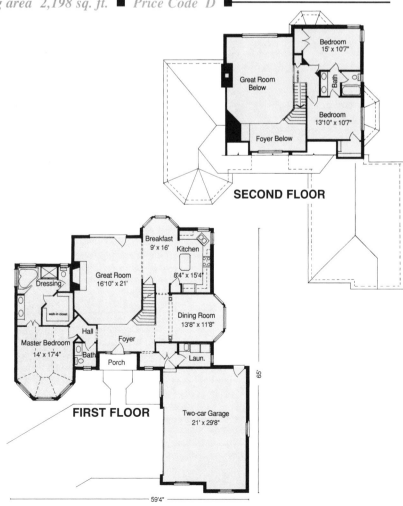

Living Large

■ Total living area 2,056 sq. ft. ■ Price Code D ■

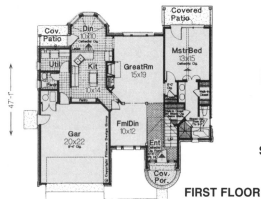

FIRST FLOOR

SECOND FLOOR

No. 98551

■ **This plan features**

- Four bedrooms

- One full, one three-quarter and one half baths

■ The luxurious, brick exterior and pleasing rooflines are full of curb appeal

■ Extra kitchen storage abounds, thanks to the wall-length Pantry

■ A recessed main Entry leads through the elegant Foyer into the open Great Room

■ Enjoy breakfast or special meals in the informal Dining Area wrapped in a full b window

■ This home is designed with crawlspace a slab foundation options

First floor — 1,359 sq. ft.
Second floor — 697 sq. ft.
Garage — 440 sq. ft.

Country Exterior

■ Total living area 2,068 sq. ft. ■ Price Code D ■

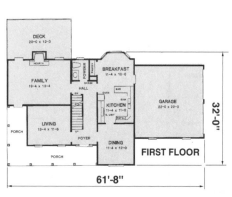

FIRST FLOOR

SECOND FLOOR

No. 90451

■ **This plan features:**

- Three bedrooms

- Two full and one half baths

■ Wraparound Porch leads into central Foy and formal Living and Dining Rooms

■ Large Family Room with a cozy fireplace and Deck access

■ Convenient Kitchen opens to Breakfast A with a bay window and built-in Pantry

■ Corner Master Bedroom with walk-in clos and appealing Bath

■ Two additional Bedrooms plus a Bonus Room share a full Bath and Laundry

■ This home is designed with basement and crawlspace foundation options

First floor — 1,046 sq. ft.
Second floor — 1,022 sq. ft.
Bonus — 232 sq. ft.

Angled Staircase

■ *Total living area 2,198 sq. ft.* ■ *Price Code D* ■

No. 99125

This plan features:

Three bedrooms

Two full and one half baths

The Kitchen has ample cabinet space and opens to the Nook, Great Room and Dining Room

Transom windows and 14-foot ceilings create a spacious Great Room

The two-story Entry has an angled staircase and views into the Dining Room and Great Room

A cathedral ceiling, walk-in closet and five-piece Bath highlight the Master Bedroom

This home is designed with a basement foundation

First floor — 1,304 sq. ft.
Second floor — 894 sq. ft.
Basement — 1,304 sq. ft.

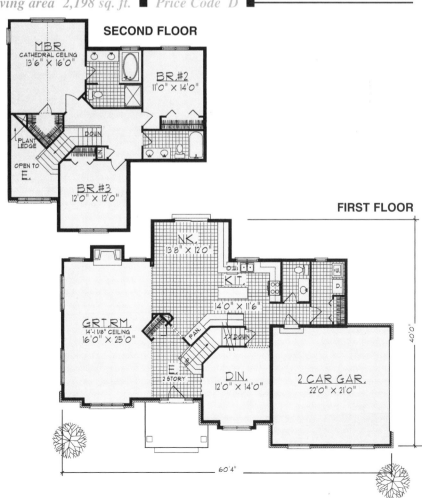

SECOND FLOOR

MBR.
CATHEDRAL CEILING
13'6" X 16'0"

BR. #2
11'0" X 14'0"

PLANT LEDGE

DOWN

OPEN TO E.

BR. #3
12'0" X 12'0"

FIRST FLOOR

NK.
13'8" X 12'0"

KIT.
14'0" X 11'6"

GRT. RM.
14'-1 1/8" CEILING
16'0" X 25'0"

PAN.

DOWN

E.
2 STORY

DIN.
12'0" X 14'0"

2 CAR GAR.
22'0" X 21'0"

40'0"

60'4"

Style and Versatility

■ *Total living area 2,257 sq. ft.* ■ *Price Code E* ■

FIRST FLOOR

SECOND FLOOR

WIDTH 57'-0"
DEPTH 56'-8"

No. 20231

■ **This plan features:**

— Four bedrooms

— Two full and one half baths

■ The covered Porch leads into th
Foyer and the two-story Great
Room beyond, which features a
fireplace and built-ins

■ The Dining Room has a tray
ceiling and opens to both the
Foyer and a short hall that lead
to the bright and efficient Kitch

■ The Master Bedroom has a
fireplace which efficiently and
cost-effectively uses the same
chimney as the fireplace in the
Living Room

■ This home is designed with
basement, slab and crawlspace
foundation options

First floor — 1,540 sq. ft.
Second floor — 717 sq. ft.
Basement — 1,545 sq. ft.
Garage — 503 sq. ft.

■ *Total living area 2,203 sq. ft.* ■ *Price Code D* ■

No. 96906

This plan features:

Three bedrooms

Two full and one half baths

Front and rear Covered Porches create outdoor living spaces

Expansive windows in the Family Room and Breakfast Room provide natural light

A utility hallway has a Laundry Room, Powder Room, closet and convenient access to the Garage and Kitchen

This home is designed with a crawlspace foundation

First floor — 1,169 sq. ft.

Second floor — 1,034 sq. ft.

Bonus — 347 sq. ft.

Garage — 561 sq. ft.

Deck — 217 sq. ft

Porch — 312 sq. ft.

WIDTH 55'-4"
DEPTH 52'-0"

Warm Contemporary

Total living area 2,205 sq. ft. ■ Price Code D

SECOND FLOOR

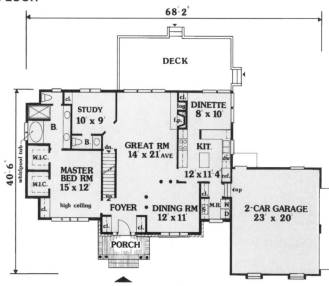

FIRST FLOOR

No. 99664

■ **This plan features:**

— Four bedrooms

— Two full and one half baths

■ Columns outline the Entry to the formal Dining Room

■ The Great Room has a built-in fireplace with adjacent log storage

■ The Kitchen has a center work island and opens to the Dinette

■ A Study and a half Bath are located off the Great Room

■ The secluded Master Suite has dual walk-in closets and a private Bath

■ This home is designed with basement, slab and crawlspace foundation options

First floor — 1,522 sq. ft.
Second floor — 683 sq. ft.
Basement — 1,522 sq. ft.
Garage — 489 sq. ft.

Beauty and Tradition

No. 24964

This plan features:

Three bedrooms

Two full and one half baths

The Foyer, with lovely open-rail staircase, is open to the Dining Room

A two-story ceiling and bay window enhance the Breakfast Room

The large Great Room includes a fireplace and offers access to two different Decks

A Bonus Room will add more living space if finished

This home is designed with basement, slab and crawlspace foundation options

First floor – 1,195 sq. ft.

Second floor – 1,045 sq. ft.

Basement – 1,195 sq. ft.

Bonus – 338 sq. ft.

Garage – 635 sq. ft.

WIDTH 55'-8"
DEPTH 46'-0"

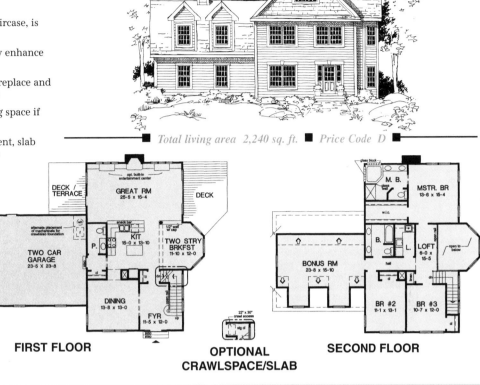

■ Total living area 2,240 sq. ft. ■ Price Code D ■

FIRST FLOOR

OPTIONAL CRAWLSPACE/SLAB

SECOND FLOOR

Volume Ceilings

No. 99169

This plan features:

Three bedrooms

Two full and one half baths

The two-story Entry has a large closet

The Kitchen has a serving island and an eating Nook and opens to the Family Room

The Family Room has a volume ceiling and a fireplace

The Master Suite has a large walk-in closet and private five-piece Bath

Two additional Bedrooms have huge closets and share a full Bath

This home is designed with a basement foundation

First floor – 1,435 sq. ft.

Second floor – 646 sq. ft.

Basement – 1,435 sq. ft.

Garage – 519 sq. ft.

■ Total living area 2,081 sq. ft. ■ Price Code D ■

FIRST FLOOR

SECOND FLOOR

Arched Accents Give Impact

■ *Total living area 2,209 sq. ft.* ■ *Price Code D* ■

FIRST FLOOR

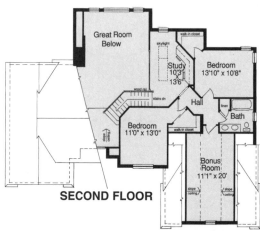

SECOND FLOOR

No. 92643

■ **This plan features:**

— Three bedrooms

— Two full and one half baths

■ The Great Room is enhanced by an entertainment center, hearth fireplace and a wall of windows

■ The angled Kitchen features a work island/snack bar and a Breakfast Area

■ The second floor has two Bedrooms with walk-in closets, skylit Study, a double vanity Bath and a Bonus Room

■ This home is designed with a basement foundation

First floor — 1,542 sq. ft.
Second floor — 667 sq. ft.
Bonus — 236 sq. ft.
Basement — 1,470 sq. ft.
Garage — 420 sq. ft.

Charming and Convenient

■ *Total living area 2,209 sq. ft.* ■ *Price Code D* ■

No. 91534

This plan features:

Three bedrooms

Two full and one half baths

The center Foyer opens to the formal Dining and Living Areas

The spacious Family Room has an inviting fireplace and backyard view

The convenient Kitchen has a peninsula counter/snack bar, a Pantry, a built-in desk, a large eating Nook and is near the Laundry/Garage Entry

The Master Suite features an arched window, a vaulted ceiling and a plush Bath with a walk-in closet and Spa tub

This home is designed with a basement foundation

First floor — 1,214 sq. ft.

Second floor — 995 sq. ft.

Bonus Room — 261 sq. ft.

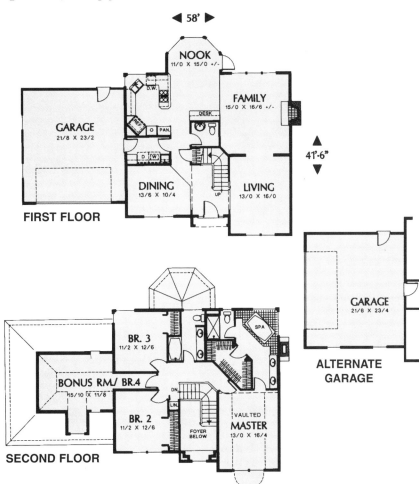

An Extraordinary Home

■ Total living area 2,082 sq. ft. ■ Price Code D

FIRST FLOOR

SECOND FLOOR

No. 92642

■ **This plan features:**

— Three bedrooms

— Two full and one half baths

■ An exciting roof line and textured exteri providing a rich solid look

■ A lovely Foyer that views the cozy firepla and stylish French doors in the Great Ro beyond

■ A grand Entry into the formal Dining Room with a volume ceiling, pulling the Great Room and Dining Room together a spacious feeling

■ A roomy, well-equipped Kitchen that includes a pass-through to the Great Roo

■ Large windows in the Breakfast Area flooding the room with natural light, making it a bright and cheery place to st your day

■ A private, first floor Master Bedroom wit luxurious, compartmented Bath

■ This home is designed with a basement foundation

First floor — 1,524 sq. ft.
Second floor — 558 sq. ft.
Basement — 1,460 sq. ft.
Bonus — 267 sq. ft.

Warm Welcome

■ Total living area 2,083 sq. ft. ■ Price Code D

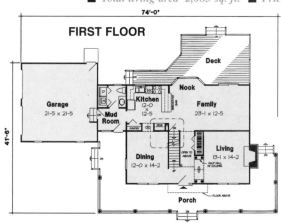

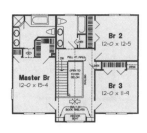

SECOND FLOOR

No. 24245

■ **This plan features:**

— Three bedrooms

— Two full and one half baths

■ Formal areas flanking the Entry hall

■ A Living Room that includes a wonderful fireplace

■ Direct access from the formal Dining Roo to the Kitchen

■ A U-shaped Kitchen including a Breakfas Bar, built-in Pantry planning desk, and a double sink

■ A Mudroom Entry that will help keep the dirt from play or muddy shoes away fro the rest of the home

■ An expansive Family Room with direct access to the rear Deck

■ A Master Suite highlighted by a walk-in closet and a private Master Bath

■ This home is designed with basement, sla and crawlspace foundation options

First floor — 1,113 sq. ft.
Second floor — 970 sq. ft.
Garage — 480 sq. ft.
Basement — 1,113 sq. ft.

■ Total living area 2,210 sq. ft. ■ Price Code D ■

No. 93437

This plan features:

Three bedrooms

Two full and one half baths

The opulent Master Suite is set apart, occupying its own private wing of the home

The Garage includes a Storage Nook, perfect for tools and equipment

The secondary Bedrooms and the Bonus Room occupy the second floor and share a double vanity Bath

This home is designed with a basement foundation

First floor — 1,670 sq. ft.
Second floor — 540 sq. ft.
Bonus — 455 sq. ft.
Basement — 1,677 sq. ft.
Garage — 594 sq. ft.

Rich Classic Lines

■ *Total living area 2,212 sq. ft.* ■ *Price Code D* ■

plant shelf

Bedrm 2
10x13

open to below

Dn

Bedrm 4
10·5x11

Bedrm 3
13x11

SECOND FLOOR

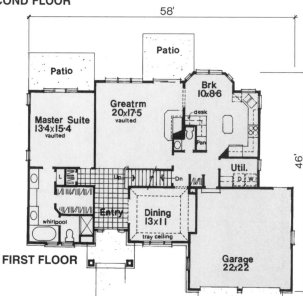

58'

Patio

Patio

Patio

Brk
10x8·6

Greatrm
20x17·5
vaulted

desk

Master Suite
13·4x15·4
vaulted

Pan

46'

Util.

L

Up

Dn

D W.

whirlpool

Entry

Dining
13x11
tray ceiling

Garage
22x22

FIRST FLOOR

No. 91901

■ **This plan features:**

— Four bedrooms

— Three full and one half baths

■ A two-story Foyer flooded by lig
through a half-round transom
window

■ A vaulted ceiling in the Great
Room that continues into the
Master Suite

■ A corner fireplace in the Great
Room and French doors to the
Breakfast/Kitchen Area

■ The Kitchen has a center island,
an angled sink, a built-in desk a
Pantry

■ This home is designed with a
basement foundation

First floor — 1,496 sq. ft.
Second floor — 716 sq. ft.
Basement — 1,420 sq. ft.
Garage — 460 sq. ft.

European Influence

■ *Total living area 2,213 sq. ft.* ■ *Price Code D* ■

No. 97205

This plan features:

Three bedrooms, with optional fourth

Two full and one half baths

The Foyer has a vaulted ceiling, decorative plant shelf and views through the house to the fireplace in the Family Room

Step-saving design highlights the Kitchen with Pantry and serving bar to the vaulted Breakfast Area

Luxurious details in the Master Suite include a tray ceiling, five-piece Bath and walk-in closet

This home is designed with basement, slab and crawlspace foundation options

First floor — 1,488 sq. ft.
Second floor — 725 sq. ft.
Basement — 1,488 sq. ft.
Garage — 460 sq. ft.

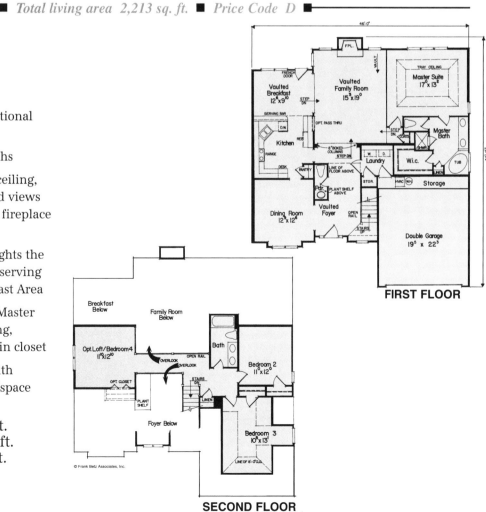

Surprising Interior

■ *Total living area 2,226 sq. ft.* ■ *Price Code D* ■

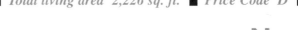

No. 24737

■ **This plan features:**

— Four bedrooms

— Two full and one half baths

■ This home has a traditional facad
but an open and modern interio

■ The Foyer features a unique
staircase and views through the
house to the fireplace in the Gre
Room

■ Centrally located, the Kitchen
opens to the Breakfast Area, Gre
Room and Dining Room

■ This home is designed with
basement, slab and crawlspace
foundation options

First floor — 1,368 sq. ft.
Second floor — 858 sq. ft.
Basement — 1,243 sq. ft.
Garage — 523 sq. ft.
Bonus — 550 sq. ft.
Deck — 120 sq. ft.
Porch — 282 sq. ft.

SECOND FLOOR

FIRST FLOOR

Accented by Quoins

No. 90471

This plan features:

- Four bedrooms
- Two full and one half baths
- Bay windows in the front and rear of the home add to its beauty
- The enormous Great Room spans an entire side of the home and offers a hearth fireplace and access to the Deck
- The Kitchen is an open layout with the Breakfast Nook
- Future expansion is provided for in the upper-level Bonus Room
- This home is designed with basement and crawlspace foundation options
- First floor — 1,048 sq. ft.
- Second floor — 1,050 sq. ft.
- Bonus — 284 sq. ft.
- Basement — 1,034 sq. ft.
- Garage — 484 sq. ft.

■ *Total living area 2,098 sq. ft.* ■ *Price Code D* ■

SECOND FLOOR

FIRST FLOOR

Great Traffic Patterns

No. 97252

This plan features:

- Four bedrooms
- Two full and one half baths
- An arched Entrance has a half circle window above and sidelights flanking it
- The Living and Dining Rooms are adjoined yet defined by columns
- The Breakfast Bay is bright and flows from the Kitchen
- A serving bar to the Family Room from the Kitchen adds convenience and allows for family interaction
- The second floor Master Suite is topped by a tray ceiling in the Bedroom and a vaulted ceiling in the Bath
- Three additional Bedrooms share the full, double vanity Bath in the hall
- This home is designed with basement, slab and crawlspace foundation options
- First floor — 1,044 sq. ft.
- Second floor — 1,057 sq. ft.
- Bonus — 107 sq. ft.
- Basement — 1,044 sq. ft.
- Garage — 420 sq. ft.

■ *Total living area 2,101 sq. ft.* ■ *Price Code D* ■

FIRST FLOOR

SECOND FLOOR

Cul-de-Sac Favorite

■ *Total living area 2,078 sq. ft.* ■ *Price Code D* ■

FIRST FLOOR

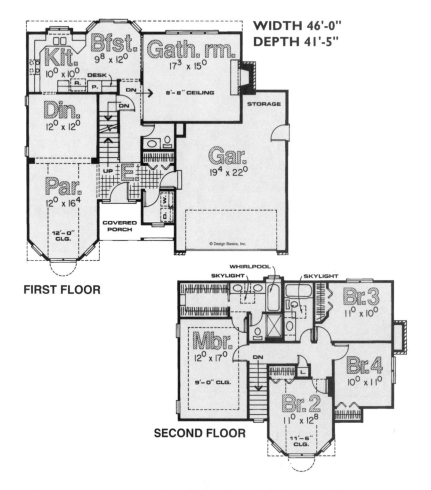

WIDTH 46'-0"
DEPTH 41'-5"

Kit. 10⁰ x 10⁰
Bfst. 9⁸ x 12⁰
Gath. rm. 17³ x 15⁰
DESK
8'-8" CEILING
DN
DN
STORAGE
Din. 12⁰ x 12⁰
R.
P.
Gar. 19⁴ x 22⁰
Par. 12⁰ x 16⁴
UP
12'-0" CLG.
COVERED PORCH
© Design Basics, Inc.

FIRST FLOOR

WHIRLPOOL
SKYLIGHT
SKYLIGHT
Br. 3 11⁰ x 10⁰
Mbr. 12⁰ x 17⁰
DN
Br. 4 10⁰ x 11⁰
9'-0" CLG.
Br. 2 11⁰ x 12⁸
11'-6" CLG.

SECOND FLOOR

No. 94936

■ **This plan features:**

— Four bedrooms

— Two full and one half baths

■ The incredible efficiency of the design of this home makes it seem much larger than it is

■ The large Parlor opens to the Dining Room

■ The fireplaced Gathering Room removed from the formal area of the house to create a real family retreat

■ This home is designed with a basement foundation

■ Alternate foundation options available at an additional charge. Please call 1-800-235-5700 for additional information.

First floor — 1,113 sq. ft.
Second floor — 965 sq. ft.
Basement — 1,113 sq. ft.
Garage — 486 sq. ft.

■ *Total living area 2,224 sq. ft.* ■ *Price Code D* ■

No. 34701

This plan features:

Four bedrooms

Two full and one half baths

Formal Living Room opens to fireplaced Family Room with access to rear yard

Center-island Kitchen provides ample counter and cabinet space and opens to sunny Breakfast Room

The second floor Master Bedroom includes a compartmentalized Bath and plenty of closet space

Three additional Bedrooms complete the second floor

This home is designed with basement, slab and crawlspace foundation options

First floor — 1,090 sq. ft.
Second floor — 1,134 sq. ft.
Basement — 1,090 sq. ft.
Garage — 576 sq. ft.

WIDTH 66'-0"
DEPTH 27'-0"

Kitchen
island
Brkfst
10-8 x 10-2
Family Rm
20 x 12-6

Garage
21-8 x 23-4

10-4 x 12-6
pan. desk

Dining Rm
13-8 x 12-6

Living
15 x 12-6

UP

FIRST FLOOR

DN

BASEMENT OPTION

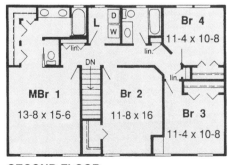

L
D
W

lin.

Br 4
11-4 x 10-8

lin.

DN

lin.

MBr 1
13-8 x 15-6

Br 2
11-8 x 16

Br 3
11-4 x 10-8

SECOND FLOOR

REAR ELEVATION

Tile Floors

■ *Total living area 2,249 sq. ft.* ■ *Price Code D* ■

OPEN TO GRT. RM.

BDR. #3
12'4" × 12'4"

DN

OPEN TO E.

BR. #2
11'2" × 10'10"

BR. #4
12'0" × 11'10"

LIN

BRICK ARCH

SECOND FLOOR

GRT. RM.
VAULTED CEILING
14'0" × 20'0"

NK.
10'10" × 12'0"

KIT.
9'10" × 12'0"

BUILT IN CAB.

ARCH

LIN

UP

E.
2-STORY

DIN.
11'0" × 13'10"

MBR.
CATHEDRAL CEILING
13'0" × 15'8"

2 CAR GAR.
19'4" × 20'2"

49'0"

56'0"

FIRST FLOOR

No. 97136

■ **This plan features:**

— Four bedrooms

— Two full and one half baths

■ Tile flooring in the Kitchen, Nook, Utility Area, Entry and Baths is easy to maintain

■ Convenient to the Kitchen and Garage, the Utility Area features Laundry Room with sink, coat closet and half Bath

■ An arched opening separates the island Kitchen and Nook with the vaulted Great Room

■ French doors lead into the Master Bedroom from the two-story Entry

■ This home is designed with a basement foundation

First floor — 1,554 sq. ft.
Second floor — 695 sq. ft.
Basement — 1,554 sq. ft.
Garage — 389 sq. ft.

Comfortable Colonial

■ *Total living area 2,102 sq. ft.* ■ *Price Code D* ■

No. 93354

This plan features:

Four bedrooms

Two full and one half baths

Entry Porch leads into central Foyer between formal Living and Dining Rooms

Comfortable Family Room with a corner gas fireplace and backyard view

Hub Kitchen with a work island, Pantry, Dinette Area with outdoor access, and nearby Laundry and Garage Entry

Corner Master Bedroom offers a walk-in closet and a double vanity Bath with a whirlpool tub

This home is designed with a basement foundation

First floor — 1,110 sq. ft.
Second floor — 992 sq. ft.
Garage — 530 sq. ft.
Basement — 1,110 sq. ft.

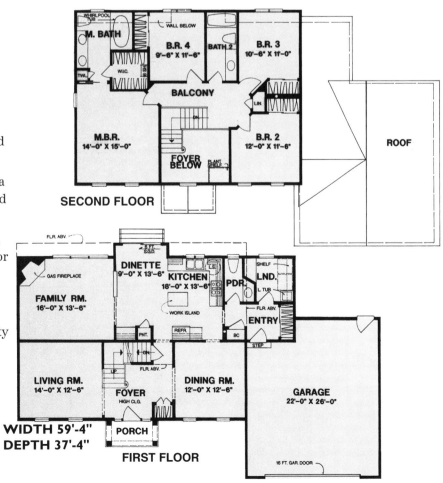

Splendid Country Home

■ *Total living area 2,089 sq. ft.* ■ *Price Code D* ■

No. 96529

■ **This plan features:**

— Four bedrooms

— Three full and one half baths

■ Terrific open plan features great use of space

■ The open formal Dining Room i defined by elegant columns

■ The large Family Room, with fireplace and rear Porch access, i open to the bay-windowed Breakfast Room and the Kitchen

■ The Bedrooms are spaced throughout the floor plan offerir a maximum of privacy

■ This home is designed with slab and crawlspace foundation options

Main floor — 2,089 sq. ft.
Garage — 541 sq. ft.
Bonus — 497 sq. ft.

WIDTH 79'-0"
DEPTH 52'-0"

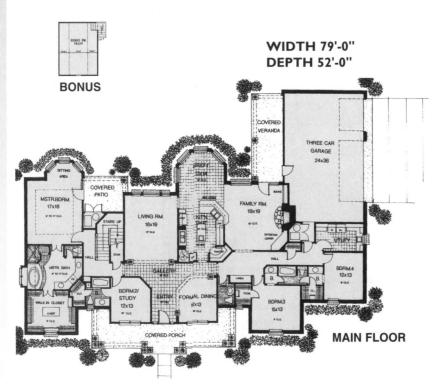

BONUS

MAIN FLOOR

■ *Total living area 2,256 sq. ft.* ■ *Price Code E* ■

No. 90475

This plan features:

- Four bedrooms

- Three full baths

- Victorian style adds to the curb appeal and charm of this home

- Built-in book shelves and a hearth fireplace highlight the Parlor

- The well-equipped galley Kitchen has a built-in desk and opens to the Dining Room and Breakfast Room

- This home is designed with basement and crawlspace foundation options

Main floor — 1,218 sq. ft.
Second floor — 1,038 sq. ft.
Basement — 1,164 sq. ft.
Deck — 144 sq. ft.
Porch — 168 sq. ft.

Sunken Living Room

■ Total living area 2,259 sq. ft. ■ Price Code E ■

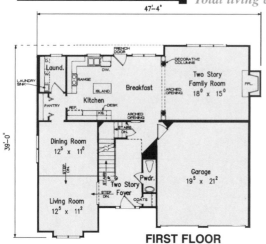

FIRST FLOOR

SECOND FLOOR   **OPTIONAL SITTING ROOM PLAN**

© Frank Betz Associates, Inc.

No. 97215

■ This plan features:

— Four bedrooms

— Two full and one half baths

■ The elegant two-story Foyer and the Dining Room open to the sunken Living Room

■ Decorative columns supporting arched opening into the Family Room create a stately view from the Kitchen and Breakfast Area

■ A open-rail balcony overlooks the two-story Family Room

■ This home is designed with basement and crawlspace foundation options

First floor — 1,167 sq. ft.
Second floor — 1,092 sq. ft.
Basement — 1,167 sq. ft.
Garage — 428 sq. ft.

■ *Total living area 2,260 sq. ft.* ■ *Price Code E* ■

No. 24732

This plan features:

Four bedrooms

Two full and one half baths

The wraparound front Porch imparts an old-fashioned appeal

The formal Dining and Living Rooms to either side of the Foyer provide for gracious entertaining

The efficient Kitchen features a Laundry closet and an extended serving counter for the eating Nook and Family Room

The expansive Master Bedroom has a huge walk-in closet and a plush whirlpool Bath

This home is designed with basement, slab and crawlspace foundation options

First floor — 1,027 sq. ft.
Second floor — 1,233 sq. ft.
Basement — 945 sq. ft.
Garage — 632 sq. ft.

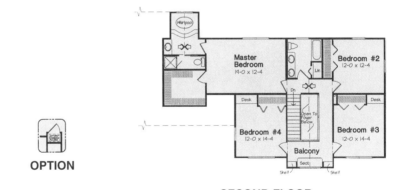

OPTION

SECOND FLOOR

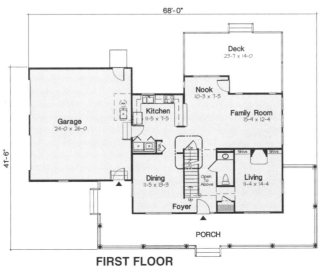

FIRST FLOOR

Elegant Formal Rooms

■ Total living area 2,201 sq. ft. ■ Price Code D ■

MAIN FLOOR

WIDTH 59'-6"
DEPTH 62'-0"

OPTIONAL BASEMENT STAIR LOCATION

No. 97228

■ **This plan features:**

— Three bedrooms

— Two full and one half baths

■ Wonderful formal spaces are a highlight this lovely home, including the elegant Living Room

■ The spacious Foyer opens up into the vaulted space of the Family Room with i tall windows, fireplace and access to the vaulted Breakfast Room

■ The secluded Master Bedroom offers his and hers walk-in closets as well as a truly luxurious Bath

■ This home is designed with basement an crawlspace foundation options

Main floor — 2,201 sq. ft.
Garage — 452 sq. ft.
Basement — 2,201 sq. ft.

Executive Two-Story

■ Total living area 2,116 sq. ft. ■ Price Code D ■

FIRST FLOOR

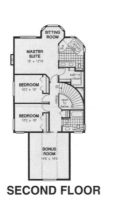

SECOND FLOOR

No. 98800

■ **This plan features:**

— Three bedrooms

— Two full and one half baths

■ Gracefully curving staircase dominating Foyer and leading to the Bedrooms

■ Kitchen and Breakfast Nook separated fr the Family Room by only a railing and a step down

■ Built-in entertainment center and a warming fireplace highlighting the sunk Family Room

■ Formal Living Room and Dining Room t adjoin and include a fireplace in the Livi Room and a built-in china cabinet area i the Dining Room

■ Lavish Master Suite boasts a Sitting Roor and a deluxe five-piece Bath

■ Bonus Room to be finished for future ne

■ This home is designed with a basement foundation

First floor — 1,258 sq. ft.
Second floor — 858 sq. ft.
Garage — 441 sq. ft.
Basement — 1,251 sq. ft.
Bonus — 263 sq. ft.

■ *Total living area 2,261 sq. ft.* ■ *Price Code E* ■

No. 98221

■ **This plan features:**

- Four bedrooms

- Two full and one half baths

■ The formal Parlor has a bay window and French doors that open to the Family Room

■ A private Sitting Room adjoins the Master Bedroom and shares a see-through fireplace

■ This home is designed with a basement foundation

First floor — 1,113 sq. ft.
Second floor — 1,148 sq. ft.
Basement — 1,113 sq. ft.
Garage — 529 sq. ft.

FIRST FLOOR

WIDTH 66'-0"
DEPTH 31'-0"

SECOND FLOOR

Stately Front Porch with Columns

■ *Total living area 2,056 sq. ft.* ■ *Price Code D* ■

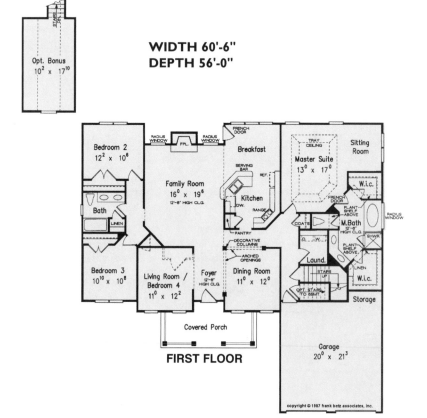

WIDTH 60'-6"
DEPTH 56'-0"

FIRST FLOOR

No. 97622

■ This plan features:

— Three bedrooms

— Two full baths

■ Formal Living Room can be turned into an additional Bedroom with ease

■ Tray ceiling crowns the secluded Master Bedroom which includes Sitting Room

■ Arched openings and columns define the entrance to the Dining Room

■ Efficient Kitchen includes built-in Pantry and peninsula serving bar

■ This home is designed with basement and crawlspace foundation options

Main floor — 2,056 sq. ft.
Bonus — 208 sq. ft.
Basement — 2,056 sq. ft.
Garage — 454 sq. ft.

Cozy Yet Spacious

■ *Total living area 2,270 sq. ft.* ■ *Price Code E* ■

No. 97293

This plan features:

- Four bedrooms

- Two full and one half baths

- The Living Room has an elegant arched opening to the Foyer and to the Dining Room

- The sunken Family Room has a fireplace and French doors to the backyard

- The Breakfast Room is enhanced by decorative columns

- This home is designed with basement, slab and crawlspace foundation options

First floor — 1,186 sq. ft.
Second floor — 1,084 sq. ft.
Garage — 440 sq. ft.

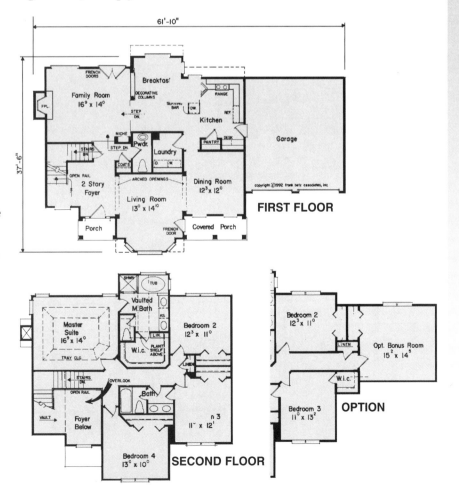

Angled Covered Porch

■ *Total living area 2,272 sq. ft.* **■** *Price Code E* **■**

Future BonusRm 16x12
Sloping Clg.
Not Included In Square Footage

Bed#4 13x11
Sloping Clg.
Skylight
DN

Bed#3 11x12

Bed#2 12x14

SECOND FLOOR

70' - 0"

Covered Patio

Covered Patio

FamilyRm 16x20

MstrBed 13x18

38' - 5"

Brkfst 10x14

Gar 20x27

Gallery

Kit 13x10

FmlDin 11x14

Ent

Pwdr
Plant Ledge

Util

UP

Covered Porch

FIRST FLOOR

No. 98595

■ This plan features:

— Four bedrooms

— Two full and one half baths

■ An angled front Porch adds to th[e] curb appeal of this home

■ The U-shaped Kitchen has an island cooktop and Pantry and opens to the Breakfast Area

■ Three additional Bedrooms shar[e] a full Bath with twin vanities

■ This home is designed with basement, slab and crawlspace foundation options

First floor — 1,572 sq. ft.
Second floor — 700 sq. ft.
Bonus — 202 sq. ft.

Dressed to Impress

No. 97970

This plan features:

Four bedrooms

Two full and one half baths

The Foyer offers access to the Master Bedroom, the formal Dining Room, and the Great Room

The Great Room, with its focal-point fireplace, includes access to the Patio, offering outdoor entertainment options

A private Master Suite offers his and her walk-in closets and a luxurious Bath

The Kitchen and adjoining Breakfast Nook provides convenience and dining options

The Secondary Bedrooms share a full Bath on the second floor

This home is designed with basement, crawlspace and slab foundation options

Alternate foundation options available at an additional charge. Please call 1-800-235-5700 for more information.

First floor — 1,593 sq. ft.

Second floor — 633 sq. ft.

Bonus — 298 sq. ft.

Garage — 526 sq. ft.

■ Total living area 2,226 sq. ft. ■ Price Code D ■

FIRST FLOOR

© Design Basics, Inc.

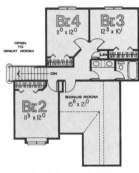

SECOND FLOOR

Open-Rail Staircase

No. 98485

This plan features:

Four bedrooms

Three full baths

The two-story Foyer has an attractive open-rail staircase

The Dining Room entrance is defined by columns

The Kitchen opens to a bay Breakfast Area and is convenient to the Laundry Room

The Family Room has a vaulted ceiling, a fireplace and access to the backyard through a French door

The Master Suite has a tray ceiling, walk-in closet and private Bath

The optional Bonus Room has potential for expansion

This home is designed with basement and crawlspace foundation options

First floor — 1,583 sq. ft.

Second floor — 543 sq. ft.

Bonus — 251 sq. ft.

Basement — 1,583 sq. ft.

Garage — 460 sq. ft.

■ Total living area 2,126 sq. ft. ■ Price Code D ■

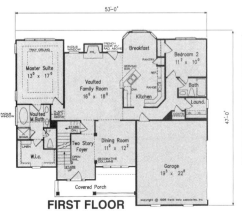

FIRST FLOOR

© 1998 Frank Betz Associates, Inc.

SECOND FLOOR

Country Charm

■ *Total living area 2,127 sq. ft.* ■ *Price Code D* ■

FIRST FLOOR

SECOND FLOOR

No. 91577

■ **This plan features:**

— Four bedrooms

— Two full and one half baths

■ This home exudes Country style and cha
due in part to the front Porch

■ The Master Bedroom has an attached Bat
with a Spa tub

■ Three upstairs Bedrooms share a full Bat
and contain ample closet space

■ The Living Room accesses the Porch
through the front or side doors

■ The Kitchen features a center island with
cooktop, a Pantry and a desk

■ This home is designed with a crawlspace
foundation

First floor — 1,037 sq. ft.
Second floor — 1,090 sq ft.
Garage — 484 sq. ft.

Easy Maintenance

■ *Total living area 2,128 sq. ft.* ■ *Price Code D* ■

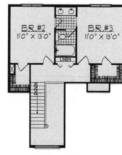

FIRST FLOOR

SECOND FLOOR

No. 99126

■ **This plan features:**

— Three bedrooms

— Two full and one half baths

■ A decorative boxed window and columns
define the style of this brick home

■ Tile flooring and a vaulted ceiling add
interest to the convenient Entry with half
Bath, coat closet and access to the Garage

■ Built-in shelves, boxed window and
fireplace create a sophisticated Great Roor

■ Special features in the Kitchen include a
built-in desk, a center island with circular
eating bar and a Nook with access to the
rear yard

■ Dual vanities and a garden tub highlight t
Master Bath

■ This home is designed with a basement
foundation

First floor — 1,565 sq. ft.
Second floor — 563 sq ft.
Basement — 1,565 sq. ft.

Striking Structure

■ *Total living area 2,277 sq. ft.* ■ *Price Code E* ■

No. 99431

This plan features:

- Four bedrooms

- Two full and one half baths

- Wraparound covered Porch and windows create a striking appearance

- Great Room features a cathedral ceiling, transom windows and huge fireplace

- Center-island Kitchen has a lazy Susan and an ample Pantry

- This home is designed with a basement foundation

- Alternate foundation options available at an additional charge. Please call 1-800-235-5700 for more information.

First floor — 1,570 sq. ft.
Second floor — 707 sq. ft.
Garage — 504 sq. ft.
Basement — 1,570 sq. ft.

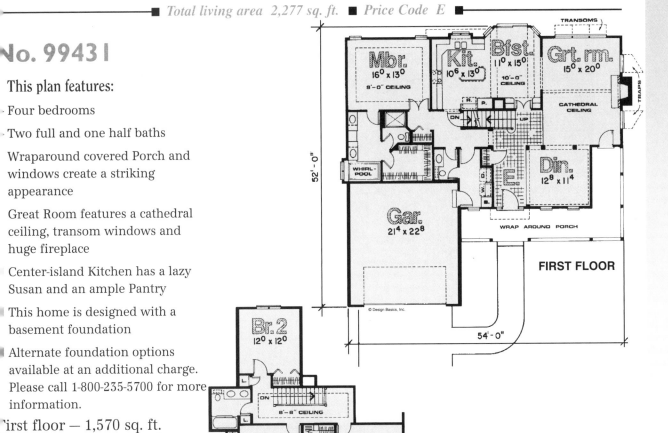

Texture Adds to Elegance

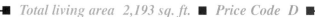

■ *Total living area 2,193 sq. ft.* ■ *Price Code D* ■

MAIN FLOOR

OPTIONAL BONUS

No. 98466

■ This plan features:

— Three or four bedrooms

— Two full baths

■ Foyer opens to Family Room with fireplace flanked by tall windows

■ The formal Living Room or the optional Bonus Room could be finished as a fourth — or perhaps fifth — Bedroom

■ The Master Bedroom is crowned by a lovely tray ceiling and includes a sunny Sitting Room

■ This home is designed with basement, slab and crawlspace foundation options

Main floor — 2,193 sq. ft.
Bonus — 400 sq. ft.
Garage — 522 sq. ft.

Triple Dormers Add Light

■ *Total living area 2,297 sq. ft.* ■ *Price Code E* ■

No. 90474

This plan features:

- Three bedrooms

- Two full and one half baths

- The Family Room has a focal-point fireplace surrounded by windows and access to the rear Deck

- The privately located Master Bedroom features large closets and a Spa Bath

- The future Bonus Room and additional Bedrooms are on the second floor

- This home is designed with basement and crawlspace foundation options

First floor — 1,580 sq. ft.
Second floor — 717 sq. ft.
Bonus — 410 sq. ft.
Basement — 1,342 sq. ft.
Garage — 484 sq. ft.

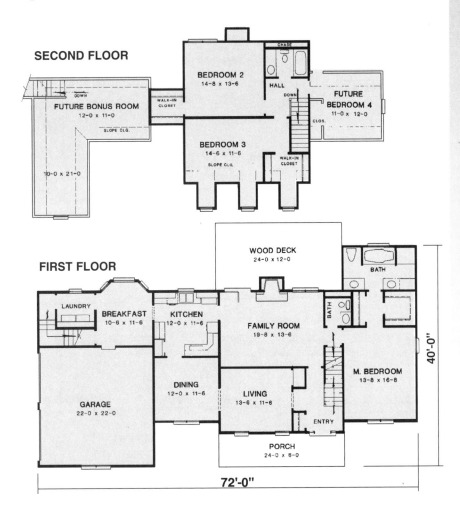

SECOND FLOOR

FUTURE BONUS ROOM
12-0 x 11-0
SLOPE CLG.
10-0 x 21-0

DOWN
WALK-IN CLOSET

CHASE
BEDROOM 2
14-8 x 13-6
HALL
DOWN
FUTURE BEDROOM 4
11-0 x 12-0
CLOS.

BEDROOM 3
14-6 x 11-6
SLOPE CLG.
WALK-IN CLOSET

FIRST FLOOR

WOOD DECK
24-0 x 12-0
BATH

LAUNDRY
BREAKFAST
10-6 x 11-6
KITCHEN
12-0 x 11-6
FAMILY ROOM
19-8 x 13-6
BATH

GARAGE
22-0 x 22-0

DINING
12-0 x 11-6
LIVING
13-6 x 11-6
M. BEDROOM
13-8 x 16-8

ENTRY

PORCH
24-0 x 6-0

40'-0"

72'-0"

Stately Manse

■ *Total living area 2,257 sq. ft.* ■ *Price Code E* ■

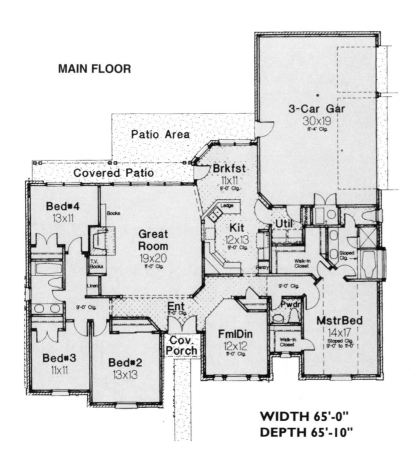

MAIN FLOOR

Patio Area

Covered Patio

3-Car Gar
30x19
8'-4" Clg.

Brkfst
11x11
9'-0" Clg.

Bed#4
13x11

Great
Room
19x20
11'-0" Clg.

Kit
12x13
9'-0" Clg.

Util

Walk-In
Closet

Ledge

Books

T.V.
Books

Linen

Ent
11'-0" Clg.

Cov.
Porch

Bed#3
11x11

Bed#2
13x13

FmlDin
12x12
11'-0" Clg.

Pwdr

Walk-in
Closet

Pantry

Sloped
Clg.

MstrBed
14x17
Sloped Clg.
9'-0" to 11'-0"

9'-0" Clg.

9'-0" Clg.

WIDTH 65'-0"
DEPTH 65'-10"

No. 98548

■ **This plan features:**

– Four bedrooms

– Two and one half full baths

■ Large fireplaced Great Room opens to sunny Breakfast Room and well-planned Kitchen

■ Covered and open Patios at the rear of the house offer the opportunity to expand the Living Space outdoors

■ The secluded Master Bedroom features abundant closet space

■ The fourth Bedroom, at the rear of the home with Patio access, could be used as a Study

■ This home is designed with slab and crawlspace foundation options

Main floor — 2,257 sq. ft.
Garage — 601 sq. ft.

Secluded Study/Bedroom

No. 97219

This plan features:

- Four bedrooms

- Three full and one half baths

- The Kitchen includes a Pantry and easy access to the formal Dining Room

- The first floor Study with Bath can be used as a fourth Bedroom

- This home is designed with basement and crawlspace foundation options

- First floor — 1,257 sq. ft.

- Second floor — 871 sq. ft.

■ Total living area 2,128 sq. ft. ■ Price Code D ■

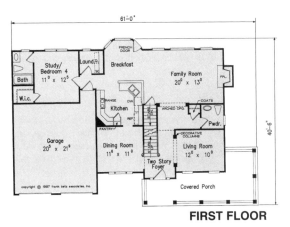

FIRST FLOOR

SECOND FLOOR

SECOND FLOOR W/BONUS ROOM

Sun Room Living

No. 99459

This plan features:

- Four bedrooms

- Two full and one half baths

- Living Room opens through French doors to fireplaced Family Room

- Formal Dining Room features an elegant bay window

- The Kitchen is open to the Breakfast Area and the Family Room

- The secluded Master Bedroom has a walk-in closet and a luxurious Bath

- This home is designed with a basement foundation

- Alternate foundation options available at an additional charge. Please call 1-800-235-5700 for additional information.

- First floor — 1,602 sq. ft.

- Second floor — 654 sq. ft.

■ Total living area 2,256 sq. ft. ■ Price Code E ■

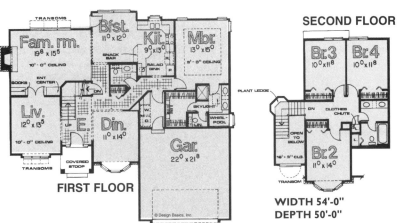

SECOND FLOOR

FIRST FLOOR

WIDTH 54'-0"
DEPTH 50'-0"

339

Everything You Need...
...to Make Your Dream Come True

You pay only a fraction of the original cost for home designs by respected professionals.

You've Picked Your Dream Home!

You can imagine your new home situated on your lot in the morning sunlight. You can visualize living there, enjoying your family, entertaining friends and celebrating holidays. All that remains are the details. That's where we can help. Whether you plan to build it yourself, act as your own general contractor or hire a professional builder, your Garlinghouse Co. home plans will provide the perfect design and specifications to help make your dream home a reality.

We can offer you an array of additional products and services to help you with your planning needs. We can supply materials lists, construction cost estimates based on your local material and labor costs and modifications to your selected plan if you would like.

For over 90 years, homeowners and builders have relied on us for accurate, complete, professional blueprints. Our plans help you get results fast... and save money, too! These pages will give you all the information you need to order. So get started now... We know you'll love your new Garlinghouse home!

Sincerely,

James D. McNair III

Chief Executive Officer

EXTERIOR ELEVATIONS

Elevations are scaled drawings of the front, rear, left, and right sides of a home. All of the necessary information pertaining to the exterior finish materials, roof pitches, and exterior he dimensions of your home are defined.

CABINET PLANS

These plans, or in some cases elevations, will detail the layout of the kitchen and bathroom cabinets at a larger scale. This gives you an accurate layout for your cabinets or an ideal star point for a modified custom cabinet design. Available for most plans. You may also show the f plan without a cabinet layout. This will allow you to start from scratch and design your own dream kitchen.

TYPICAL WALL SECTION

This section is provided to help your builder understand the structural components and mater. used to construct the exterior walls of your home. This section will address insulation, roof components, and interior and exterior wall finishes. Your plans will be designed with either 2x 2x6 exterior walls, but most professional contractors can easily adapt the plans to the wall thickness you require.

FIREPLACE DETAILS

If the home you have chosen includes a fireplace, the fireplace detail will show typical method to construct the firebox, hearth and flue chase for masonry units, or a wood frame chase for a zero-clearance unit. Available for most plans.

FOUNDATION PLAN

These plans will accurately dimension the footprint of your home including load bearing points and beam placement if applicable. The foundation style will vary from plan to plan. Your local climatic conditions will dictate whether a basement, slab or crawlspace is best suited for your area. In most cases, if your plan comes with one foundation style, a professional contractor ca easily adapt the foundation plan to an alternate style.

ROOF PLAN

The information necessary to construct the roof will be included with your home plans. Some plans will reference roof trusses, while many others contain schematic framing plans. These framing plans will indicate the lumber sizes necessary for the rafters and ridgeboards based c the designated roof loads.

TYPICAL CROSS SECTION

A cut-away cross-section through the entire home shows your building contractor the exact correlation of construction components at all levels of the house. It will help to clarify the load bearing points from the roof all the way down to the basement. Available for most plans.

DETAILED FLOOR PLANS

The floor plans of your home accurately dimension the positioning of all walls, doors, windows stairs and permanent fixtures. They will show you the relationship and dimensions of rooms, closets and traffic patterns. The schematic of the electrical layout may be included in the plan. This layout is clearly represented and does not hinder the clarity of other pertinent information shown. All these details will help your builder properly construct your new home.

STAIR DETAILS

If stairs are an element of the design you have chosen, the plans will show the necessary infor mation to build these, either through a stair cross section, or on the floor plans. Either way, the information provides your builders the essential reference points that they need to build the stairs.

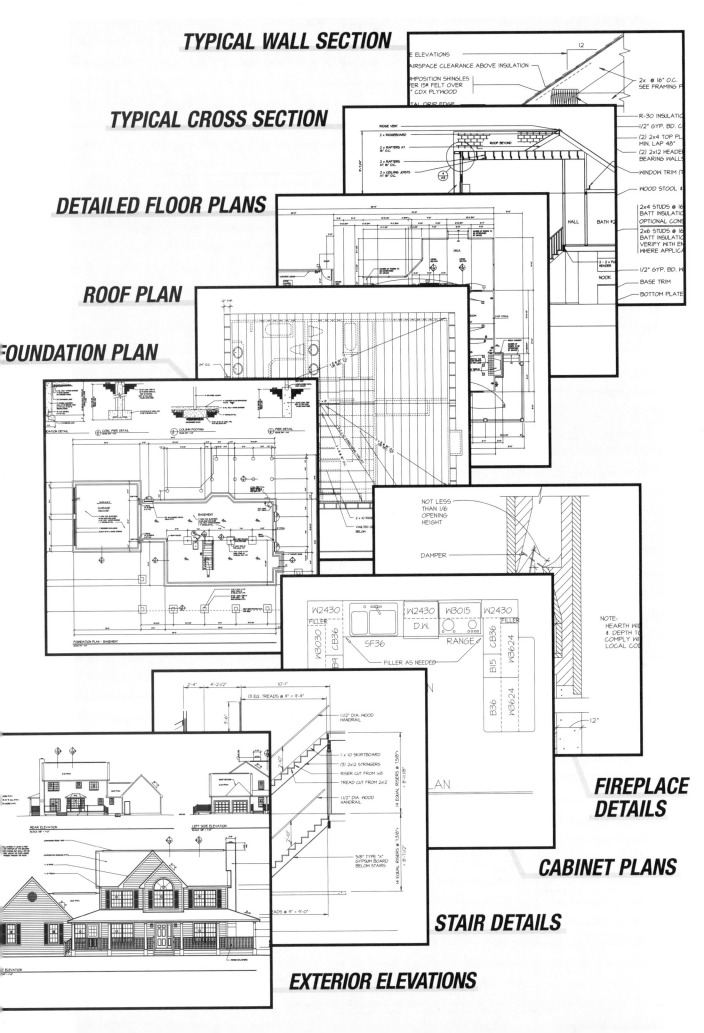

TYPICAL WALL SECTION

TYPICAL CROSS SECTION

DETAILED FLOOR PLANS

ROOF PLAN

FOUNDATION PLAN

FIREPLACE DETAILS

CABINET PLANS

STAIR DETAILS

EXTERIOR ELEVATIONS

Garlinghouse Options & Extras ...Make Your Dream A Home

Reversed Plans Can Make Your Dream Home Just Right!

"That's our dream home...if only the garage were on the other side!"

You could have exactly the home you want by flipping it end-for-end. Check it out by holding your dream home page of this book up to a mirror. Then simply order your plans "reversed." We'll send you one full set of mirror-image plans (with the writing backwards) as a master guide for you and your builder.

The remaining sets of your order will come as shown in this book so the dimensions and specifications are easily read on the job site...but most plans in our collection come stamped "REVERSED" so there is no construction confusion.

We can only send reversed plans with multiple-set orders. There is a $50 charge for this service.

Some plans in our collection are available in Right Reading Reverse. Right Reading Reverse plans will show your home in reverse, with the writing on the plan being readable. This easy-to-read format will save you valuable time and money. Please contact our Customer Service Department at (860) 659-5667 to check for Right Reading Reverse availability. *(There is a $135 charge for this service.)*

As Shown   Reversed

Specifications & Contract Form

We send this form to you free of charge with your home plan order. The form is designed to be filled in by you or your contractor with the exact materials to use in the construction of your new home. Once signed by you and your contractor it will provide you with peace of mind throughout the construction process.

$19.95 per set
(includes postage)

Remember To Order Your Materials List

It'll help you save money. Available at a modest additional charge, the Materials List gives the quantity, dimensions, and specifications for the major materials needed to build your home. You will get faster, more accurate bids from your contractors and building suppliers — and avoid paying for unused materials and waste. Materials Lists are available for all home plans except as otherwise indicated, but can only be ordered with a set of home plans. Due to differences in regional requirements and homeowner or builder preferences... electrical, plumbing and heating/air conditioning equipment specifications are not designed specifically for each plan. However, non-plan specific detailed typical prints of residential electrical, plumbing and construction guidelines can be provided. Please see below for additional information.

Detail Plans Provide Valuable Information About Construction Techniques

Because local codes and requirements vary greatly, we recommend that you obtain drawings and bids from licensed contractors to do your mechanical plans. However, if you want to know more about techniques — and deal more confidently with subcontractors — we offer these remarkably useful detail sheets. These detail sheets will aid in your understanding of these technical subjects. **The detail sheets are not specific to any one home plan and should be used only as a general reference guide.**

RESIDENTIAL CONSTRUCTION DETAILS

Ten sheets that cover the essentials of stick-built residential home construction. Details foundation options — poured concrete basement, concrete block, or monolithic concrete slab. Shows all aspects of floor, wall and roof framing. Provides details for roof dormers, overhangs, chimneys and skylights. Conforms to requirements of Uniform Building code or BOCA code. Includes a quick index and a glossary of terms.

RESIDENTIAL PLUMBING DETAILS

Eight sheets packed with information detailing pipe installation methods, fittings, and sized. Details plumbing hook-ups for toilets, sinks, washers, sump pumps, and septic system construction. Conforms to requirements of National Plumbing code. Color coded with a glossary of terms and quick index.

RESIDENTIAL ELECTRICAL DETAILS

Eight sheets that cover all aspects of residential wiring, from simple switch wiring to service entrance connections. Details distribution panel layout with outlet and switch schematics, circuit breaker and wiring installation methods, and ground fault interrupter specifications. Conforms to requirements of National Electrical Code. Color coded with a glossary of terms.

Modifying Your Favorite Design, Made EASY!

OPTION #1

Modifying Your Garlinghouse Home Plan

Simple modifications to your dream home, including minor non-structural changes and material substitutions, can be made between you and your builder by marking the changes directly on your blueprints. However, if you are considering making significant changes to your chosen design, we recommend that you use the services of The Garlinghouse Design Staff. We will help take your ideas and turn them into a reality, just the way you want. Here's our procedure!

When you place your Vellum order, you may also request a free Garlinghouse Modification Kit. In this kit, you will receive a red marking pencil, furniture cut-out sheet, ruler, a self addressed mailing label and a form for specifying any additional notes or drawings that will help us understand your design ideas. Mark your desired changes directly on the Vellum drawings. NOTE: Please use only a **red pencil** to mark your desired changes on the Vellum. Then, return the redlined Vellum set in the original box to us. **IMPORTANT**: Please roll the Vellums for shipping, **do not fold** the Vellums for shipping.

We also offer modification estimates. We will provide you with an estimate to draft your changes based on your specific modifications before you purchase the vellums, for a $50 fee. After you receive your estimate, if you decide to have us do the changes, the $50 estimate fee will be deducted from the cost of your modifications. If, however, you choose to use a different service, the $50 estimate fee is non-refundable. (Note: Personal checks cannot be accepted for the estimate.)

Within 5 days of receipt of your plans, you will be contacted by the Design Staff with an estimate for the design services to draw those changes. A 50% deposit is required before we begin making the actual modifications to your plans.

Once the design changes have been completed to your vellum plan, a representative will call to inform you that your modified Vellum plan is complete and will be shipped as soon as the final payment has been made. For additional information call us at 1-860-659-5667. Please refer to the Modification Pricing Guide for estimated modification costs.

OPTION #2

Reproducible Vellums for Local Modification Ease

If you decide not to use Garlinghouse for your modifications, we recommend that you follow our same procedure of purchasing our Vellums. You then have the option of using the services of the original designer of the plan, a local professional designer, or architect to make the modifications to your plan.

With a Vellum copy of our plans, a design professional can alter the drawings just the way you want, then you can print as many copies of the modified plans as you need to build your house. And, since you have already started with our complete detailed plans, the cost of those expensive professional services will be significantly less than starting from scratch. Refer to the price schedule for Vellum costs.

IMPORTANT RETURN POLICY: Upon receipt of your Vellums, if for some reason you decide you do not want your modified plan, then simply return the Kit and the unopened Vellums. Reproducible Vellum copies of our home plans are copyright protected and only sold under the terms of a license agreement that you will receive with your order. Should you not agree to the terms, then the Vellums may be exchanged, less the shipping and handling charges, and a 20% exchange fee. For any additional information, please call us at 1-860-659-5667.

MODIFICATION PRICING GUIDE

CATEGORIES	ESTIMATED COST
KITCHEN LAYOUT — PLAN AND ELEVATION	$175.00
BATHROOM LAYOUT — PLAN AND ELEVATION	$175.00
FIREPLACE PLAN AND DETAILS	$200.00
INTERIOR ELEVATION	$125.00
EXTERIOR ELEVATION — MATERIAL CHANGE	$140.00
EXTERIOR ELEVATION — ADD BRICK OR STONE	$400.00
EXTERIOR ELEVATION — STYLE CHANGE	$450.00
NON BEARING WALLS (INTERIOR)	$200.00
BEARING AND/OR EXTERIOR WALLS	$325.00
WALL FRAMING CHANGE — 2X4 TO 2X6 OR 2X6 TO 2X4	$240.00
ADD/REDUCE LIVING SPACE — SQUARE FOOTAGE	QUOTE REQUIRED
NEW MATERIALS LIST	QUOTE REQUIRED
CHANGE TRUSSES TO RAFTERS OR CHANGE ROOF PITCH	$300.00
FRAMING PLAN CHANGES	$325.00
GARAGE CHANGES	$325.00
ADD A FOUNDATION OPTION	$300.00
FOUNDATION CHANGES	$250.00
RIGHT READING PLAN REVERSE	$575.00
ARCHITECTS SEAL (Available for most states.)	$300.00
ENERGY CERTIFICATE	$150.00
LIGHT AND VENTILATION SCHEDULE	$150.00

Questions?
Call our customer service department at 1-860-659 5667

"How to obtain a construction cost calculation based on labor rates and building material costs in <u>your</u> Zip Code area!

ZIP-QUOTE!
HOME COST CALCULATOR

ZIP QUOTE
HOME COST CALCULATOR

WHY?

Do you wish you could quickly find out the building cost for your new home without waiting for a contractor to compile hundreds of bids? Would you like to have a benchmark to compare your contractor(s) bids against? **Well, Now You Can!!,** with **Zip-Quote** Home Cost Calculator. Zip-Quote is only available for zip code areas within the United States.

HOW?

Our new **Zip-Quote** Home Cost Calculator will enable you to obtain the calculated building cost to construct your new home, based on labor rates and building material costs within your zip code area, without the normal delays or hassles usually associated with the bidding process. Zip-Quote can be purchased in two separate formats, an itemized or a bottom line format.

"How does **Zip-Quote** actually work?" When you call to order, you must choose from the options available, for your specific home, in order for us to process your order. Once we receive your **Zip-Quote** order, we process your specific home plan building materials list through our Home Cost Calculator which contains up-to-date rates for all residential labor trades and building material costs in your zip code area. "The result?" A calculated cost to build your dream home in your zip code area. This calculation will help you (as a consumer or a builder) evaluate your building budget. This is a valuable tool for anyone considering building a new home.

All database information for our calculations is furnished by Marshall & Swift, L.P. For over 60 years, Marshall & Swift L.P. has been a leading provider of cost data to professionals in all aspects of the construction and remodeling industries.

OPTION 1

The **Itemized Zip-Quote** is a detailed building material list. Each building material list line item will separately state the labor cost, material cost and equipment cost (if applicable) for the use of that building material in the construction process. Each category within the building material list will be subtotaled and the entire Itemized cost calculation totaled at the end. This building materials list will be summarized by the individual building categories and will have additional columns where you can enter data from your contractor's estimates for a cost comparison between the different suppliers and contractors who will actually quote you their products and services.

OPTION 2

The **Bottom Line Zip-Quote** is a one line summarized total cost for the home plan of your choice. This cost calculation is also based on the labor cost, material cost and equipment cost (if applicable) within your local zip code area.

COST

The price of your **Itemized Zip-Quote** is based upon th pricing schedule of the plan you have selected, in addition to t price of the materials list. Please refer to the pricing schedule on our order form. The price of your initial **Bottom Line Z Quote** is $29.95. Each additional **Bottom Line Zip-Quote** ordered in conjunction with the initial order is only $14.95. **Bottom Line Zip-Quote** may be purchased separately and does NOT have to be purchased in conjunction with a home plan order.

FYI

An **Itemized Zip-Quote** Home Cost Calculation can ONLY be purchased in conjunction with a Home Plan order. The **Itemized Zip-Quote** can not be purchased separately. The **Bottom Line Zip-Quote** can be purchased separately and doesn't have to be purchased in conjunction with a home plan order. Please consult with a sales representative for current availability. If you find within 60 days of your order da that you will be unable to build this home, then you may exchange the plans and the materials list towards the price of new set of plans (see order info pages for plan exchange policy The **Itemized Zip-Quote** and the **Bottom Line Zip-Quot** are NOT returnable. The price of the initial **Bottom Line Zip-Quote** order can be credited towards the purchase of an **Itemized Zip-Quote** order only. Additional **Bottom Line Zip-Quote** orders, within the same order can not be credited Please call our Customer Service Department for more information.

Itemized Zip-Quote is available for plans where you see this symbol. ZIP

Bottom Line Zip-Quote is available for all plans under 4,00 square feet. BL

SOME MORE INFORMATION

Itemized and Bottom Line Zip-Quotes give you approxima ed costs for constructing the particular house in your area. These costs are not exact and are only intended to be used as preliminary estimate to help determine the affordability of a ne home and/or as a guide to evaluate the general competitivenes of actual price quotes obtained through local suppliers and cor tractors. However, Zip-Quote cost figures should never be relied upon as the only source of information in either case. Land, sewer systems, site work, landscaping and other expense are not included in our building cost figures. Garlinghouse and Marshall & Swift L.P. can not guarantee any level of data accura or correctness in a Zip-Quote and disclaim all liability for loss with respect to the same, in excess of the original purchase price of the Zip-Quote product. All Zip-Quote calculations ar based upon the actual blueprints and do not reflect any differences or options that may be shown on the published house renderings, floor plans, or photographs.

What Garlinghouse Offers

Home Plan Blueprint Package

By purchasing a multiple set package of blueprints or a vellum from Garlinghouse, you not only receive the physical blueprint documents necessary for construction, but you are also granted a license to build one, and only one, home. You can also make simple modifications, including minor non-structural changes and material substitutions, to our design, as long as these changes are made directly on the blueprints purchased from Garlinghouse and no additional copies are made.

Home Plan Vellums

By purchasing vellums for one of our home plans, you receive the same construction drawings found in the blueprints, but printed on vellum paper. Vellums can be erased and are perfect for making design changes. They are also semi-transparent making them easy to duplicate. But most importantly, the purchase of home plan vellums comes with a broader license that allows you to make changes to the design (ie, create a hand drawn or CAD derivative work), to make an unlimited number of copies of the plan, and to build one home from the plan.

License To Build Additional Homes

With the purchase of a blueprint package or vellums you automatically receive a license to build one home and only one home, respectively. If you want to build more homes than you are licensed to build through your purchase of a plan, then additional licenses may be purchased at reasonable costs from Garlinghouse. Inquire for more information.

IMPORTANT INFORMATION TO READ BEFORE YOU PLACE YOUR ORDER

How Many Sets Of Plans Will You Need?

The Standard 8-Set Construction Package

Our experience shows that you'll speed every step of construction and avoid costly building errors by ordering enough sets to go around. Each tradesperson wants a set — the general contractor and all subcontractors; foundation, electrical, plumbing, heating/air conditioning and framers. Don't forget your lending institution, building department and, of course, a set for yourself. * Recommended For Construction *

The Minimum 4-Set Construction Package

If you're comfortable with arduous follow-up, this package can save you a few dollars by giving you the option of passing down plan sets as work progresses. You might have enough copies to go around if work goes exactly as scheduled and no plans are lost or damaged by subcontractors. But for only $60 more, the 8-set package eliminates these worries. * Recommended For Bidding *

The Single Study Set

We offer this set so you can study the blueprints to plan your dream home in detail. They are stamped "study set only-not for construction", and you cannot build a home from them. In pursuant to copyright laws, it is illegal to reproduce any blueprint.

An Important Note About Building Code Requirements:

All plans are drawn to conform to one or more of the industry's major national building standards. However, due to the variety of local building regulations, your plan may need to be modified to comply with local requirements — snow loads, energy loads, seismic zones, etc. Do check them fully and consult your local building officials.

A few states require that all building plans used be drawn by an architect registered in that state. While having your plans reviewed and stamped by such an architect may be prudent, laws requiring non-conforming plans like ours to be completely redrawn forces you to unnecessarily pay very large fees. If your state has such a law, we strongly recommend you contact your state representative to protest.

The rendering, floor plans, and technical information contained within this publication are not guaranteed to be totally accurate. Consequently, no information from this publication should be used either as a guide to construct a home or for estimating the cost of building a home. Complete blueprints must be purchased for such purposes.

Order Form

Plan prices guaranteed until 3/20/04— After this date call for updated pricing

Order Code No. **CHP2**

_____ set(s) of blueprints for plan #_____ $_____

_____ Vellum & Modification kit for plan #_____ $_____

_____ Additional set(s) @ $30 each for plan #_____ $_____

_____ Mirror Image Reverse @ $50 each $_____

_____ Right Reading Reverse @ $135 each $_____

_____ Materials list for plan #_____ $_____

_____ Detail Plans @ $19.95 each
   ❑ Construction ❑ Plumbing ❑ Electrical $_____

_____ Bottom line ZIP Quote @ $29.95 for plan #_____ $_____

_____ Additional Bottom Line Zip Quote
   @ $14.95 for plan(s) #_____

_____ $_____

_____ Itemized ZIP Quote for plan(s) #_____ $____

Shipping (see charts on opposite page) $____

Subtotal $____

Sales Tax (CT residents add 6% sales tax) $____

TOTAL AMOUNT ENCLOSED $____

Send your check, money order or credit card information to:
(No C.O.D.'s Please)

Please submit all United States & Other Nations orders to:

Garlinghouse Company
174 Oakwood Drive
Glastonbury, CT. 06033

ADDRESS INFORMATION:

NAME:_____

EMAIL ADDRESS:_____

STREET:_____

CITY:_____

STATE:_____ ZIP:_____

DAYTIME PHONE:_____

Credit Card Information

Charge To: ❑ Visa   ❑ Mastercard

Card # | | | | | | | | | | | | | | | | | |

Signature _____ Exp. _____/_____

ORDER TOLL FREE — 1-800-235-5700
Monday-Friday 8:00 a.m. to 8:00 p.m. Eastern Time
or FAX your Credit Card order to 1-860-659-5692
All foreign residents call 1-800-659-5667

Please have ready: 1. Your credit card number 2. The plan number 3. The order code number ⟳ *CHP28*

Garlinghouse 2002 Blueprint Price Code Schedule

Additional sets with original order $50

	1 Set	4 Sets	8 Sets	Vellums	ML	Itemized ZIP Quote
A	$345	$385	$435	$525	$60	$50
B	$375	$415	$465	$555	$60	$50
C	$410	$450	$500	$590	$60	$50
D	$450	$490	$540	$630	$60	$50
E	$495	$535	$585	$675	$70	$60
F	$545	$585	$635	$725	$70	$60
G	$595	$635	$685	$775	$70	$60
H	$640	$680	$730	$820	$70	$60
I	$685	$725	$775	$865	$80	$70
J	$725	$765	$815	$905	$80	$70
K	$765	$805	$855	$945	$80	$70
L	$800	$840	$890	$980	$80	$70

BEST PLAN VALUE IN THE INDUSTRY!

Shipping — (Plans 1-59999)

	1-3 Sets	4-6 Sets	7+ & Vellums
Standard Delivery (UPS 2-Day)	$25.00	$30.00	$35.00
Overnight Delivery	$35.00	$40.00	$45.00

International Shipping & Handling

	1-3 Sets	4-6 Sets	7+ & Vellums
Regular Delivery Canada (7-10 Days)	$25.00	$30.00	$35.00
Express Delivery Canada (5-6 Days)	$40.00	$45.00	$50.00
Overseas Delivery Airmail (2-3 Weeks)	$50.00	$60.00	$65.00

Shipping — (Plans 60000-99999)

	1-3 Sets	4-6 Sets	7+ & Vellums
Ground Delivery (7-10 Days)	$15.00	$20.00	$25.00
Express Delivery (3-5 Days)	$20.00	$25.00	$30.00

Our Reorder and Exchange Policies:

If you find after your initial purchase that you require additional sets of plans you may purchase them from us at special reorder prices (please call for pricing details) provided that you reorder within 6 months of your original order date. There is a $28 reorder processing fee that is charged on all reorders. For more information on reordering plans please contact our Customer Service Department. Your plans are custom printed especially for you once you place your order. For that reason we cannot accept any returns.

If for some reason you find that the plan you have purchased from us does not meet your needs, then you may exchange that plan for any other plan in our collection. We allow you sixty days from your original invoice date to make an exchange. At the time of the exchange you will be charged a processing fee of 20% of the total amount of your original order plus the difference in price between the plans (if applicable) plus the cost to ship the new plans to you. Call our Customer Service Department for more information. Please Note: reproducible vellums can only be exchanged if they are unopened.

Important Shipping Information

Please refer to the shipping charts on the order form for service availability for your specific plan number. Our delivery service must have a street address or Rural Route Box number — never a post office box. (PLEASE NOTE: Supplying a P.O. Box number only will delay the shipping of your order.) Use a work address if no one is home during the day.

Orders being shipped to APO or FPO must go via First Class Mail.

For our International Customers, only Certified bank checks and money orders are accepted and must be payable in U.S. currency. For speed, we ship international orders Air Parcel Post. Please refer to the chart for the correct shipping cost.

Index

Option Key

| **BL** Bottom-line Zip Quote | **ML** Materials List Available | **ZIP** Itemized Zip Quote | **RRR** Right Reading Reverse | **DUP** Duplex Plan |

Index

Option Key

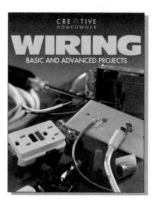
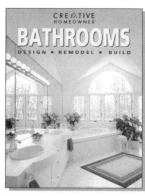

the Home Planner, Builder & Owner

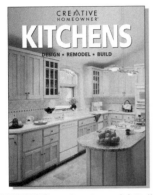

KITCHENS: Design, Remodel, Build

This is the reference book for modern kitchen design, with more than 100 full-color photos to help homeowners plan the layout. Step-by-step instructions illustrate basic plumbing and wiring techniques; how to finish walls and ceilings; and more.

BOOK #: 277065   192pp.   8½"x10⅞"

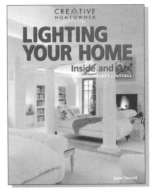

LIGHTING YOUR HOME: Inside and Out

Lighting should be selected with care. This book thoroughly explains lighting design for every room as well as outdoors. It is also a step-by-step manual that shows how to install the fixtures. More than 125 photos and 400 drawings.

BOOK #: 277583   176pp.   8½"x10⅞"

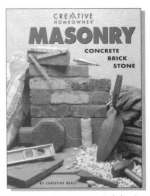

MASONRY: Concrete, Brick, Stone

Concrete, brick, and stone choices are detailed with step-by-step instructions and over 35 color photographs and 460 illustrations. Projects include a brick or stone garden wall, steps and patios, a concrete-block retaining wall, a concrete sidewalk.

BOOK #: 277106   176pp.   8½"x10⅞"

The Smart Approach to KITCHEN DESIGN

Transform a dated kitchen into the spectacular heart of your home. Learn how to create a better layout and more efficient storage. Find out about the latest equipment and materials. Savvy tips explain how to create style like a pro. More than 150 color photos.

BOOK #: 279935   176 pp.   9"x10"

PLANNING YOUR ADDITION

Planning an addition to your home involves a daunting number of choices, from choosing a contractor to selecting bathroom tile. Using 280 color drawings and photographs, architect/author Jerry Germer helps you make the right decision.

BOOK #: 277004   192pp.   8½"x10⅞"

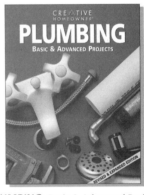

PLUMBING: Basic & Advanced Projects

Take the guesswork out of plumbing repair and installation for old and new systems. Projects include replacing faucets, unclogging drains, installing a tub, replacing a water heater, and much more. 500 illustrations and diagrams.

BOOK #: 277620   176pp.   8½"x10⅞"

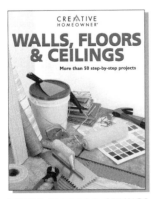

WALLS, FLOORS & CEILINGS

Here's the definitive guide to interiors. It shows you how to replace old surfaces with new professional-looking ones. Projects include installing molding, skylights, insulation, flooring, carpeting, and more. Over 500 color photos and drawings.

BOOK #: 277697   176pp.   8½"x10⅞"

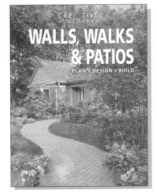

WALLS, WALKS & PATIOS

Learn how to build a patio from concrete, stone, or brick and complement it with one of a dozen walks. Learn about simple mortarless walls, landscape timber walls, and hefty brick and stone walls. 50 photographs and 320 illustrations, all in color.

BOOK #: 277994   192pp.   8½"x10⅞"

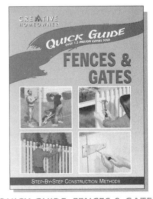

QUICK GUIDE: FENCES & GATES

Learn how to build and install all kinds of fences and gates for your yard, from hand-built wood privacy and picket fences to newer prefabricated vinyl and chain-link types. Over 200 two-color drawings illustrate step-by-step procedures.

BOOK #: 287732   80pp.   8½"x10⅞"

Place Your Order ....

CERAMIC TILE

Design and complete interior and exterior tile projects on walls, floors, countertops, shower enclosures, more. Over 350 color photographs and illustrations.

BOOK #: 277524   160pp.   8½"x10⅞"

COLOR IN THE AMERICAN HOME

Find out how to make the most of color in your home. Over 150 photographs of traditional and contemporary interiors.

BOOK #: 287264   176pp.   9"x10"

The Smart Approach to HOME DECORATING

Learn how to work with space, color, pattern, and texture with the flair of a professional designer. More than 300 color photos.

BOOK #: 279667   256pp.   9"x10"

CREATIVE HOMEOWNER®

BOOK ORDER FORM   *Please Print*

SHIP TO:

Name:

Address:

City: State: Zip: Phone Number:

(Should there be a problem with your order)

Quantity	Title	Price	CH #	Cost
	375 Southern Home Plans	$9.95	277037	
	380 Country & Farmhouse Home Plans	9.95	277035	
	400 Affordable Home Plans	9.95	277012	
	408 Vacation & Second Home Plans	8.95	277036	
	508 One-Story Home Plans	9.95	277030	
	508 Two-Story Home Plans	9.95	277031	
	600 Most Popular Home Plans	9.95	277029	
	Adding Value to Your Home	16.95	277006	
	Advanced Home Gardening	24.95	274465	
	Annuals, Perennials, and Bulbs	19.95	274032	
	Bathrooms: Design, Remodel, Build	19.95	277053	
	Better Lawns, Step by Step	14.95	274359	
	Bird Feeders	10.95	277102	
	Build a Kids' Play Yard	14.95	277662	
	Cabinets & Built-Ins	14.95	277079	
	Ceramic Tile	16.95	277524	
	Color in the American Home	19.95	287264	
	Complete Guide to Wallpapering	14.95	278910	
	Complete Guide to Water Gardens	19.95	274452	
	Complete Home Landscaping	24.95	274615	
	Creating Good Gardens	16.95	274244	
	Custom Closets	12.95	277132	
	Decks: Planning, Designing, Building	16.95	277162	
	Decorating with Architectural Trimwork	19.95	277495	
	Decorating with Paint & Paper	19.95	279723	
	Decorating with Tile	19.95	279824	
	Decorative Paint Finishes	10.95	287371	
	Drywall: Pro Tips for Hanging & Finishing	14.95	278315	
	Easy-Care Guide to Houseplants	19.95	275243	
	Fences, Gates & Trellises	14.95	277981	
	Furniture Repair & Refinishing	19.95	277335	
	Gazebos & Other Outdoor Structures	14.95	277138	
	Home Book	40.00	267855	
	Home Landscaping: California Reg.	19.95	274267	
	Home Landscaping: Mid-Atlantic Reg.	19.95	274537	
	Home Landscaping: Midwest Reg./S Can.	19.95	274385	
	Home Landscaping: Northeast Reg./SE Can.	19.95	274618	
	Home Landscaping: Southeast Reg.	19.95	274762	
	House Framing	19.95	277655	
	Kitchens: Design, Remodel, Build (New Ed.)	16.95	277065	
	Lighting Your Home Inside & Out	16.95	277583	
	Lyn Peterson's Real Life Decorating	27.95	279382	
	Masonry: Concrete, Brick, Stone	16.95	277106	
	Mastering Fine Decorative Paint Techniques	27.95	279550	
	Planning Your Addition	16.95	277004	
	Plumbing: Basic and Advanced Projects	14.95	277620	
	Remodeling Basements, Attics & Garages	16.95	277680	

Quantity	Title	Price	CH #	Cost
	Smart Approach to Bath Design	$19.95	287225	
	Smart Approach to Home Decorating	24.95	279667	
	Smart Approach to Kid's Rooms	19.95	279473	
	Smart Approach to Kitchen Design	19.95	279935	
	Smart Approach to Window Decor	19.95	279431	
	Trees, Shrubs & Hedges for Home Landscaping	19.95	274238	
	Walls, Floors & Ceilings	16.95	277697	
	Walls, Walks & Patios	14.95	277994	
	Wiring: Basic and Advanced Projects	19.95	277049	
	Yard and Garden Furniture (Plans & Projects)	19.95	277462	

Quick Guide Series

Quantity	Title	Price	CH #	Cost
	Quick Guide - Attics	$7.95	287711	
	Quick Guide - Basements	7.95	287242	
	Quick Guide - Ceramic Tile	7.95	287730	
	Quick Guide - Decks	7.95	277344	
	Quick Guide - Fences & Gates	7.95	287732	
	Quick Guide - Floors	7.95	287734	
	Quick Guide - Garages & Carports	7.95	287785	
	Quick Guide - Gazebos	7.95	287757	
	Quick Guide - Insulation & Ventilation	7.95	287367	
	Quick Guide - Interior & Exterior Painting	7.95	287784	
	Quick Guide - Masonry Walls	7.95	287741	
	Quick Guide - Patios & Walks	7.95	287778	
	Quick Guide - Plumbing	7.95	287863	
	Quick Guide - Ponds & Fountains	7.95	287804	
	Quick Guide - Pool & Spa Maintenance	7.95	287901	
	Quick Guide - Roofing	7.95	287807	
	Quick Guide - Siding	7.95	287892	
	Quick Guide - Stairs & Railings	7.95	287755	
	Quick Guide - Storage Sheds	7.95	287815	
	Quick Guide - Trim (Crown Molding, Base & more)	7.95	287745	
	Quick Guide - Walls & Ceilings	7.95	287792	
	Quick Guide - Windows & Doors	7.95	287812	
	Quick Guide - Wiring, Fourth Edition	7.95	287884	

Number of Books Ordered _____   Total for Books _____

NJ Residents add 6% tax _____

Prices subject to change without notice.   Subtotal _____

Postage/Handling Charges
$3.75 for first book / $1.25 for each additional book _____

Total _____

Make checks (in U.S. currency only) payable to:

CREATIVE HOMEOWNER®
P.O. BOX 38, 24 Park Way
Upper Saddle River, New Jersey 07458-9960

Please visit us at our Web site: **www.creativehomeowner.com**